Essentials of
Computer Architecture

Essentials of Computer Architecture

DOUGLAS E. COMER

Department of Computer Sciences
Purdue University
West Lafayette, IN 47907

PEARSON EDUCATION INTERNATIONAL

If you purchased this book within the United States or Canada
you should be aware that it has been wrongfully imported without
the approval of the Publisher or the Author.

Vice President and Editorial Director, ECS: *Marcia Horton*
Publisher: *Alan Apt*
Associate Editor: *Toni Holm*
Editorial Assistant: *Patrick Lindner*
Vice President and Director of Production and Manufacturing, ESM: *David W. Riccardi*
Executive Managing Editor: *Vince O'Brien*
Managing Editor: *Camille Trentacoste*
Production Editor: *Irwin Zucker*
Manufacturing Manager: *Trudy Pisciotti*
Manufacturing Buyer: *Lisa McDowell*
Director of Creative Services: *Paul Belfanti*
Creative Director: *Carole Anson*
Art Director: *Maureen Eide*
Cover Designer: *John Christiana*
Cover Art: *KJA-Artists.com*
Executive Marketing Manager: *Pamela Hersperger*
Marketing Assistant: *Barrie Reinhold*

 © 2005 by Pearson Education, Inc.
Pearson Prentice Hall
Pearson Education, Inc.
Upper Saddle River, New Jersey 07458

Pearson Prentice Hall® is a trademark of Pearson Education, Inc.

The author and publisher of this book have used their best efforts in preparing this book. These efforts include the development, research, and testing of the theories and programs to determine their effectiveness. The author and publisher make no warranty of any kind, expressed or implied, with regard to these programs or the documentation contained in this book. The author and publisher shall not be liable in any event for incidental or consequential damages in connection with, or arising out of, the furnishing, performance, or use of these programs.

TRADEMARK INFORMATION: Company and product names used in this text may be trademarks or registered trademarks of the individual companies, and are respectfully acknowledged. SPARC is a registered trademark of SPARC International, Inc. in the United States and other countries. MIPS is a registered trademark of MIPS Technologies, Inc. in the United States and other countries. Itanium and Xeon are trademarks of, and Intel and Pentium are registered trademarks of Intel Corporation.

Printed in the United States of America

10 9 8 7 6 5 4 3 2 1

ISBN 0-13-196426-7

Pearson Education Ltd., *London*
Pearson Education Australia Pty. Ltd., *Sydney*
Pearson Education Singapore Pte. Ltd.
Pearson Education North Asia Ltd. *Hong Kong*
Pearson Education Canada Inc., *Toronto*
Pearson Educación de Mexico, S.A. de C.V.
Pearson Education—Japan, Inc., *Tokyo*
Pearson Education—Malaysia Pte. Ltd.
Pearson Education Inc., *Upper Saddle River, New Jersey*

To Chris, who makes all the
bits of life meaningful

Contents

PART I   Basics

PART II   Processors

Chapter 4   The Variety Of Processors And Computational Engines   47

Chapter 5   Processor Types And Instruction Sets   61

Chapter 6   Operand Addressing And Instruction Representation   83

Chapter 7   CPUs: Microcode, Protection, And Processor Modes   95

PART III   Memories

Chapter 10   Physical Memory And Physical Addressing   143

Chapter 11   Virtual Memory Technologies And Virtual Addressing   163

Chapter 12   Caches And Caching   185

PART IV   I/O

Chapter 15   Programmed And Interrupt-Driven I/O   237

Chapter 16   A Programmer's View Of Devices, I/O, And Buffering   255

PART V   Advanced Topics

Chapter 17   Parallelism   279

Chapter 18   Pipelining   299

Chapter 19   Assessing Performance   **311**

Chapter 20   Architecture Examples And Hierarchy   **319**

Appendix 1   Lab Exercises For A Computer Architecture Course   **331**

Preface

This book began when I was assigned to help salvage an undergraduate computer organization course. The course had suffered years of neglect: it had been taught by a series of professors, mostly visitors, who had little or no interest or background in digital hardware, and the curriculum had deteriorated to a potpourri of topics that were only loosely related to hardware architectures. In some semesters, students spent the entire class studying Boolean Algebra, without even the slightest connection to actual hardware. In others, students learned the arcane details of one particular assembly language, without a notion of alternatives.

Is a computer organization course worth saving? Absolutely! In many Computer Science programs, the computer organization course is the only time students are exposed to fundamental concepts that explain the structure of the computer they are programming. Understanding the hardware makes it possible to construct programs that are more efficient and less prone to errors. In a broad sense, a basic knowledge of architecture helps programmers improve program efficiency by understanding the consequences of programming choices. Knowing how the hardware works can also improve the programming process by allowing programmers to pinpoint the source of bugs quickly. Finally, graduates need to understand basic architectural concepts to pass job application tests given by firms like Intel and Microsoft.

One of the steps in salvaging our architecture course consisted in looking at textbooks. We discovered the texts could be divided into roughly two types: texts aimed at beginning engineering students who would go on to design hardware, and texts written for CS students that attempt to include topics from compilers, operating systems, and (in at least one case) a complete explanation of how Internet protocols operate. Neither approach seemed appropriate for a single, introductory course on the subject. We wanted a book that (1) focused on the concepts rather than engineering details (because our students are not focused on hardware design); (2) explained the subject from a programmer's point of view, and emphasized consequences for programmers; and (3) did not try to cover several courses' worth of material. When no text was found, it seemed that the only solution was to create one.

The text is divided into five parts. Part 1 covers the basics of digital logic, gates, and data representation. We emphasize the representation chapter because notions of two's-compliment arithmetic and ranges of integer values are essential in programming. Parts 2, 3, and 4 cover the three essential areas of architecture: processors, memories, and I/O systems. In each case, the chapters give students enough background to understand how the mechanisms operate and the consequences for programmers. Finally, Part 5 covers advanced topics like parallelism, pipelining, and performance.

An Appendix describes an important aspect of the course: a hands-on lab where students can learn by doing. Although most lab problems focus on programming, students should spend the first few weeks in lab wiring a few gates on a breadboard. The equipment is inexpensive (we spent less than fifteen dollars per student on permanent equipment; students purchase their own set of chips for under twenty dollars).

We have set up a web site to accompany the book at:

http://www.eca.cs.purdue.edu

Rajesh Subraman has agreed to manage the site, which contains a set of class presentation materials created by the author as well as a set created by Rajesh. We invite other instructors to contribute their materials.

The text and lab exercises have been used at Purdue; students have been extremely positive about both. We received notes of thanks for the text and course. For many students, the lab is their first experience with hardware, and they are enthusiastic.

My thanks to the many individuals who contributed to the book. Bernd Wolfinger provided extensive reviews and made several important .suggestions about topics and direction. Dan Ardelean, James Cernak, and Tim Korb gave detailed comments on many chapters. Dave Capka reviewed early chapters. Rajesh Subraman taught from the book and provided his thoughts about the content. In the CS 250 class at Purdue, the following students each identified one or more typos in the manuscript: Nitin Alreja, Alex Cox, David Ehrmann, Roger Maurice Elion, Andrew Lee, Stan Luban, Andrew L. Soderstrom, and Brandon Wuest.

Finally, I thank my wife, Chris, for her patient and careful editing and valuable suggestions that improve and polish each book.

Douglas E. Comer

June, 2004

About The Author

Dr. Douglas Comer has an extensive background in computer systems, and has worked with both hardware and software. Comer's work on software spans most aspects of systems, including compilers and operating systems. He created a complete operating system, including a process manager, a memory manager, and device drivers for both serial and parallel interfaces. Comer has also implemented network protocol software and network device drivers for conventional computers and network processors. Both his operating system, Xinu, and TCP/IP protocol stack have been used in commercial products.

Comer's experience with hardware includes work with discrete components, building circuits from logic gates, and experience with basic silicon technology. He has written popular textbooks on network processor architectures, and at Bell Laboratories, Comer studied VLSI design and fabricated a VLSI chip.

Comer is a Distinguished Professor of Computer Science at Purdue University, where he develops and teaches courses and does research on computer organization, operating systems, networks, and Internets. Comer has created innovative laboratories in which students can build and measure systems such as operating systems and IP routers; all of Comer's courses include hands-on lab work. He continues to consult and lecture at universities, industries, and conferences around the world.

In addition to writing a series of internationally acclaimed technical books on computer operating systems, networks, TCP/IP, and computer technologies, Comer serves as the editor-in-chief of the journal *Software — Practice and Experience*. He is a Fellow of the ACM, a Fellow of the Purdue Teaching Academy, and a recipient of numerous awards, including a Usenix Lifetime Achievement award.

Additional information can be found at:

www.cs.purdue.edu/people/comer

and information about Comer's books can be found at:

www.comerbooks.com

1

Introduction And Overview

1.1 The Importance Of Architecture

Computers are everywhere. Cell phones, video games, and automobiles all contain computer systems. Each of these systems depends on software, which brings us to an important question: why should someone interested in building software study computer architecture? The answer is that understanding the hardware makes it possible to write smaller, faster code that is less prone to errors. A basic knowledge of architecture also helps programmers appreciate the relative cost of operations (e.g., the time required for an I/O operation compared to the time required for an arithmetic operation) and the effects of programming choices. Finally, understanding how hardware works helps programmers debug — someone who is aware of the hardware has more clues to help spot the source of bugs. In short, the more a programmer understands about the underlying hardware the better they will be at creating software.

1.2 Learning The Essentials

As any hardware engineer will tell you, digital hardware used to build computer systems is incredibly complex. In addition to myriad technologies and intricate sets of electronic components that constitute each technology, engineers must master design rules that dictate how the components can be constructed and how they can be interconnected to form systems. Furthermore, the technologies continue to evolve, and newer, smaller, faster components appear continuously.

Fortunately, as this text demonstrates, it is possible to understand architectural components without knowing low-level technical details. The text focuses on essentials, and explains computer architecture in broad, conceptual terms — it describes each of the major components and examines their role in the overall system. Thus, readers do not need a background in electronics or electrical engineering to understand the subject.

1.3 Organization Of The Text

What are the major topics we will cover? The text is organized into five parts.

Basics. The first section covers two topics that are essential to the rest of the book: digital logic and data representation. We will see that in each case, the issue is the same: the use of electronic mechanisms to represent and manipulate digital information.

Processors. One of the three principle areas of architecture, processing concerns both computation (e.g., arithmetic) and control (e.g., executing a sequence of steps). We will learn about the basic building blocks, and see how the blocks are used in a modern Central Processing Unit (CPU).

Memory. The second principle area of architecture, memory systems, focuses on the storage and access of digital information. We will examine both physical and virtual memory systems, and understand one of the most important concepts in computing: caching.

I/O. The third principle area of architecture, input and output, focuses on the interconnection of computers and devices such as keyboards, mice, displays, disks, and networks. We will learn about bus technology, see how a processor uses a bus to communicate with a device, and understand the role of device driver software.

Advanced Topics. The final section focuses on two important topics that arise in many forms: parallelism and pipelining. We will see how either parallel or pipelined hardware can be used to improve overall performance.

1.4 What We Will Omit

Boiling a topic down to essentials means choosing items to omit. In the case of this text, we have chosen breadth rather than depth — when a choice is required, we have chosen to focus on concepts instead of details. Thus, the text covers the major topics in architecture, but omits lesser-known variants and low-level engineering details. For example, our discussion of how a basic nor-gate operates gives a simplistic description without discussing the exact internal structure or discussing exactly how a gate dissipates the electrical current that flows into it. Similarly, our discussion of processors and memory systems avoids quantitative analysis of performance that an engineer needs. Instead, we take a high-level view aimed at helping the reader understand the overall design and the consequences for programmers rather than preparing the reader to build hardware.

1.5 Terminology: Architecture And Design

Throughout the text we will use the term *architecture* to refer to the overall organization of a computer system. A computer architecture is analogous to a blueprint — the architecture specifies the interconnection among major components and the overall functionality of each component without giving many details. Before a digital system can be built that implements a given architecture, engineers must translate the overall architecture into a practical *design* that accounts for details that the architectural specification omits. For example, the design must specify how components are grouped onto circuit boards and how power is distributed to each board. Eventually, a design must be implemented, which entails choosing specific hardware from which the system will be constructed. A design represents one possible way to realize a given architecture, and an implementation represents one possible way to realize a given design. The point is that architectural descriptions are abstractions, and we must remember that many designs can be used to satisfy a given architecture and many implementations can be used to realize a given design.

1.6 Summary

This text covers the essentials of computer architecture: digital logic, processors, memories, I/O, and advanced topics. The text does not require a background in electrical engineering or electronics. Instead, topics are explained by focusing on concepts, avoiding low-level details, and concentrating on items that are important to programmers.

Basics Of Digital Logic And Data Representation

The Fundamentals From Which Computers Are Built

2

Fundamentals Of Digital Logic

2.1 Introduction

This chapter covers the basics of digital logic. The goal is straightforward — provide a background that is sufficient for a reader to understand remaining chapters. Thus, we will not need to delve into electrical details, discuss the underlying physics, or learn the design rules that engineers follow to interconnect devices. Instead, we will learn a few basics that will allow us to understand how complex digital systems work.

2.2 Electrical Terminology: Voltage And Current

Engineers use the terms *voltage* and *current* to refer to quantifiable properties of electricity: the *voltage* between two points (measured in *volts*) represents the potential force, and the *current* (measured in *amperes* or *amps*) represents the flow of electrons along a path (e.g., along a wire). A good analogy can be made with water: voltage corresponds to water pressure, and current corresponds to the amount of water flowing through a pipe at a given time. There is also an analogy in the relationship between water pressure and water flow and the relationship between voltage and current. If a hole appears that allows water to flow, water pressure drops; if current starts flowing through a wire, voltage drops.

The most important thing to know about electrical voltage is that voltage can only be measured as the difference between two points (i.e., the measurement is relative). Thus, a *voltmeter*, which is used to measure voltage, always has two probes; the meter

7

does not register a voltage until both probes have been connected. To simplify measurement, we assume one of the two points represents zero volts, and express the voltage of the second point relative to zero. Electrical engineers use the term *ground* to refer to the point that is assumed to be at zero volts. In all digital circuits shown in this text, for example, we will assume that electrical power is supplied by two wires: one wire is a ground wire, which is assumed to be at zero volts, and a second wire is at five volts.

Fortunately, we can understand the essentials of digital logic without knowing more about voltage and current. We only need to understand how electrical flow can be controlled and how electricity can be used to represent digital values.

2.3 The Transistor

The mechanism used to control flow of electrical current is a semiconductor device that is known as a *transistor*†. At the lowest level, all digital systems are composed of transistors.

Each individual transistor functions like a miniature switch that can be operated electrically. A transistor has three connections: two through which a large current can flow and one for a small current that controls the flow. When a small, positive current flows through the control connection, a large current can flow through the other two connections; when the small current stops flowing through the control connection, the large current also stops flowing. Figure 2.1 shows the diagram engineers use to denote a transistor‡.

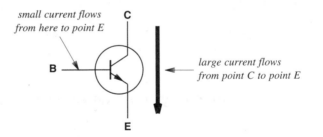

Figure 2.1 A transistor. When a small current flows between points *B* and *E*, a large current can flow between points *C* and *E*.

It may seem that a single transistor — a device that controls electrical current — is irrelevant to digital circuits and computer architecture. We will see, however, how transistors can be used to build more complex components that are used to build digital systems.

---

†Although other semiconductors can be used, most transistors are made from silicon.
‡Technically, the diagram shows an NPN transistor because the emitter and collector (labeled *E* and *C*) are made from N-type silicon and the base (labeled *B*) is made from P-type silicon.

2.4 Logic Gates

How are digital circuits built? The answer lies in Boolean algebra. Programmers are familiar with the three basic Boolean functions: *and*, *or*, and *not*. Figure 2.2 lists the possible input values and the result of each function.

A	B	A and B		A	B	A or B		A	not A
0	0	0		0	0	0		0	1
0	1	0		0	1	1		1	0
1	0	0		1	0	1			
1	1	1		1	1	1			

Figure 2.2 Boolean functions and the result for each possible set of inputs. A logical value of zero represents *false*, and a logical value of one represents *true*.

Boolean functions are used in building digital hardware. More important, it is possible to use transistors to construct circuits that implement each of the Boolean functions. Thus, Boolean functions can be translated directly into hardware.

To understand the relationship between Boolean functions and hardware, consider the Boolean *not*. If we use five volts to represent a Boolean *1* and zero volts to represent a Boolean *0*, a single transistor plus a component known as a resistor can implement the Boolean *not*. That is, the output is the opposite of the input — when five volts is placed on the input, the output drops to zero volts; when zero volts is placed on the input, the output rises to five volts†. Figure 2.3 illustrates a circuit that implements Boolean *not*.

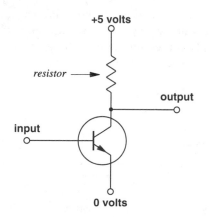

Figure 2.3 A transistor and a resistor used to implement the Boolean function *not*. When the input is zero volts, the output is five volts, and vice versa.

---

†In practice, the resistor limits the amount of current that can flow, which means the two values for voltage are not exactly zero and five. However, the voltages are close enough that we can think of them as exact.

To understand how the circuit operates, imagine the transistor to be a switch. When it is turned on, the transistor connects the output to zero volts; when it is turned off, the transistor disconnects the output from zero volts, and the output registers five volts. An input of five volts causes the transistor to turn on, and an input of zero volts causes the transistor to turn off. Thus, the output is always the opposite of the input.

Boolean circuits are fundamental to digital systems, and are given the name *logic gates*. Engineers do not construct gates from individual transistors because manufacturers sell electronic parts (actually *integrated circuits*) that contain all the circuitry for a gate.

A detail adds a minor complication: because of the way electronic circuits work, it takes fewer transistors to provide the inverse of Boolean functions. Thus, electronic parts that implement logic gates provide the inverse of *and* and *or*: *nand* (which stands for *not and*) and *nor* (which stands for *not or*). Figure 2.4 shows how *truth tables* can be used to list the functions that logic gates provide.

A	B	A nand B
0	0	1
0	1	1
1	0	1
1	1	0

A	B	A nor B
0	0	1
0	1	0
1	0	0
1	1	0

Figure 2.4 The *nand* and *nor* functions implemented by logic gates. Using the inverse simplifies the circuitry required.

2.5 Symbols Used For Gates

When they design circuits, engineers do not think about individual transistors. Instead, they represent each gate by a symbol, and draw circuits by interconnecting gates. Figure 2.5 shows the symbols used for the three basic Boolean functions that hardware provides. Engineers use the term *inverter* for a gate that performs the Boolean *not* operation.

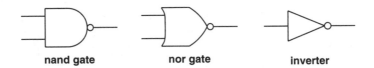

nand gate   nor gate   inverter

Figure 2.5 The symbols for *nand*, *nor*, and *inverter* gates. Inputs are shown on the left, and the output is shown on the right.

2.6 Construction Of Gates From Transistors

For our purposes, the internal details of gates are unimportant. All we need to understand is how gates are used. However, it is interesting to see that transistors can be used to create a gate. Figure 2.6 provides an example by showing the internal structure of a *nor* gate composed of transistors, resistors, and components known as *diodes*. The diagram reveals the underlying complexity: six transistors, five resistors, and three diodes are needed to form a single *nor* gate.

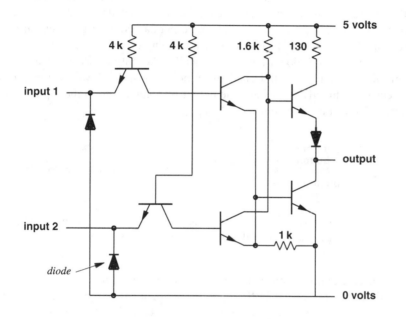

Figure 2.6 The internal structure of a *nor* gate formed from transistors and other components. A solid dot indicates an electrical connection between two wires. Resistors are labeled with a value in ohms, with *k* indicating multiplication by 1000.

The drawing in the figure is known as a *schematic diagram*. Each line on a schematic corresponds to a wire that connects one component to another. In addition, the schematic shows wires that correspond to two inputs, an output, power (five volts), and ground (zero volts).

The diagram in Figure 2.6 uses a common convention: two lines that cross do not indicate an electrical connection unless a solid dot appears. That is, two lines that cross without a dot correspond to a situation in which there is no physical connection; we can imagine that the wires are positioned so an air gap exists between them (i.e., the wires do not touch).

Now that we have seen an example of how a gate can be created out of transistors, we do not need to consider individual transistors again. Throughout the rest of the chapter, we will discuss gates without referring to their internal mechanisms; later chapters discuss larger, more complex mechanisms that are composed of gates.

2.7 Example Interconnection Of Gates

The electronic parts that implement gates are classified as *Transistor-Transistor Logic (TTL)* because the output transistors in each gate are designed to connect directly to input transistors in other gates. In fact, an output can connect to several inputs†. For example, suppose a circuit is needed in which the output is true if a disk is spinning and the user presses a power-down button. Logically, the output is a Boolean *and* of two inputs, but none of the gates described above provides *and*. However, the *and* function can be created by directly connecting the output of a *nand* gate to the input of an *inverter*. Figure 2.7 illustrates the connection.

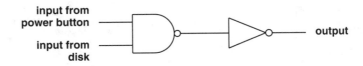

Figure 2.7 Illustration of gate interconnection. The output from one logic gate can connect directly to the inputs of other gates.

As another example, consider the circuit in Figure 2.8 that shows three inputs. What function does the circuit in the figure implement? There are two ways to answer the question: we can determine the Boolean formula to which the circuit corresponds, or we can enumerate the value that appears on each wire for all eight possible combinations of input values.

To derive a Boolean formula, observe that input *Y* is connected directly to an inverter. Thus, the value on wire *A* corresponds to the Boolean function *not Y*. The *nor* gate takes inputs *not Y* (from the inverter) and *Z*, so the value on wire *B* corresponds to the Boolean function:

$$Z \text{ nor (not } Y)$$

---

†The technology limits the number of inputs that can be supplied from a single output; we use the term *fanout* to specify the number of inputs to which an output connects.

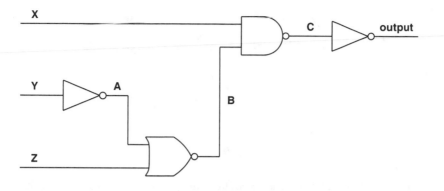

Figure 2.8 An example of a circuit with three inputs labeled X, Y, and Z. Internal interconnections are also labeled to allow us to discuss intermediate values.

Finally, from Figure 2.7, we know that the combination of a *nand* gate followed by an inverter produces the Boolean *and* of the two inputs. Thus, the output value corresponds to:

$$X \text{ and } (Z \text{ nor } (\text{not } Y))$$

which can also be expressed:

$$X \text{ and not } (Z \text{ or } (\text{not } Y)) \tag{2.1}$$

In practice, engineers spend more time constructing new circuits than analyzing existing circuits. The equivalence between Boolean expressions and digital logic circuits is also used in design. An engineer can start by finding a Boolean expression that solves the problem, and then translate the expression into equivalent hardware. More important, tools are available that optimize Boolean expressions. That is, an engineer can create a Boolean expression that specifies the behavior of a circuit, and then use a tool that automatically transforms the expression into an equivalent expression that requires fewer gates.

A second technique used to understand a logic circuit consists of enumerating all possible inputs, and then finding the corresponding values at each point in the circuit. For example, because the circuit in Figure 2.8 has three inputs, eight possible combinations of input exist. The table in Figure 2.9 lists the input combinations on wires X, Y, and Z along with the resulting values on the wires labeled A, B, C, and output.

X	Y	Z	A	B	C	output
0	0	0	1	0	1	0
0	0	1	1	0	1	0
0	1	0	0	1	1	0
0	1	1	0	0	1	0
1	0	0	1	0	1	0
1	0	1	1	0	1	0
1	1	0	0	1	0	1
1	1	1	0	0	1	0

Figure 2.9 A truth table that enumerates values for three inputs for the circuit in Figure 2.8, and the resulting values at various points in the circuit.

To make the output easier to understand, it can be converted to conventional Boolean operations. The resulting Boolean expression is equivalent to both the truth table in the figure and expression (2.1) above†:

X and Y and (not Z))

2.8 Multiple Gates Per Integrated Circuit

The table in Figure 2.9 is generated by starting with the eight possible values in columns *X*, *Y*, and *Z*, and then filling in the remaining columns one at a time. For example, point *A* in the circuit represents the output from the first inverter, which is the inverse of input *Y*. Thus, column *A* can be filled in by reversing the values in column *Y*. Similarly, column *B* represents the *nor* of columns *A* and *Z*.

Because the logic gates described above do not require many transistors, multiple gates that use TTL can be manufactured on a single, inexpensive electronic component. One popular set of TTL components that implement logic gates is known as the *7400 family*‡; each component in the family is assigned a part number that begins with *74*. Physically, many of the parts in the 7400 family consist of a rectangular package approximately one-half inch long with fourteen copper wires (called *pins*) that are used to connect the part to a circuit. Part number 7400 contains four *nand* gates, part number 7402 contains four *nor* gates, and part number 7404 contains six inverters. Figure 2.10 illustrates how the inputs and outputs of individual logic gates connect to pins in each case.

---

†Both Boolean equations and truth tables are useful. Boolean equations tend to be used during design, and truth tables tend to be used when debugging circuits.

‡In addition to the logic gates described in this section, the 7400 family also includes more sophisticated mechanisms, such as flip-flops, counters, and demultiplexors, that are described later in the chapter.

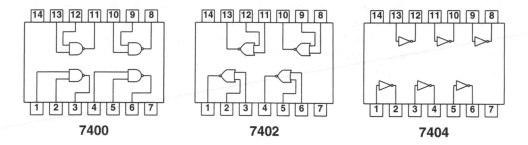

Figure 2.10 Illustration of the pin connections on three commercially available integrated circuits that implement logic gates. Pins 7 and 14 supply power (zero volts and five volts) to run the circuit.

2.9 The Need For More Than Combinatorial Circuits

The circuits described above are classified as *combinatorial* because the output is a Boolean combination of input values. In a combinatorial circuit, the output only changes when an input value changes. Although combinatorial circuits are essential, they are not sufficient — computation requires circuits that can take action without waiting for inputs to change. For example, when a user presses a button to power on a computer, hardware must perform a sequence of operations, and the sequence must proceed without further input from the user. The hardware does not require a user to hold the power button continuously — the startup sequence must continue even after the user releases the button. Furthermore, pressing the same button again causes the hardware to initiate a shutdown sequence.

How can digital logic perform a sequence of operations without requiring the input values to change? How can a digital circuit continue to operate after an input reverts to its initial condition? The answers involve additional mechanisms. The first case is handled by circuits that are more sophisticated than Boolean logic gates, and the second case is handled by a *clock*. The next sections present examples of sophisticated circuits, and later sections explain clocks.

2.10 Circuits That Maintain State

In addition to Boolean gates, electronic parts are available that maintain *state*. Such a part responds to the history of inputs, not just the current input values. The most trivial state maintaining mechanism is a *flip-flop*. One form of flip-flop acts exactly like the power switch on a computer: the first time its input becomes *1*, the flip-flop turns on the output, and the second time its input becomes *1*, the flip-flop turns off the output. That is, receiving an input of 1 causes the flip-flop to change the output from the current state to the opposite. Like a push-button switch used to control power, a flip-flop does not respond to a continuous input — the input must return to *0* before a value of 1 will cause the flip-flop to change state. Figure 2.11 shows a sequence of inputs and the resulting output.

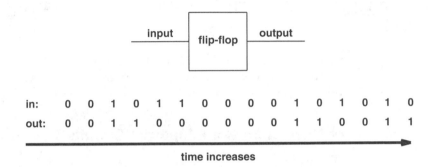

Figure 2.11 Illustration of how one type of flip-flop reacts to a sequence of inputs. The flip-flop output changes when the input transitions from 0 to 1 (i.e., from zero volts to five volts).

2.11 Transition Diagrams

To understand how a flip-flop works, it is helpful to plot the input and output in graphical form as a function of time. Engineers use the term *transition diagram* for such a plot. Figure 2.12 illustrates a transition diagram for the flip-flop values from Figure 2.11.

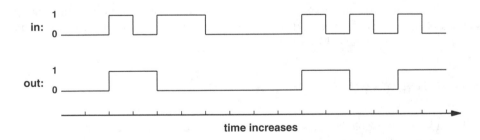

Figure 2.12 Illustration of a transition diagram that shows how a flip flop reacts to the series of inputs in Figure 2.11. Marks along the x-axis indicate times; each corresponds to one bit.

The transition diagram shows that for the example flip-flop, the output only changes when the input transitions from zero to one. Engineers say that the output transition occurs on the *leading edge* of the input change; circuits that transition when the input changes from one to zero are said to occur on the *falling edge*.

In practice, additional details complicate flip-flops. For example, most flip-flops include an additional input named *reset* that places the output in a 0 state. In addition, several variants of flip-flops exist. For example, some flip-flops provide a second output that is the inverse of the main output (in some circuits, having the inverse available results in fewer gates).

2.12 Binary Counters

A single flip-flop only offers two possible output values: 0 or 1. An alternative mechanism, called a *counter* accumulates a numeric total. Like a flip-flop, a counter's output changes whenever the input transitions from 0 to 1. Unlike a flip-flop, however, a counter has multiple outputs that represent the total transition count in binary†. Figure 2.13 illustrates how a counter with three outputs responds to input changes.

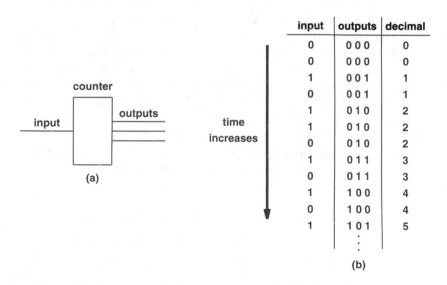

input	outputs	decimal
0	0 0 0	0
0	0 0 0	0
1	0 0 1	1
0	0 0 1	1
1	0 1 0	2
1	0 1 0	2
0	0 1 0	2
1	0 1 1	3
0	0 1 1	3
1	1 0 0	4
0	1 0 0	4
1	1 0 1	5

(b)

Figure 2.13 Illustration of (a) a binary counter, and (b) a sequence of input values and the corresponding outputs. The column labeled *decimal* gives the decimal equivalent of the outputs.

Like our description of a flip-flop, our description of a binary counter lacks several details. For example, counters have an additional input used to reset the count to zero.

†The next chapter considers data representation in more detail; for now it is sufficient to understand that the outputs represent a number.

Because it has a fixed number of output pins, a counter has a maximum value it can represent. When the accumulated count exceeds the maximum value, the counter resets the output to zero, and has an additional output that is used to indicate that an overflow occurred.

2.13 Clocks And Sequences

We said that a mechanism known as a *clock* allows hardware to operate without requiring the input to change. In fact, most digital logic circuits are said to be *clocked*, which means that a clock, rather than a set of inputs, controls and synchronizes the operation of individual components and subassemblies to ensure that they work together as intended.

What is a clock? In terms of digital circuits, we can imagine that a clock is a mechanism that emits an alternating sequence of 0 and 1 values at a regular rate. The speed of a clock is measured in *Hertz (Hz)* (the number of times per second the clock cycles through a 1 followed by a 0). Most clocks in high-speed digital computers operate at a speed of one hundred megahertz (100 MHz) or several gigahertz (GHz). For example, at present, the clock in a high-speed PC operates at 3 GHz.

It is difficult for a human to imagine clocks that operate at such high rates. To make the concept clear, let's assume a clock is available that operates at an extremely slow rate of 1Hz. Such a clock might be used to control an interface for a human. For example, if a computer contains an LED that flashes on and off to indicate that the computer is active, a slow clock is needed to control the LED. Note that a clock rate of 1Hz means the clock completes an entire cycle in one second. That is, the clock emits a logical 1 for one-half cycle followed by a logical zero for one-half cycle. If a circuit arranges to turn on an LED whenever the clock emits a logical 1, the LED will remain on for one-half second, and then will be off for one-half second.

How does an alternating sequence of 0 and 1 make digital circuits more powerful? To understand, we will consider a simple clocked circuit. Suppose that during startup, a computer must perform the following sequence of steps:

- Test the battery
- Power on and test the memory
- Start the disk spinning
- Power up the CRT
- Read the boot sector from disk into memory
- Start the CPU

Furthermore, to simplify the explanation, we will assume that one second must pass after starting a step before the circuit starts the next step. Thus, we desire a circuit that, once it has been started, will perform the six steps in sequence, at one-second intervals with no further changes in input.

For now, we will focus on the essence of the circuit, and consider how it can be started later. A circuit to handle the task of performing six steps in sequence can be built from three building blocks: a clock, a binary counter, and a device known as a *demultiplexor*, often abbreviated *demux*. We have already considered a counter, and we will assume that a clock is available that generates digital output at a rate of exactly one cycle per second. The last component, a demultiplexor, is a single integrated circuit that maps between a binary value and a set of outputs. That is, a demultiplexor takes a binary value as input, and uses the value to choose an output. Only one output of a demultiplexor is on at any time; all others are off — when the input lines represent the value i in binary, the demultiplexor selects the ith output. Figure 2.14 illustrates the concept.

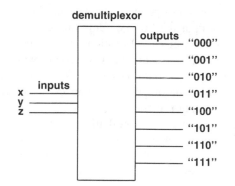

Figure 2.14 Illustration of a demultiplexor with three input lines and eight output lines. When inputs x, y, and z have the values 0, 1, and 1, the fourth output from the top is selected.

A demultiplexor provides the last piece needed for our simplistic sequencing mechanism — if we combine a clock, counter, and demultiplexor, the resulting circuit can execute a series of steps. For example, Figure 2.15 shows the interconnection in which the output of a clock is used as input to a binary counter, and the output of a binary counter is used as input to a demultiplexor.

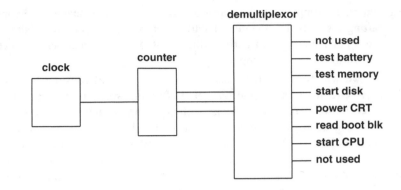

Figure 2.15 An illustration of how a clock can be used to create a circuit that performs a sequence of six steps. Output lines from the counter connect directly to input lines of the demultiplexor.

To understand how the circuit operates, assume that the counter has been reset to zero. Because the counter output is 000, the demultiplexor selects the topmost output, which is not used (i.e., not connected). Operation starts when the clock changes from logical 0 to logical 1. The counter accumulates the count, which changes its output to 001. When its input changes, the demultiplexor selects the second output, which is labeled test battery. Presumably, the output wire connects to a circuit that performs the necessary test. The second output remains selected for one second. During the second, the clock output remains at logical 1 for one-half second, and then reverts to logical 0 for one-half second. When the clock output changes back to logical 1, the counter output lines change to 010, and the demultiplexor selects the third output, which is connected to circuitry that tests memory.

Of course, details are important. For example, to be compatible with other devices, the clock must use five volts for logical 1, and zero volts for logical 0. Furthermore, to be directly connected, the output lines of the binary counter must use the same binary representation as the input lines of the demultiplexor. The next chapter considers representation in more detail; for now, we assume they are compatible.

2.14 The Important Concept Of Feedback

The simplistic circuit in Figure 2.15 lacks an important feature: there is no way to control operation (i.e., to start or stop the sequence). Because a clock runs forever, the counter in the figure counts from zero through its maximum value, and then starts again at zero. As a result, the demultiplexor will repeatedly cycle through its outputs, with each output being held for one second before moving on to the next.

Few digital circuits perform the same series of steps repeatedly. How can we arrange to stop the sequence after the six steps have been executed? The solution lies in a fundamental concept: *feedback*. Feedback lies at the heart of complex digital circuits because it allows the results of processing to affect the way a circuit behaves. In the computer startup sequence, feedback is needed for each of the steps. If the disk cannot be started, for example, the boot sector cannot be read from the disk.

To see a trivial example of feedback, consider how we might use the final output, call it *F*, from the demultiplexor to stop the process. An easy way consists of using the value of F to prevent clock pulses from reaching the counter. That is, instead of connecting the clock output directly to the counter input, we insert logic gates that only allow the counter pulses to continue when F has the value 0. In terms of Boolean algebra, the counter input should be:

CLOCK *and* (*not* F)

That is, as long as F is false, the counter input should be equal to the clock; when F is true, however, the counter input changes to (and remains) zero; Figure 2.16 shows how two inverters and a nand gate can be used to implement the necessary function.

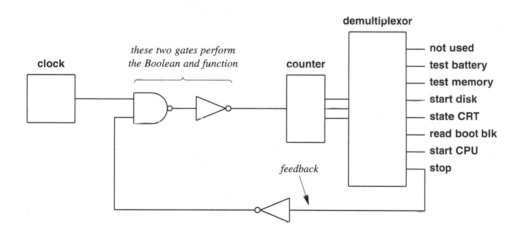

Figure 2.16 A modification of the circuit in Figure 2.15 that includes feedback to stop processing after one pass through each output.

The feedback in Figure 2.16 is fairly obvious because there is an explicit physical connection between the last output and the combinatorial circuit on the input side. The figure also makes it easy to see why feedback mechanisms are sometimes called *feedback loops†*.

---

†A feedback loop is also present among the gates used to construct a flip-flop.

2.15 Starting A Sequence

Figure 2.16 shows that it is possible to use feedback to terminate a process. However, the circuit is still incomplete because it does not contain a mechanism that allows the sequence to start. Fortunately, adding a starting condition is trivial. To understand why, recall that a counter contains a separate input line that resets the count to zero. All that is needed to make our circuit start running is another input (e.g., from a button that a user pushes) connected to the counter reset.

When the user pushes the button, the counter resets to zero, which causes the counter's output to become 000. When it receives an input of all zeros, the demultiplexor turns on the first output, and turns off the last output. When the last output turns off, the nand gate allows the clock pulses through, and the counter begins to run.

Although it does indeed start the sequence, allowing a user to reset the counter can cause problems. For example, consider what happens if a user becomes impatient during the startup sequence and presses the button a second time. Once the counter resets, the sequence starts again from the beginning. In some cases, performing an operation twice simply wastes time. In other cases, however, repeating an operation causes problems (e.g., some disk drives require that only one command be issued at a time). Thus, a production system uses complex combinatorial logic to prevent a sequence from being interrupted or restarted before it completes.

2.16 Iteration In Software Vs. Replication In Hardware

One of the fundamental differences between software and hardware arises from the way software and hardware handle operations that must be applied to a set of items. In software, the fundamental paradigm for handling multiple items consists of *iteration* — a programmer writes code that repeatedly finds the next item in a set and applies the operation to the item. That is, because the underlying system can only apply the operation to one item at a time, a programmer must explicitly specify the number of items in the set and the order in which they are to be processed. Iteration is so essential to programming that most programming languages provide a compact syntax that allows the programmer to express the iteration clearly (e.g., a *for loop*).

Although hardware can be built to perform iteration, doing so is difficult, and the resulting hardware is clumsy. Instead, the fundamental hardware paradigm for handling multiple items consists of *replication* — a hardware engineer creates multiple copies of the underlying gates, and allows each copy to act on one item. For example, suppose we need to compute a Boolean operation on a set of thirty-two Boolean values. The ideal hardware solution consists of replicating the necessary gate thirty-two times, and allowing each instance to operate on one of the thirty-two items. For example, to compute the Boolean *not* of thirty-two values, a hardware designer might use thirty-two inverters.

Replication is difficult for programmers to understand and appreciate because replication is antithetical to good programming — a programmer is taught to avoid duplicating code. In the hardware world, however, replication has two distinct advantages. First, as we mentioned above, replication often makes the resulting hardware more elegant than hardware that uses iteration because replication avoids the extra hardware needed to select an individual item, move it into place, and move the result back. Second, and more important, replication increases performance dramatically. In addition to avoiding the overhead of selecting and moving items, replication allows multiple operations to be performed simultaneously. For example, thirty-two inverters working at the same time can invert thirty-two bits in exactly the same amount of time that it takes one inverter to invert a single bit. To put it another way: thirty-two inverters working simultaneously are more than thirty-two times faster than a single inverter iteratively solving the same problem. The notion of hardware replication and parallel operation appears throughout the text; a later chapter explains how parallelism applies on a larger scale.

2.17 Gate And Chip Minimization

We have glossed over many of the underlying engineering details. For example, once they choose a general design and the amount of replication that will be used, engineers seek ways to minimize the amount of hardware needed. There are two issues: minimizing gates and minimizing integrated circuits. The first issue involves general rules of Boolean algebra. For example, consider the Boolean expression:

not (*not* z)

A circuit to implement the expression consists of two inverters connected together. Of course, we know that two *not* operations are the identity function, so the expression can be replaced by z. That is, a pair of directly connected inverters can be removed from a circuit without affecting the result.

As another example of Boolean expression optimization, consider the expression:

x *nor* (*not* x)

Either *x* will have the value 1, or *not x* will have the value 1, which means the *nor* function will always produce the same value, a logical 0. Therefore, the entire expression can be replaced by the value 0. In terms of a circuit, it would be foolish to use a *nor* gate and an inverter to compute the expression because the two gates will always yield the same output. Thus, once an engineer writes a Boolean expression formula, the formula can be analyzed to look for instances of subexpressions that can be reduced or eliminated without changing the result.

Although Boolean formulas can be optimized, further optimization is needed because the overall goal is minimization of integrated circuits. To understand the complexity, recall that some integrated circuits contain multiple copies of a given type of gate. Thus, minimizing the number of Boolean operations may not help if the optimization increases the types of gates required. For example, suppose a Boolean expression requires four *nand* gates, and consider an optimization that reduces the requirements to three gates: two *nand* gates and a *nor* gate. Unfortunately, although the total number of gates is lower, the optimization increases the number of integrated circuits required (because a single integrated circuit contains four *nand* gates, but two circuits are required for a *nand* and a *nor* gate).

2.18 Using Spare Gates

Consider the circuit in Figure 2.16 carefully†. Assuming the clock, counter, and demultiplexor each require one integrated circuit, how many additional integrated circuits are required? The obvious answer is two: one is needed for the *nand* gate (e.g., a 7400) and another for the two inverters (e.g., a 7404). However, a hardware engineer can implement the circuit with only one additional integrated circuit. To see how, observe that although the 7400 contains four *nand* gates, only one is needed. How can the spare gates be used? The trick lies in observing that *nand* of 1 and 0 is 1, and *nand* of 1 and 1 is 0. That is,

$$1\ nand\ x$$

is equivalent to:

$$not\ x$$

So, to use a *nand* gate as an inverter, an engineer simply connects one of the two inputs to five volts.

2.19 Power Distribution And Heat Dissipation

In addition to planning digital circuits that correctly perform the intended function and minimizing the number of components used, engineers must contend with the underlying power and cooling requirements. For example, although the diagrams in this chapter only depict the logical inputs and outputs of gates, every gate consumes power. By everyday standards, the amount of power used by a single integrated circuit is insignificant. However, because hardware designers tend to use replication instead of iteration, complex digital systems contain many circuits. An engineer must calculate the total power required, construct the appropriate power supplies, and plan additional wiring that carries power to each chip.

The laws of physics dictate that any device that consumes power will generate heat. The amount of heat generated is proportional to the amount of power consumed, so a small integrated circuit generates a small amount of heat. Because a digital system uses hundreds of circuits that operate in a small, enclosed space, the total heat generated can be significant. Unless engineers plan a mechanism to dissipate heat, high tempera-

---

†Figure 2.16 can be found on page 21.

tures will cause the circuits to fail. For small systems, engineers add holes to the chassis that allow hot air to escape and be replaced by cooler air from the surrounding room. For intermediate systems, such as personal computers, fans are added to move air through the system more quickly. For the largest digital systems, cool air is insufficient — a refrigeration system with liquid coolant must be used.

2.20 Timing

Our quick tour of digital logic omits another important aspect that engineers must consider: *timing*. A gate does not act instantly. Instead a gate takes time to *settle* (i.e., to change the output once the input changes). In our examples, timing is irrelevant because the clock runs at the incredibly slow rate of 1Hz and all gates settle in less than a microsecond. Thus, the gates settle long before the clock pulses.

In practice, timing is an essential aspect of engineering because digital circuits are designed to operate at high speed. To ensure that a circuit will operate correctly, an engineer must calculate the time required for all gates to settle.

Engineers must also calculate the time required to propagate signals throughout an entire system, and must ensure that the system does not fail because of *clock skew*. To understand clock skew, consider Figure 2.17 that illustrates a circuit board with a clock that controls three of the integrated circuits in the system.

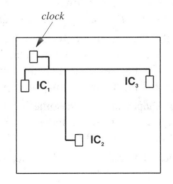

Figure 2.17 Illustration of three integrated circuits in a digital system that are controlled by a single clock. The length of wire between the clock and an integrated circuit determines when a clock signal arrives.

In the figure, the three integrated circuits are physically distributed (presumably, other integrated circuits occupy the remaining space). Unfortunately, a finite time is required for a signal from the clock to reach each of the circuits, and the time is proportional to the length of wire between the clock and a given circuit. As a result, the clock signal will arrive at some of the integrated circuits sooner than it arrives at others. As a rule of thumb, a signal requires one nanosecond to propagate across one foot of wire. Thus, for a system that measures eighteen inches across, the clock signal can reach locations near the clock a nanosecond before the signal reaches the farthest location. Obviously, clock skew can cause a problem if parts of the system must operate before other parts. An engineer needs to calculate the length of each path and design a layout that avoids the problem of clock skew.

As a consequence of clock skew, engineers seldom use a single global clock to control a large system. Instead, several clocks are used, with each clock controlling one part of the system. In particular, clocks that run at the highest rates are used in small physical areas. Although using multiple clocks avoids the problems of clock skew, multiple clocks introduce another problem, *clock synchronization*: all clocks must be engineered to coordinate.

2.21 Physical Size And Process Technologies

Most digital circuits are built from integrated circuits (*ICs*), a technology that permits many transistors to be placed on a single silicon chip along with wiring that interconnects them. The idea is that the components on an IC form a useful circuit.

ICs are often created by using *Complementary Metal Oxide Semiconductor* (*CMOS*) technology. Silicon is doped with impurities to give it negative or positive ionization. The resulting substances are known as *N-type silicon* or *P-type silicon*. When arranged in layers, N-type and P-type silicon form transistors.

IC manufacturers do not create a single IC at a time. Instead, a manufacturer creates a round *wafer* that is a few inches in diameter and contains many copies of a given IC design. Once the wafer has been created, the vendor cuts out the individual chips, and packages each chip in a plastic case along with pins that connect to the chip.

ICs come in a variety of shapes and sizes; some have only eight external connections (i.e., *pins*), and others have over four hundred†. Some ICs contain dozens of transistors, others contain millions.

Depending on the number of transistors on the chip, ICs can be divided into four broad categories:

Name	Example Use
Small Scale Integration (SSI)	Basic Boolean gates
Medium Scale Integration (MSI)	Intermediate logic, such as counters
Large Scale Integration (LSI)	Small, embedded processors
Very Large Scale Integration (VLSI)	Complex processors

---

†Engineers use the term *pinout* to describe the purpose of each pin on a chip.

For example, integrated 7400, 7402, and 7404 circuits described in this chapter are classified as SSI. A binary counter or flip-flop is classified as MSI.

The definition of VLSI keeps changing as manufacturers devise new ways to increase the density of transistors per square area. Gordon Moore, a cofounder of Intel Corporation, is attributed with having observed that the density of silicon circuits, measured in the number of transistors per square inch, would double every year. The observation, known as *Moore's Law*, was revised in the 1970s, when the rate slowed to doubling every eighteen months.

In addition to general-purpose ICs that are designed and sold by vendors, it has become possible to build special-purpose ICs. Known as *Application Specific Integrated Circuits (ASICs)*, the ICs are designed by a private company, and then the designs are sent to a vendor to be manufactured. Although designing an ASIC is expensive and time-consuming — approximately a million dollars and nearly two years — once the design is completed, copies of the ASIC are inexpensive to produce. Thus, high-end digital systems often use ASIC chips.

2.22 Circuit Boards And Layers

Most digital systems are built using a *printed circuit board* that consists of a fiberglass board with thin metal strips attached to the surface and holes for mounting integrated circuits and other components. In essence, the metal strips on the circuit board form the wiring that interconnects components.

Can a circuit board be used for complex interconnections that require wires to cross? Interestingly, engineers have developed *multilayer* circuit boards that solve the problem. In essence, a multilayer circuit board allows wiring in three dimensions — when a wire must cross another, the designer can arrange to pass the wire up to a higher layer, make the crossing, and then pass the wire back down.

It may seem that a few layers will suffice for any circuit. However, large complex circuits with thousands of interconnections may need additional layers. It is not uncommon for engineers to design circuit boards that have eighteen layers; the most advanced boards can have twenty-four layers.

2.23 Levels Of Abstraction

As this chapter illustrates, it is possible to view digital logic at various levels of abstraction. At the lowest level, a transistor is created from silicon. At the next level, multiple transistors are used along with components, such as resistors and diodes, to form gates. At the next level, multiple gates are combined to form intermediate scale units, such as flip flops. In later chapters, we will discuss more complex mechanisms, such as processors, memory systems, and I/O devices, that are each constructed from multiple intermediate scale units. Figure 2.18 summarizes the levels of abstraction.

Abstraction	Implemented With
Computer	Circuit board(s)
Circuit board	Components such as processor and memory
Processor	VLSI chip
VLSI chip	Many gates
Gate	Many transistors
Transistor	Semiconductor implemented in silicon

Figure 2.18 An example of levels of abstraction in digital logic. An item at one level is implemented using items at the next lower level.

The important point is that moving up the levels of abstraction allows us to hide more details and talk about larger and larger pieces without giving internal details. When we describe processors, for example, we can consider how a processor works without examining the internal structure at the level of gates or transistors.

An important consequence of abstraction arises in the diagrams architects and engineers use to describe digital systems. As we have seen, schematic diagrams can represent the interconnection of transistors, resistors, and diodes. Diagrams can also be used to represent an interconnection among gates. In later chapters, we will use high-level diagrams that represent the interconnection of processors and memory systems. In such diagrams, a small rectangular box will represent a processor or a memory without showing the interconnection of gates. When looking at an architectural diagram, it will be important to understand the level of abstraction, and to remember that a single item in a high-level diagram can correspond to an arbitrarily large number of gates.

2.24 Summary

Digital logic refers to the pieces of hardware used to construct digital systems such as computers. As we have seen, Boolean algebra is an important tool in digital circuit design; there is a direct relationship between Boolean functions and the gates used to implement combinatorial digital circuits. We have also seen that Boolean logic values can be described using truth tables.

A clock is a straightforward mechanism that emits pulses at regular intervals. A clock allows a digital circuit to change without requiring inputs to change, and can be used to provide synchronization among multiple parts of a circuit.

Although we think of digital logic from a mathematical point of view, building practical circuits involves understanding the underlying hardware details. In particular, besides basic correctness, engineers must contend with problems of power distribution, heat dissipation, and clock skew.

3

Data And Program
Representation

3.1 Introduction

The previous chapter introduces digital logic, and describes basic hardware building blocks that are used to create digital systems. This chapter continues the discussion of fundamentals by explaining how digital systems encode programs and data. We will see that representation is important for programmers as well as for hardware engineers because software must understand the underlying representation.

3.2 Digital Logic And Abstraction

As we have seen, digital logic circuits contain many low-level details. The circuits use transistors and electrical voltage to perform basic operations. The main point of digital logic, however, is *abstraction* — we want to hide the underlying details and use high-level abstractions whenever possible. For example, we have seen that each input or output of a digital logic circuit is restricted to two possible conditions: *off*, which is often represented by zero volts, or *on*, which is often represented by five volts. When they use logic gates to design computers, however, computer architects do not think about such details. Instead, they assign abstract names to the two conditions, and use the names. For example, an architect might choose to use a pair of names, such as *low* and *high* or *true* and *false*, to label the conditions†. As a result, complex digital systems, such as memories and processors, can be described, built, and used without thinking about individual transistors or voltages.

---

†The previous chapter shows another alternative: the two Boolean values of logical 0 and logical 1.

To a programmer, the most important abstractions consist of those that are visible to the software: the representations used for data and programs. The next sections consider data representation, and discuss how it is visible to programs; later sections describe program representation.

3.3 Bits And Bytes

All data representation builds on digital logic. We use the abstraction *binary digit* (*bit*) to describe a digital entity that can have two possible values, and assign the mathematical names *0* and *1* for the two values.

Multiple bits are used to represent more complex data items. For example, each computer system defines a *byte* to be the smallest data item larger than a bit that the hardware can manipulate.

How big is a byte? Technically, the size of a byte is not standard for all computers. Instead, the size is chosen by the architect who designs the computer. Early computer designers experimented with a variety of byte sizes, and some special-purpose computers still use unusual byte sizes. For example, an early computer manufactured by CDC corporation used a six-bit byte, and a computer manufactured by BB&N used a ten-bit byte. However, most modern computer systems define a byte to contain eight bits — the size has become so widely accepted that engineers usually assume a byte size equal to eight bits, unless told otherwise†.

3.4 Byte Size And Possible Values

The number of bits per byte is especially important to programmers because computer programs use bytes to store values. The size of the byte determines the maximum value that can be stored. A byte that contains k bits can represent one of 2^k values (i.e., exactly 2^k unique strings of 1s and 0s exist that have length k). Thus, a six-bit byte can represent 64 possible values, and an eight-bit byte can represent 256 possible values. As an example, consider the eight possible values that correspond to a set of three bits as Figure 3.1 illustrates.

000	010	100	110
001	011	101	111

Figure 3.1 The eight unique combinations that can be assigned to three bits.

What does a given pattern of bits represent? The most important thing to understand is that the bits themselves have no intrinsic meaning — the interpretation of the value is determined by the way hardware and software use the bits. For example, com-

---

†We will follow the practice in the text by assuming that a byte contains eight bits.

puter hardware can be designed in which a set of three bits represents the status of three peripheral devices:

- The first bit has the value 1 if a disk is connected
- The second bit has the value 1 if a printer is connected
- The third bit has the value 1 if a keyboard is connected

Alternatively, hardware can be designed in which a set of three bits represent the current status of three pushbutton switches: the ith bit is 1 if a user is currently pushing switch i.

3.5 Binary Arithmetic

One of the most common abstractions used to associate a meaning with each combination of bits is taken from mathematics: the set of bits is interpreted as a binary integer. To understand the interpretation, remember that in base ten, the possible digits are 0 through 9, and that the number 123 represents 1 times 100 plus 2 times 10 plus 3 times 1. Like the decimal number system, the binary number system uses positional information in which each position represents the next highest power of the base. Thus, positions in the binary number system represent successive powers of two: 2^0, 2^1, 2^2, and so on. Figure 3.2 illustrates the positional concept.

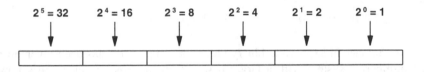

Figure 3.2 The value associated with each of the first six positions of the binary number system. Each binary digit corresponds to the next power of two.

As an example, consider the binary number:

$$0\ 1\ 0\ 1\ 0\ 1$$

According to the figure, the value can be interpreted as:

$$0\times2^5 + 1\times2^4 + 0\times2^3 + 1\times2^2 + 0\times2^1 + 1\times2^0 = 21$$

We will discuss more about integer representation later in the chapter. For now, it is sufficient to observe an important consequence of conventional positional notation: the binary numbers that can be represented in k bits start at zero instead of one. If we use the positional interpretation illustrated in Figure 3.2, the binary numbers that can be represented with three bits range from zero through seven. Similarly, the binary numbers that can be represented with eight bits range from zero through two hundred fifty-five. We can summarize:

> *A set of k bits can be interpreted to represent a binary integer. When conventional positional notation is used, the values that can be represented with k bits range from 0 through 2^k-1.*

3.6 Hexadecimal Notation

Although a binary number can be translated to an equivalent decimal number, programmers and engineers sometimes find the decimal equivalent difficult to understand. For example, if a programmer needs to test the fifth bit from the right, using the binary constant 010000 makes the correspondence between the constant and the bit much clearer than the equivalent decimal constant 16.

Unfortunately, long strings of bits are as unwieldy and difficult to understand as a decimal equivalent. For example, to determine whether the sixteenth bit is set in the following binary number, a human needs to count individual bits:

$$1\ 1\ 0\ 1\ 1\ 1\ 1\ 0\ 1\ 1\ 0\ 0\ 1\ 0\ 0\ 1\ 0\ 0\ 0\ 0\ 1\ 0\ 0\ 1\ 0\ 1\ 0\ 0\ 1\ 0\ 0\ 1$$

To aid humans in expressing binary values, a compromise has been invented: a positional numbering system with a larger base. If the base is chosen to be a power of two, translation to binary is trivial. Base sixteen is especially popular, and the numbering system is known as *hexadecimal*. Hexadecimal offers two advantages. First, because the representation is substantially more compact than binary, the resulting strings are shorter. Second, because sixteen is a power of two, conversion between binary and hexadecimal is straightforward and does not involve a complex arithmetic calculation.

In essence, hexadecimal encodes each group of four bits as a single hex digit between zero and fifteen†. Figure 3.3 lists the sixteen hex digits along with the binary and decimal equivalent of each.

---

†Programmers use the term *hex* as an abbreviation for *hexadecimal*.

Hex Digit	Binary Value	Decimal Equivalent
0	0000	0
1	0001	1
2	0010	2
3	0011	3
4	0100	4
5	0101	5
6	0110	6
7	0111	7
8	1000	8
9	1001	9
A	1010	10
B	1011	11
C	1100	12
D	1101	13
E	1110	14
F	1111	15

Figure 3.3 The sixteen hexadecimal digits and their equivalent binary and decimal values. Each hex digit encodes four bits of a binary value.

As an example of hexadecimal encoding, look at Figure 3.4, which illustrates how a binary string corresponds to its hexadecimal equivalent.

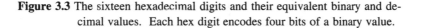

```
1 1 0 1  1 1 1 0  1 1 0 0  1 0 0 1  0 0 0 0  1 0 0 1  0 1 0 0  1 0 0 1
   D        E        C        9        0        9        4        9
```

Figure 3.4 Illustration of the relationship between binary and hexadecimal. Each hex digit represents four bits.

3.7 Notation For Hexadecimal And Binary Constants

Because the digits used in binary, decimal, and hexadecimal number systems overlap, constants can be ambiguous. To solve the ambiguity, an alternate notation is needed. Mathematicians and some textbooks add a subscript to denote a base other than ten (e.g., 135_{16} specifies that the constant is hexadecimal). Computer architects and programmers tend to follow programming language notation: hex constants begin with prefix *0x*, and binary constants begin with prefix *0b*. Thus, to denote 135_{16}, engineers write 0x135. Similarly, the 32-bit constant from Figure 3.4 is written:

$$0xDEC90949$$

3.8 Character Sets

We said that bits have no intrinsic meaning, and that the hardware or software must determine what each bit represents. More important, more than one interpretation can be used — a set of bits can be created and used with one abstraction, and later used with another.

As an example, consider character data that has both a numeric and symbolic interpretation. Each computer system defines a *character set* to be a set of symbols that the computer and I/O devices understand. A typical character set contains uppercase and lowercase letters, digits, and punctuation marks. More important, computer architects choose a character set such that each character fits into a byte (i.e., each of the bit patterns in a byte is assigned one character). Thus, a computer that uses an eight-bit byte has two hundred fifty-six (2^8) characters in its character set, and a computer that uses a six-bit byte has sixty four (2^6) characters. In fact, the relationship between the byte size and the character set is so strong that many programming languages refer to a byte as a *character*.

What bit values are used to encode each character? The computer architect must decide. In the 1960s, for example, IBM Corporation chose the *Extended Binary Coded Decimal Interchange Code (EBCDIC)*† representation as the character set used on IBM computers. CDC Corporation chose a six-bit character set for use on their computers. The two character sets were completely incompatible.

As a practical matter, computer systems connect to devices such as keyboards, printers, or modems, and such devices are often built by separate companies. To interoperate correctly, peripheral devices and computer systems must agree on which bit pattern corresponds to a given symbolic character. To help vendors build compatible equipment, the *American National Standards Institute (ANSI)* defined a character representation known as the *American Standard Code for Information Interchange (ASCII)*‡. The ASCII character set specifies the representation of one hundred twenty-eight characters, including the usual letters, digits, and punctuation marks; it is widely accepted.

Figure 3.5 lists the ASCII representation of characters by giving a hexadecimal value and the corresponding symbolic character. Of course, the hexadecimal notation is merely a shorthand notation for a binary string. For example, the lowercase letter *a* has hexadecimal value 0x61, which corresponds to the binary value 0b01100001.

We said that a conventional computer uses eight-bit bytes, and that ASCII defines one hundred twenty-eight characters (i.e., a seven-bit character set). Thus, when ASCII is used on a conventional computer, one-half of the byte values are unassigned (numeric values 128 through 255). How are the additional values used? In some cases, they are not — peripheral devices that accept or deliver characters merely ignore the eighth bit in a byte. In other cases, the computer architect or a programmer extends the character set (e.g., by adding punctuation marks for alternate languages).

---

†EBCDIC is pronounced *ebb'se-dick*.
‡ASCII is pronounced *ass'key*.

00 nul	01 soh	02 stx	03 etx	04 eot	05 enq	06 ack	07 bel
08 bs	09 ht	0A lf	0B vt	0C np	0D cr	0E so	0F si
10 dle	11 dc1	12 dc2	13 dc3	14 dc4	15 nak	16 syn	17 etb
18 can	19 em	1A sub	1B esc	1C fs	1D gs	1e rs	1F us
20 sp	21 !	22 "	23 #	24 $	25 %	26 &	27 '
28 (	29)	2A *	2B +	2C ,	2D –	2E .	2F /
30 0	31 1	32 2	33 3	34 4	35 5	36 6	37 7
38 8	39 9	3A :	3B ;	3C <	3D =	3E >	3F ?
40 @	41 A	42 B	43 C	44 D	45 E	46 F	47 G
48 H	49 I	4A J	4B K	4C L	4D M	4E N	4F O
50 P	51 Q	52 R	53 S	54 T	55 U	56 V	57 W
58 X	59 Y	5A Z	5B [	5C \	5D]	5E ^	5F _
60 `	61 a	62 b	63 c	64 d	65 e	66 f	67 g
68 h	69 i	6A j	6B k	6C l	6D m	6E n	6F o
70 p	71 q	72 r	73 s	74 t	75 u	76 v	77 w
78 x	79 y	7A z	7B {	7C		7D }	7E ~	7F del

Figure 3.5 The ASCII character set. Each entry shows a hexadecimal value and the graphical representation of the character associated with the value.

3.9 Unicode

Although a seven-bit character set and an eight-bit byte work well for English and some European languages, they do not suffice for all languages. Chinese, for example, contains thousands of symbols and glyphs. To accommodate such languages, extensions and alternatives have been proposed.

One of the promising proposals is named *Unicode*. Unicode extends ASCII and plans to accommodate all languages, including languages from the Far East. Originally designed as a sixteen-bit character set, later versions of Unicode have been extended to accommodate larger representations. Thus, future computers may base their character set on Unicode.

3.10 Unsigned Integers, Overflow, And Underflow

The positional representation of binary numbers illustrated in Figure 3.2† is said to produce *unsigned integers*. That is, each of 2^k combinations of bits is associated with a nonnegative numeric value. Because the unsigned integers used in a computer have finite size, operations like addition and subtraction can have unexpected results. For ex-

---

†Figure 3.2 can be found on page 31.

ample, computing the difference between two k-bit unsigned integers can yield a negative (i.e., signed) result. Similarly, adding two k-bit unsigned integers can produce a value that requires more than k bits to represent.

Hardware to perform unsigned arithmetic handles the problem in an interesting way. First, the hardware produces a result by using *wraparound* (i.e., the hardware adds two k-bit integers, and takes the k low-order bits of the answer). Second, the hardware sets *overflow* or *underflow* conditions to indicate whether the result exceeded k bits or was negative†. For example, an overflow indicator corresponds to the value that would appear in the $k+1^{st}$ bit (i.e., the value commonly known as *carry*). Figure 3.6 illustrates an addition with three-bit arithmetic that results in a carry.

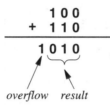

Figure 3.6 Illustration of addition with unsigned integers that produces overflow. The overflow indicator, which tells whether wraparound occurred, is equal to the carry bit.

3.11 Numbering Bits And Bytes

How should set of bits be numbered? If we view the set as a string, it makes sense to start numbering from the left, but if we view the set as a binary number, it makes sense to start numbering from the right (i.e., from the least significant bit). Numbering is especially important when data is transferred. For example, when sending a byte of data over a network, both the sending and receiving computers must agree on whether the least-significant or most-significant bit will be transferred first.

The issue of numbering becomes more complicated if we consider data items that span multiple bytes. For example, consider transferring a thirty-two bit integer. If the computer uses eight-bit bytes, the integer will span four bytes, which can be transferred starting with the least-significant or the most-significant.

We use the term *little endian* to characterize a system that numbers bytes of an integer from least-significant to most-significant, and the term *big endian* to characterize a system that numbers bytes of an integer from most-significant to least-significant. Similarly, we use the terms *bit little endian* and *bit big endian* to characterize systems that number bits within a byte starting at the least-significant bit and most-significant bit, respectively. Figure 3.7 illustrates the two styles of numbering.

---

†We use the term *underflow* to denote a value that is less than the representation can hold. In particular, a negative result from unsigned integer arithmetic is classified as an underflow because negative values cannot be represented.

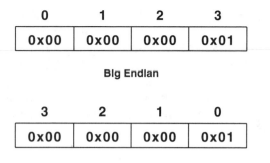

Figure 3.7 Illustration of big endian and little endian byte numbering for a thirty-two bit integer equal to 1. Little endian numbers the least significant byte zero; big endian numbers the most significant byte zero.

In the figure, both the big endian and little endian forms contain the number 1 expressed as a thirty-two bit, unsigned value on a computer that uses eight bits per byte. Thus, only the least-significant bit is set to one; all other bits are zero. The values in each byte give the contents of the byte in hexadecimal; the labels on the top of each byte give the byte numbering.

3.12 Signed Integers

The positional representation considered above cannot accommodate negative numbers. To do so, we need an alternative interpretation of bit values. Three interpretations have been used:

- *Sign-Magnitude*. The sign is kept separate from the value: a set of bits stores the absolute value of an integer and a separate bit stores the sign (i.e., the sign bit is set to 1 if the integer is negative).

- *One's Complement*. A single set of bits is used. To form a negative of any value, reverse each bit (i.e., change from 0 to 1 or vice versa).

- *Two's Complement*. A single set of bits is used. To form a negative number, start with a positive number, subtract one, and then reverse each bit.

Each interpretation has interesting quirks. For example, the sign-magnitude interpretation makes it possible to create a value of *negative zero*, even though the concept does not correspond to a valid mathematical notion. The one's comple-

ment interpretation provides two values for zero: all zero bits and the complement, all one bits. Finally, the two's complement interpretation includes one
more negative value than positive values (to accommodate zero).

Which interpretation is best? Programmers can debate the issue because
each interpretation works well in some cases. However, computer architects
make the decision, and many choose the two's complement scheme because two's
complement makes it possible to build low-cost, high-speed hardware to perform
arithmetic operations.

3.13 An Example Of Two's Complement Numbers

We said that k bits can represent 2^k possible combinations. Unlike the unsigned representation in which the combinations correspond to a continuous set of
integers starting at zero, two's complement divides the combinations in half.
Each combination in the first half (zero through $2^{k-1}-1$ is assigned the same
value as in the unsigned representation. Combinations in the second half, each of
which has the high-order bit equal to one, correspond to negative integers. Thus,
at exactly one-half of the way through the possible combinations, the value
changes from the largest possible positive integer to the largest possible negative
integer.

An example will clarify the two's complement assignment. To keep the example small, we will consider a four-bit integer. Figure 3.8 lists the sixteen possible bit combinations, the decimal equivalent when using the two's complement
representation, and the decimal equivalent when using the unsigned representation.

The assignment of values in the figure provides an interesting advantage: except for overflow, the same hardware operations work for either representation.
For example, adding one to the binary value 1001 produces 1010. In the unsigned interpretation, adding one to nine produces ten; in the two's complement
interpretation, adding one to negative seven produces negative six. The important
point is:

> *A computer can use a single piece of hardware to provide un-
> signed or two's complement integer arithmetic; software run-
> ning on the computer can choose an interpretation for each in-
> teger.*

Binary Value	Unsigned Equivalent	Two's Complement Equivalent
1111	15	-1
1110	14	-2
1101	13	-3
1100	12	-4
1011	11	-5
1010	10	-6
1001	9	-7
1000	8	-8
0111	7	7
0110	6	6
0101	5	5
0100	4	4
0011	3	3
0010	2	2
0001	1	1
0000	0	0

Figure 3.8 The value assigned to each combination of four bits when using unsigned or two's complement representations.

3.14 Sign Extension

Although Figure 3.8 shows a four-bit two's complement representation, the four-bit representation is easily extended to arbitrary size. Many computers include hardware for multiple sizes (e.g., a single computer can offer sixteen bit, thirty-two bit, and sixty-four bit representations), and allow a programmer to choose one of the sizes for each integer data item.

If a computer does contain multiple sizes of integers, a situation can arise in which a value is copied from a smaller-size integer to a larger-size integer. For example, consider copying a value from a sixteen-bit integer to a thirty-two-bit integer. How should the extra bits be used? In two's complement, the solution consists of copying the least significant bits and then extending the sign bit — if the original value is positive, extending the high-order bit fills the most significant bits of the larger number with zeros; if the original value is negative, extending the high-order bit fills the most significant bits of the larger number with ones. In either case, the larger number will have the same numeric value as the smaller number†.

---

†Sign extension also occurs during a right-shift operation: the hardware replicates the high-order bit; doing so means that either a positive or negative value is divided by a power of two. For example, because division by a power of two can be implemented by a right shift, applying a right shift of one bit to an integer that represents -14 results in -7, and applying a right shift of one bit to an integer that represents +14 results in +7.

We can summarize:

> *Sign extension: in two's complement arithmetic, when an integer Q composed of k bits is copied to an integer of more than k bits, the additional high-order bits are made equal to the top bit of Q. Extending the sign bit means the numeric value remains the same.*

We said that it is possible to create software that either uses an unsigned or two's complement representation. However, sign extension provides another exception: the hardware always performs sign extension. Thus, if an unsigned integer is copied to a larger unsigned integer, the copy may not have the same numeric value as the original†. The point is:

> *Because two's complement hardware performs sign extension; copying an unsigned integer to a larger unsigned integer can change the value.*

3.15 Floating Point

In addition to hardware that performs signed and unsigned integer arithmetic, general purpose computers provide hardware that performs arithmetic on *floating point* values. Floating point representation used in computers derives from *scientific notation* in which each value is represented by a *mantissa* and an *exponent*. For example, scientific notation expresses the value 12345 as 1.2345×10^4. Similarly, a chemist might write a well-known constant, such as Avogadro's number, as:

$$6.022 \times 10^{23}$$

Unlike conventional scientific notation, the floating point representation used in computers is based on binary. Thus, a floating point value consists of two sets of bits: one set that encodes a mantissa and another set that encodes an exponent.

To further optimize space, many floating point representations include optimizations:

- The value is normalized
- The leading bit is implicit
- The exponent is biased to allow negative values

---

†The value changes in cases where the high-order bit is set in the original unsigned integer (i.e., if the value is greater than one-half the maximum unsigned integer).

The first two optimizations are related. A floating point number is *normalized* by adjusting the exponent to eliminate leading zeros from the mantissa. In decimal, for example, 0.003×10^4 can be normalized to 3×10^1. Interestingly, normalizing a binary floating point number always produces a leading bit of 1 (expect in the special case of zero). Therefore, to increase the number of bits available to hold values, floating point representations do not store the leading bit of the mantissa. Instead, they simply assume the leading bit is one.

An example will clarify the concepts. The example we will use is IEEE† standard 754, which is widely used in the computer industry. The standard specifies both *single precision* and *double precision* numbers. According to the standard, a single precision value occupies thirty-two bits, and a double precision value occupies sixty-four bits. Figure 3.9 illustrates how the IEEE standard divides a floating point number into three fields.

Figure 3.9 The format of a single precision and a double precision floating point number, according to IEEE standard 754, with the lowest bit in each field labeled. Field *S* denotes a sign bit, and other fields contain the exponent and mantissa.

IEEE uses bit little endian numbering for the bits, which means that the least significant bit is assigned number zero. In single precision, for example, the twenty-three rightmost bits, which constitute a mantissa, are numbered zero through twenty-two. The next eight bits, which comprise an exponent, are numbered twenty-three through thirty, and the most significant bit, which contains a sign, is number thirty-one. For double precision, the mantissa increases to fifty-two bits and the exponent increases to eleven.

The IEEE standard specifies that the value stored in the exponent field consists of the true exponent plus a *bias constant*. For example, the bias constant used with single precision is one hundred twenty-seven‡. Thus, if the true exponent is two, the exponent field in a single precision value is assigned the value one hundred twenty-nine. Using a bias allows exponents to be negative (e.g., an exponent of negative four is stored as one hundred twenty-three).

---

†IEEE stands for Institute of Electrical and Electronic Engineers, an organization that creates standards used in electronic digital systems.

‡The bias constant is $2^{k-1} - 1$ (e.g., the double precision bias constant is one thousand twenty-three), where k is the number of bits in the exponent field.

3.16 Special Values

Like most floating point representations, the IEEE standard follows the implicit leading bit assumption — a mantissa is assumed to have a leading one bit that is not stored. Of course, any representation that strictly enforces the assumption of a leading one bit is useless because the representation cannot store the value zero. To handle zero, the IEEE standard makes an exception — when all bits are zero, the implicit assumption is ignored, and the stored value is taken to be zero.

The IEEE standard includes two other special values that are reserved to represent positive and negative infinity: the exponent contains all ones and the mantissa contains all zeros. The point of including values for infinity is that some digital systems do not have facilities to handle errors such as arithmetic overflow. On such systems, it is important that a value be reserved so the software can determine that a floating point operation failed.

3.17 Range Of IEEE Floating Point Values

The IEEE standard for single precision floating point allows normalized values in which the exponent ranges from negative one hundred twenty-seven through one hundred twenty-eight. Thus, the approximate range of values that can be represented is:

$$2^{-126} \text{ to } 2^{127}$$

which is approximately:

$$10^{-38} \text{ to } 10^{38}$$

For a double precision value, the range is considerably greater. The approximate range is:

$$10^{-308} \text{ to } 10^{308}$$

3.18 Data Aggregates

So far, we have only considered the representation for individual data items such as characters, integers, or floating point numbers. Most programming languages allow a programmer to specify *aggregate* values that contain multiple data items, such as *arrays*, *records*, or *structures*. How are such values stored? In general, an aggregate value occupies contiguous bytes. Thus, on a computer that uses an eight-bit byte, a data aggregate that consists of three sixteen-bit integers occupies six contiguous bytes as Figure 3.10 illustrates.

0	1	2	3	4	5
integer #1		integer #2		integer #3	

Figure 3.10 A data aggregate consisting of three sixteen-bit integers arranged in contiguous bytes. In the figure, the six bytes have been numbered in big endian order.

We will see later that some memory systems do not permit arbitrary data types to be contiguous. Thus, we will reconsider data aggregates when we discuss memory architecture.

3.19 Program Representation

Modern computers are classified as *stored program computers* because programs as well as data are placed in memory. We will discuss program representation and storage in the next chapters, including the structure of instructions the computer understands and their storage in memory. For now, it is sufficient to understand that each computer defines a specific set of operations and a format in which each is stored. On some computers, for example, each instruction is the same size as other instructions; on other computers, the instruction size varies. We will see that on a typical computer, an instruction occupies multiple bytes. Thus, the bit and byte numbering schemes that the computer uses for data values also apply to instructions.

3.20 Summary

The underlying digital hardware has two possible output values; we think of the output as a binary digit (bit), and use bits to represent data and programs. Each computer defines a byte size, and current systems typically use eight bits per byte.

A set of bits can be used to represent a character from the computer's character set, an unsigned integer, a single or double precision floating point value, or a computer program. Representations are chosen carefully to maximize the flexibility and speed of the hardware while keeping the cost low. The two's complement representation for signed integers is particularly popular because a single piece of hardware can be constructed that performs operations on either two's complement integers or unsigned integers.

Organizations, such as ANSI and IEEE, have created standards for representation; such standards allow hardware manufactured by two separate organizations to interoperate and exchange data.

EXERCISES

3.1 Give a mathematical proof that a string of k bits can represent 2^k possible values (hint: argue by induction on the number of bits).

3.2 What is the value of the following binary string in hexadecimal?

1101 1110 1010 1101 1011 1110 1110 1111

3.3 Write a computer program that determines whether the computer on which it is running uses big endian or little endian representation for integers.

3.4 Write a computer program that prints a string of zeros and ones that represent the bits of an integer. Place a blank between each bit, and add extra space after every four bits.

3.5 Write a computer program that determines whether the computer on which it is running uses one's complement, two's complement, or (possibly) some other representation for signed integers.

3.6 Write a computer program that determines whether the computer on which it is running uses the ASCII or EBCDIC character set.

3.7 Write a computer program that adds one to the largest possible positive integer to determine whether the computer uses two's complement arithmetic.

3.8 Write a computer program to display the value of a byte in hexadecimal, and apply the program to an array of bytes. Add extra space after every four bytes to make the output easier to read.

3.9 Extend the hexadecimal dump program in the previous exercise to also print the character representation of any printable character. For characters that do not have a printable representation, arrange for the program to print a period.

Processors

The Engines That Drive Computation

4

The Variety Of Processors
And Computational Engines

4.1 Introduction

Previous chapters describe the basic building blocks used to construct computer systems: digital logic and representations used for data types such as characters, integers, and floating point numbers. This chapter begins an investigation of one of three key elements of any computer system: a processor. The chapter introduces the general concept, describes the variety of processors, and discusses the relationship between clock rate and processing rate. The next chapters extend the basic description by explaining instruction sets, addressing modes, and the functions of a general-purpose CPU.

4.2 Von Neumann Architecture

One organization of computer hardware has proven to be so valuable that it is now pervasive: most computers follow the same general organization. We use the term *Von Neumann architecture* to characterize the approach†.

In essence, a computer that follows the Von Neumann architecture uses the *stored program* approach in which a program resides in memory. The hardware for a Von Neumann machine consists of three principle components that interact: processor, memory, and I/O facilities. Figure 4.1 illustrates the concept.

---

†The name is taken from John Von Neumann, a mathematician who first proposed the architecture.

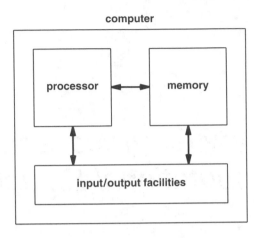

Figure 4.1 Illustration of the Von Neumann architecture. Both programs and data can be stored in memory.

4.3 Definition Of A Processor

Although programmers tend to think of a conventional computer and often use the term *processor* as a synonym for the *Central Processing Unit* (*CPU*), computer architects have a much broader meaning that includes the processors used in small devices like cell phones and portable CD players, the specialized processors used in video games and other graphics equipment, and the powerful processors used for scientific computing. To an architect, a *processor* refers to a digital device that can perform a computation involving multiple steps. Individual processors are not complete computers; they are merely one of the building blocks that an architect uses to construct a computer system. Thus, although it can compute more than the combinatorial Boolean logic circuits we examined in Chapter 2, a processor need not be extensive or powerful. In particular, some processors are significantly less powerful than the general-purpose CPU found in a typical PC. The next sections help clarify the definition by examining characteristics of processors and explaining some of the ways they can be used.

4.4 The Range Of Processors

Because processors span a broad range of functionality and many variations exist, no single description adequately captures all the properties of processors. Instead, to help us appreciate the many designs, we need to divide processors into categories according to functionality and intended use. For example, we can use four categories to explain whether a processor can be adapted to new computations. The categories are listed in order of flexibility:

- Fixed logic

- Selectable logic

- Parameterized logic

- Programmable logic

A *fixed logic processor*, which is the least flexible, performs a single operation. More important, all the functionality needed to perform the operation is built in when the processor is created, and the functionality cannot be altered without changing the underlying hardware†. For example, a fixed logic processor can be designed to compute a function, such as *sine(x)*, or to perform a graphics operation needed in a video game.

A *selectable logic processor* has slightly more flexibility than a fixed logic processor. In essence, a selectable logic processor contains facilities needed to perform more than one function; the exact function is specified when the processor is invoked. For example, a selectable logic processor might be designed to compute either *sine(x)* or *cosine(x)*.

A *parameterized logic processor* offers additional flexibility because although it only computes a predetermined function, the processor accepts a set of parameters that control the computation. For example, consider a parameterized processor that computes a hash function, *h(x)*. The hash function uses two constants, *p* and *q*, and computes the hash of *x* by computing the remainder of *x* when multiplied by *p* and divided by *q*. A parameterized processor for such a hash function allows constants *p* and *q* to be changed each time the processor is invoked. That is, in addition to the input, *x*, the processor accepts additional parameters, *p* and *q*, that control the operation.

A *programmable logic processor* offers the most flexibility because it allows the sequence of steps to be changed each time the processor is invoked — the processor can be given a program to run, typically by placing the program in memory.

4.5 Hierarchical Structure And Computational Engines

A large processor, such as a modern, general-purpose CPU, is so complex that no human can understand the entire processor as a single unit. To control the complexity, computer architects use a hierarchical approach in which subparts of the processor are designed and tested independently before being combined into the final design.

Some of the independent subparts of a large processor are so sophisticated that they fit our definition of a processor — the subpart can perform a computation that involves multiple steps. For example, a general-purpose CPU that has instructions for *sine* and *cosine* might be constructed by first building and testing a trigonometry processor, and then combining the trigonometry processor with other pieces to form the final CPU.

---

†Engineers use the term *hardwired* for functionality that cannot be changed without altering the underlying wiring.

How do we describe a subpiece of a large, complex processor that acts independently and performs a computation? Some engineers use the terms *computational engine*. The term *engine* usually implies that the subpiece fills a specific role and is less powerful than the overall unit. For example, Figure 4.2 illustrates a CPU that contains several engines.

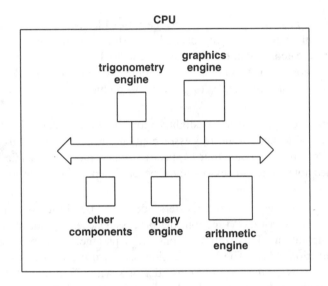

Figure 4.2 An example of a CPU that includes multiple engines plus other components. The large arrow in the center of the figure indicates a central interconnect mechanism that the components use to coordinate.

The CPU in the figure includes a special-purpose *graphics engine*. Graphics engines are common because many computers have graphics displays, and a graphics engine can perform common operations at high speed. For example, a graphics engine might include facilities to move a rectangle across a bit-mapped display (e.g., in response to mouse input) or to repaint the surface of a graphical figure after it has been moved (e.g., in response to a joystick movement).

As another example of engines, the CPU in Figure 4.2 also includes a *query engine*. Query engines and closely related *pattern engines* are used in database processors. A query engine examines a database record at high speed to determine if the record satisfies the query; a pattern engine examines a string of bits to determine if the string matches a specified pattern (e.g., to test whether a document contains a particular word).

4.6 Structure Of A Conventional Processor

Although the imaginary CPU described above contains many engines, most processors do not. Two questions arise, what engine(s) are found in a conventional processor, and how are they interconnected? This section answers the questions broadly, and later sections give more detail.

Although a practical processor contains many subcomponents with complex interconnections among them, we can view a processor has having five conceptual units:

- Controller
- Computational engine (ALU)
- Local data storage
- Internal interconnection(s)
- External interface

Figure 4.3 illustrates the concept.

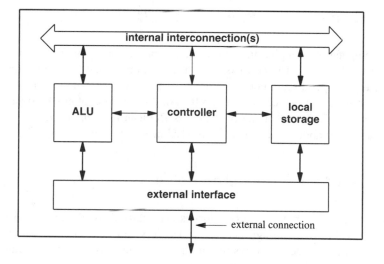

Figure 4.3 The five major units found in a conventional processor. The external interface connects to the rest of the computer system.

Controller. The controller forms the heart of a processor. Controller hardware has overall responsibility for program execution. That is, the controller steps through the program and coordinates the actions of all other hardware units to perform the specified operations.

Computational Engine. As the next section explains, the computational engine in a processor performs all computational tasks, including arithmetic operations and Boolean (logical) operations. The computational engine does not perform multiple steps or initiate activities. Instead, the engine only operates at the request of the controller.

Local Data Storage. A processor must have at least some local storage to hold data values such as operands given to the computational engine or the results of a computation. As we will see, local storage usually takes the form of hardware *registers* — values must be loaded into the hardware registers before they can be used in computation.

Internal Interconnection(s). A processor contains one or more hardware mechanisms that are used to transfer values between the other hardware units. For example, the interconnection hardware is used to move data values from the local storage to the computational engine or to move results from the computation engine to local storage. Architects sometimes use the term *data path* to describe an internal interconnection.

External Interface. The external interface unit handles all communication between the processor and the rest of the computer system. In particular, the external interface manages communication between the processor and external memory.

4.7 Definition Of An Arithmetic Logic Unit (ALU)

The computational engine in a conventional processor is known as the *Arithmetic Logic Unit (ALU)*. An ALU consists of a single, complex hardware unit that can perform a variety of operations. For example, besides integer arithmetic, an ALU provides operations on bits, such as left or right shift. An ALU also contains hardware that performs logical (i.e. Boolean) operations such as Boolean *and*, *or*, *exclusive or*, and *not*. We will learn more about functions that an ALU provides later.

4.8 Processor Categories And Roles

Understanding the range of processors is especially difficult for someone who has not encountered hardware design because processors can be used in a variety of roles. It may help if we consider the ways that hardware devices use processors and how processors function in each role. Here are five examples:

- Coprocessors
- Microcontrollers
- Microsequencers
- Embedded system processors
- General-purpose processors

Coprocessors. A coprocessor operates in conjunction with and under the control of another processor. Usually, a coprocessor consists of a special-purpose processor that performs a single task at high speed. For example, some CPUs use a coprocessor known as a *floating point accelerator* to speed the execution of arithmetic operations when a floating point operation occurs, the CPU automatically passes the necessary values to the coprocessor, obtains the result, and then continues execution. In architectures where a running program does not know which operations are performed directly by the CPU and which operations are performed by a coprocessor, we say that the operation of a coprocessor is *transparent* to the software. Typical coprocessors use fixed or selectable logic, which means that the functions the coprocessor can perform are determined when the coprocessor is designed.

Microcontrollers. A microcontroller consists of a programmable device dedicated to the control of a physical system. For example, microcontrollers run physical systems such as the engine in a modern automobile, the landing gear on an airplane, and the automatic door in a grocery store. In many cases, a microcontroller performs a trivial function that does not require computation in the usual sense. Instead, a microcontroller tests sensors and sends signals to control devices. Figure 4.4 lists an example of the steps a typical microcontroller can be programmed to perform:

```
do forever {
        wait for the sensor to be tripped;
        turn on power to the door motor;
        wait for a signal that indicates the
            door is open;
        wait for the sensor to reset;
        delay ten seconds;
        turn off power to the door motor;
}
```

Figure 4.4 Example of the steps a microcontroller performs. In most cases, microcontrollers are dedicated to trivial control tasks.

Microsequencers. A microsequencer acts like a microcontroller except instead of controlling external hardware, a microsequencer controls coprocessors and other engines within a larger processor. To understand the function, imagine a processor in which a set of coprocessors do almost all the work — the microsequencer does not perform any operation itself. Instead, the microsequencer merely invokes other hardware units, and each unit performs the appropriate task. Hardware units invoked by a microsequencer are usually quite basic (e.g., integer arithmetic, floating point arithmetic, data movement, or delay timing). Thus, a program for a microsequencer specifies which hardware unit to invoke at any time. For example, a microsequencer might request the data movement unit to move two data values into the floating point unit, request the floating point unit to perform an addition, and then request the data movement unit to move the result into memory.

Embedded System Processors. An embedded system processor runs sophisticated electronic devices such as a DVD player or a television. For example, a dialup modem might contain an embedded system processor that handles communication details (e.g., printing messages for a user) as well as control details (e.g., sensing whether the phone line is connected or whether a dialtone is present). The processors used for embedded systems are usually more powerful than the processors used as microcontrollers, but may not contain all the functions found on general-purpose CPUs.

General-Purpose Processors. General-purpose processors are the most familiar and need little explanation. For example, the CPU in a PC is a general-purpose processor.

4.9 Processor Technologies

How are processors created? Originally, a processor was created from digital logic circuits. Individual circuits were connected together on a circuit board, which then plugged into a chassis to form a working computer. By the 1970s, large-scale integrated circuit technology arrived, which meant that the smallest and least powerful processors — such as those used for microcontrollers — could each be implemented on a single integrated circuit. As integrated circuit technology improved and the number of transistors on a chip increased, a single chip became capable of holding more powerful processors. Today, many of the most powerful general-purpose processors consist of a single integrated circuit.

4.10 Stored Programs

We said that a processor performs a computation that involves multiple steps. Although some processors have the series of steps built into the hardware, most do not. Instead, they are *programmable* (i.e., they rely on a mechanism known as *programming*). That is, the sequence of steps to be performed comprise a program that is placed in a location the processor can access; the processor accesses the program and follows the specified steps.

Computer programmers are familiar with conventional computer systems that use main memory as the location that holds a program. The program is loaded into memory each time a user runs the application. The chief advantage of using main memory to hold programs lies in the ability to change the program. The next time a user runs a program after it has been changed, the altered version will be used.

Although our conventional notion of programming works well for general-purpose processors, other types of processors use alternative mechanisms that are not as easy to change. For example, the program for a microcontroller usually resides in hardware known as *Read Only Memory* (*ROM*†). In fact, the ROM that contains the program may reside on an integrated circuit along with a microcontroller that runs the program. For example, the microcontroller used in an automobile may reside on a single integrated circuit that also contains the program the microcontroller runs.

The important point is that programming is a broad notion·

> *To a computer architect, a processor is classified as programmable if at some level of detail, the processor is separate from the program it runs. To a user, it may appear that the program and processor are integrated, and it may not be possible to change the program without replacing the processor.*

4.11 The Fetch-Execute Cycle

How does a programmable processor access and perform steps of a program? Although the details vary among processors, all programmable processors follow the same fundamental paradigm. The underlying mechanism is known as the *fetch-execute cycle*.

To implement fetch-execute, a processor automatically moves through a program, performing each step. That is, each programmable processor executes two basic functions repeatedly. Algorithm 4.1 gives the two fundamental steps‡.

Algorithm 4.1

Repeat forever {

       Fetch: access the next step of the program from the location in which the program has been stored.

       Execute: Perform the step of the program.

}

Algorithm 4.1

---

†Later chapters describe memory in more detail.

‡Note that the algorithm presented here is a simplified form; when we discuss I/O, we will see how the algorithm is extended to handle device interrupts.

The important point is:

> *At some level, every programmable processor implements a fetch-execute cycle.*

Several questions arise. Exactly how is the program represented? How does a processor identify the "next" step of a program? What are the possible operations that can be performed during the execution phase of the fetch-execute cycle? How does the processor perform each operation? The next chapters will answer each of these questions in more detail. The remainder of this chapter concentrates on three questions: how does a processor begin with the first step of a program, what happens when the processor reaches the end of a program, and how fast does a processor operate?

4.12 Clock Rate And Instruction Rate

One of the primary questions about processors concerns speed: how fast does the fetch-execute cycle operate? The answer depends on the processor, the technology used to store a program, and the time required to execute each instruction. On one hand, a processor used as a microcontroller to actuate a physical device (e.g., an electric door) can be relatively slow because a response time under one-tenth of a second seems fast to a human. On the other hand, a processor used in the highest-speed computers must be as fast as possible because the goal is maximum performance.

As we saw in Chapter 2, a clock is used to control the rate at which the underlying digital logic operates, and anyone who has purchased a computer knows that a salesperson implies that a faster clock rate will produce higher performance. However, it is important to realize that the clock rate does not give the rate at which the fetch-execute cycle proceeds. In particular, the time required for the *execute* portion of the cycle depends on the instruction being executed. We will see later that operations involving memory access or I/O require more time (i.e., more clock cycles) than those that do not. The time also varies among basic arithmetic operations: integer multiplication or division requires more time than integer addition or subtraction. Floating point computation is especially costly because floating point operations usually require more clock cycles than equivalent integer operations. Floating point multiplication or division stands out as especially costly — a single floating point division can require orders of magnitude more clock cycles than an integer addition.

For now, it is sufficient to remember the general principle:

> *The fetch-execute cycle does not proceed at a fixed rate because the time taken to execute an instruction depends on the operation being performed. An operation such as multiplication requires more time than an operation such as addition.*

4.13 Control: Getting Started And Stopping

So far, we have discussed a processor running a fetch-execute cycle without giving details. We now need to answer two basic questions. How does the processor start running the fetch-execute cycle? What happens after the processor executes the last step in a program?

The issue of program termination is the easiest to understand: processor hardware is not designed to stop. Instead, the fetch-execute cycle continues indefinitely. Of course, a processor can be permanently halted, but such a sequence is only used to power down a computer — in normal operations, the processor continues to execute one instruction after another.

In some cases, a program uses a loop to delay. For example, a microcontroller may need to wait for a sensor to indicate an external condition has been met before proceeding. The processor does not merely stop to wait for the sensor. Instead, the program contains a loop that repeatedly tests the sensor. Thus, from a hardware point of view, the fetch-execute cycle continues.

The notion of an indefinite fetch-execute cycle has a direct consequence for programming: software must be planned so a processor always has a next step to execute. In the case of a dedicated system such as a microcontroller that controls a physical device, the program consists of an infinite loop — when it finishes the last step of the program, the processor starts again at the first step. In the case of a general-purpose computer, an operating system is always present. The operating system can load an application into memory, and then direct the processor to run the application. To keep the fetch-execute cycle running, the operating system must arrange to regain control when the application finishes. When no application is running, the operating system enters a loop to wait for input (e.g., from a keyboard or mouse).

To summarize:

> *Because a processor runs the fetch-execute cycle indefinitely, a system must be designed to ensure that there is always a next step to execute. In a dedicated system, the same program executes repeatedly; in a general-purpose system, an operating system runs when no application is running.*

4.14 Starting The Fetch-Execute Cycle

How does a processor start the fetch-execute cycle? The answer is complex because it depends on the underlying hardware. For example, some processors have a hardware *reset*. On such processors, engineers arrange for a combinatorial circuit to apply voltage to the reset line until all system components are ready to operate. When voltage is removed from the reset line, the processor begins executing a program from a fixed location. For example, many processors start executing a program found at location zero in memory. The system architect must design the hardware to guarantee that a valid program will be placed in location zero before the processor starts.

The steps used to start a processor are known as a *bootstrap*. In an embedded environment, the program to be run usually resides in ROM. On a conventional computer, the hardware reads a copy of the operating system from disk and places the copy into memory before starting the processor. In either case, hardware assist is needed for bootstrap because a signal must be passed to the processor that causes the fetch-execute cycle to begin.

Many devices have a *soft power switch*, which means that the power switch does not actually turn power on or off. Instead, the switch acts like a sensor — the processor can interrogate the switch to determine its current position. Booting a device that has a softswitch is no different than booting other devices. When power is first applied, the processor boots, but then enters a loop that interrogates the soft power switch. Later, when the user presses the soft power switch, the hardware completes the bootstrap process.

4.15 Summary

A processor is a digital device that can perform a computation involving multiple steps. Processors can use fixed, selectable, parameterized or programmable logic. We use the term *engine* to identify a processor that is a subpiece of a more complex processor.

Processors are used in various roles, including coprocessors, microsequencers, microcontrollers, embedded system processors, and general-purpose processors. Although early processors were created from discrete logic, a modern processor is implemented as a single VLSI chip.

A processor is classified as programmable if at some level, the processor hardware is separate from the sequence of steps that the processor performs; from the point of view of the end user, however, it might not be possible to change the program without replacing the processor. All programmable processors follow a fetch-execute cycle; the time required for one cycle depends on the operation performed. Because fetch-execute processing continues indefinitely, a designer must construct a program in such a way that the processor always has an instruction to execute.

EXERCISES

4.1 Write a computer program that measures the difference in execution times between integer addition and integer division. Execute each operation 100,000 times, and compare the difference in running times. Repeat the experiment, and verify that no other activities on the computer interfere with the measurement.

4.2   Extend the measurement in the previous exercise to compare the difference between sixteen bit, thirty-two bit, and sixty-four bit integer addition.

4.3   Write a computer program that compares the difference in execution times between an integer division and a floating point division. To test the program, execute each operation 100,000 times, and compare the difference in running times.

5

Processor Types And Instruction Sets

5.1 Introduction

The previous chapter introduces a variety of processors and explains the fetch-execute cycle that programmable processors use. This chapter continues the discussion by focusing on the set of operations that a processor can perform. The chapter explains various approaches computer architects have chosen, and discusses the advantages and disadvantages of each. The next chapters extend the discussion by describing the various ways processors access operands.

5.2 Mathematical Power, Convenience, And Cost

What operations should a processor offer? From a mathematical point of view, a wide variety of computational models provide equivalent computing power. In theory, as long as a processor offers a few basic operations, the processor has sufficient power to compute any computable function†.

Programmers understand that although only a minimum set of operations are necessary, a minimum is neither convenient nor practical. That is, to a programmer, the set of available operations determines convenience rather than functionality. For example, it is possible to compute a quotient by repeated subtraction. However, writing a program that divides numbers for a processor that only provides subtraction is difficult, and the resulting code runs slowly. Thus, processors designed for arithmetic operations include hardware for division as well as hardware that performs subtraction.

---

†In a mathematical sense, only three operations are needed to compute any computable function: add one, subtract one, and branch if a value is nonzero.

To a computer architect, choosing a set of operations that the processor will perform represents a tradeoff. On one hand, adding an additional arithmetic operation, such as multiplication or division, provides convenience for the programmer. On the other hand, each additional operation adds more hardware and makes the processor design more difficult. Adding hardware also increases engineering considerations such as chip size, power consumption, and heat dissipation. Thus, because a laptop computer needs to conserve battery power and does not have an efficient cooling system, a processor designed for use in a laptop usually has fewer built-in operations than a processor designed for a desktop computer.

The point is that when considering the set of operations a given processor provides, we need to remember that the choice is a complex tradeoff. We can summarize:

The set of operations a processor provides represents a tradeoff among the cost of the hardware, the convenience for a programmer, and engineering considerations such as power consumption.

5.3 Instruction Set And Representation

When an architect designs a programmable processor, the architect must make two key decisions:

- The set of operations the hardware recognizes.
- The representation that the hardware uses for each operation.

We use the term *instruction set* to refer to the set of operations the hardware recognizes, and refer to each operation as an *instruction* (more precisely, a *type of instruction*). On each iteration of the fetch-execute cycle, the processor *executes* one instruction.

The definition of an instruction set includes an exact specification of how each instruction operates: the values on which the instruction acts and the results the instruction produces. In addition, the definition specifies allowable values (e.g., the division instruction requires the divisor to be nonzero) and error conditions (e.g., what happens if an addition results in an overflow). That is, the definition of an instruction set specifies the semantics or meaning.

The term *instruction format* refers to the binary representation that the hardware uses for instructions. The instruction format is important because it defines the boundary between hardware and software — a program must be encoded in the exact instruction format that a processor expects before the processor can execute the instructions. Thus, the instruction format defines the syntactic aspects of an instruction set.

5.4 Opcodes, Operands, And Results

Conceptually, each instruction contains three parts that specify: the exact operation to be performed, the value(s) to use, and where to place the result(s). The following paragraphs define the idea more precisely.

Opcode. The term *opcode* refers to the exact operation to be performed. An opcode is a number; when the instruction set is designed, each operation must be assigned a unique opcode. For example, integer addition might be assigned opcode five, and integer subtraction might be assigned opcode twelve.

Operands. The term *operand* refers to a value that is needed to perform an operation. The definition of an instruction set specifies the exact number of operands for each instruction, and the possible values (e.g., addition takes two signed integers).

Results. In some architectures, one or more of the operands specify where the processor should place results of an instruction (e.g., the result of an arithmetic operation); in others, the location of the result is determined automatically.

5.5 Typical Instruction Format

Each instruction is represented as a binary string. On most processors, an instruction begins with a field that contains the opcode, followed by fields that contain the operands. Figure 5.1 illustrates the general format.

Figure 5.1 The general instruction format that many processors use. The opcode at the beginning of an instruction determines how many operands follow.

5.6 Variable-Length Vs. Fixed-Length Instructions

The question arises: should each instruction be the same size (i.e., occupy the same number of bits) or should the length depend on the quantity and type of the operands? For example, consider integer arithmetic operations. Addition or subtraction operate on two values, but negation operates on a single value. Furthermore, a processor can handle multiple sizes of operands (e.g., a processor can have an instruction that adds a pair of sixteen-bit integers as well as an instruction that adds a pair of thirty-two bit integers). Should one instruction be shorter than another?

We use the term *variable-length* to characterize an instruction set that includes multiple instruction sizes, and the term *fixed-length* to characterize an instruction set in which every instruction is the same size.

From a programmer's point of view, variable-length instructions seem most appropriate because they make optimal use of memory — there are no wasted bits in the instruction because each instruction is exactly as long as it needs to be. From a hardware point of view, however, variable-length instructions require complex hardware to decode. As an alternative, fixed-length instructions require less complex hardware. Fixed-length instructions also allow a processor to operate at higher speed because the hardware can fetch and decode instructions without examining the opcode in each. Thus, processors optimized for high speed or low cost use fixed-length instructions. The point is:

> *Although the idea may seem inefficient to a programmer, using fixed-length instructions can make processor hardware less complex and faster.*

How does a processor that uses fixed-length instructions handle cases where an instruction does not need all operands? For example, how does a fixed-length instruction set accommodate both addition and negation? Interestingly, the hardware is designed to ignore fields that are unneeded for a given operation. Thus, an instruction set may specify that in some instructions, specific bits are *unused*†. To summarize:

> *When a fixed-length instruction set is employed, some instructions contain extra fields that the hardware ignores. The unused fields should be viewed as part of a hardware optimization, not as an indication of a poor design.*

5.7 General-Purpose Registers

A *register* is a high-speed hardware device that has a fixed size and supports two basic operations: *fetch* and *store*. We will see later that registers can operate in a variety of roles, including as a *program counter* that gives the address of the next instruction to execute. For now, however, we will restrict our attention to a simple case that is well-known to programmers: *general-purpose registers* that act as a temporary storage facility. A processor usually has a small number of general-purpose registers (e.g., fewer than one hundred), and each register is usually large enough to hold an integer. For example, on a processor that provides thirty-two bit arithmetic, each general-purpose register holds thirty-two bits. As a result, a general-purpose register can hold an operand needed for an arithmetic instruction or the result of such an instruction.

General-purpose registers are numbered from 0 through $N-1$. The processor provides instructions that can store a value into (or fetch a value from) a specified register. General-purpose registers have the same semantics as memory: a *fetch* operation returns

---

†Alternatively, some hardware requires unused bits to be zero.

the value specified in the previous *store* operation. Similarly, a *store* operation replaces the contents of the register with a new value.

5.8 Floating Point Registers And Register Identification

Processors that support floating point arithmetic often use a separate set of registers to hold floating point values. Confusion can arise because both general purpose registers and floating point registers are usually numbered starting at zero — the instruction determines which registers are used. For example, if registers 3 and 6 are specified as operands for an integer instruction, the processor will extract the operands from the general-purpose registers. However, if registers 3 and 6 are specified as operands for a floating point instruction, the floating point registers will be used.

5.9 Programming With Registers

Many processors require operands to be placed in general-purpose registers before an instruction is executed. Some processors also place the results of an instruction in a general-purpose register. Thus, to add two integers X and Y and place the result in Z, a programmer must create a series of instructions that move values to the corresponding registers. For example, if general-purpose registers 3, 6, and 7 are available, the program might contain four instructions that perform the following steps:

- Load a copy of X into register 3
- Load a copy of Y into register 6
- Add the value in register 3 to the value in register 6, and place the result in register 7
- Store a copy of the value in register 7 in Z

We will see that moving a value between memory and a register is relatively expensive, so performance is optimized by leaving values in registers if the value will be used again. Because a processor only contains a small number of registers, however, a programmer must decide which values to keep in the registers at any time; other values are kept in memory†. The process of choosing which values the registers contain is known as *register allocation*.

Many details complicate register allocation. One of the most common arises if an instruction generates a large result, called an *extended value*. For example, integer multiplication can produce a result that contains twice as many bits as either operand. Some processors offer facilities for *double precision* arithmetic (e.g., if a standard integer is thirty-two bits wide, a double precision integer occupies sixty-four bits).

To handle extended values, the hardware treats registers as consecutive. On such processors, for example, an instruction that loads a double precision integer into register

---

†The term *register spilling* refers to moving a value from a register into memory to make the register available for a new value.

4 will place half the integer in register 4 and the other half in register 5 (i.e., the value of register 5 will change even though the instruction contains no explicit reference). When choosing registers to use, a programmer must plan for instructions that place extended data values in consecutive registers.

5.10 Register Banks

An additional hardware detail complicates register allocation: some architectures divide registers into multiple *banks*, and require the operands for an instruction to come from separate banks. For example, on a processor that uses two register banks, an integer *add* instruction may require the two operands to be from separate banks.

To understand register banks, we must examine the underlying hardware. In essence, register banks allow the hardware to operate faster because each bank has a separate physical access mechanism and the mechanisms operate simultaneously. Thus, when the processor executes an instruction that accesses two operands in registers, both operands can be obtained at the same time. Figure 5.2 illustrates the concept.

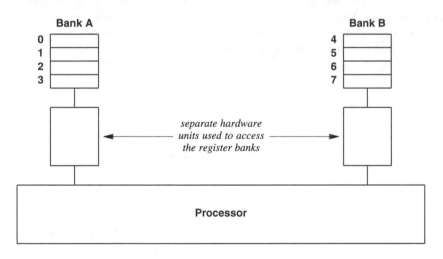

Figure 5.2 Illustration of eight registers divided into two banks. Hardware allows the processor to access both banks at the same time.

Register banks have an interesting consequence for programmers: it may not be possible to permanently assign data values to registers. To understand why, consider the following assignment statements that are typical of those used in a conventional programming language, and assume we want to implement the statements on a processor that has two register banks as Figure 5.2 illustrates.

$$R \leftarrow X + Y$$
$$S \leftarrow Z - X$$
$$T \leftarrow Y + Z$$

If the values in the above assignment statements are located in registers, each assignment statement corresponds to a single instruction. A programmer must ensure that the operands for each instruction come from separate register banks. For example, in the first addition, X and Y must be placed in registers from opposite banks: if we assume X is in a register in bank A, Y must be in a register in bank B. For the subtraction, Z must be a different bank than X (i.e., Z must be in a register in bank B). For the third assignment, Y and Z must be in different banks. Unfortunately, the first two assignments mean that Y and Z are located in the same bank. Thus, there is no possible assignment of X, Y, and Z to registers that works with all three instructions. We say that a *conflict* occurs.

What happens when a register conflict arises? The programmer must either reassign registers or insert an instruction to copy values. For example, suppose we insert an instruction to copy the value of Z into a register in bank A, Z'. The third assignment statement can be coded by referencing the register that contains Y and the register that contains Z'.

5.11 Complex And Reduced Instruction Sets

Computer architects divide instruction sets into two broad categories that are used to classify processors†:

- Complex Instruction Set Computer (CISC)
- Reduced Instruction Set Computer (RISC)

A *CISC processor* usually includes many instructions (typically hundreds), and each instruction can perform an arbitrarily complex computation. Intel's Pentium processor is classified as CISC because the processor provides hundreds of instructions, including complex instructions that require a long time to execute (e.g., one instruction manipulates graphics in memory and others compute the *sine* and *cosine* functions).

A *RISC processor* is constrained. Instead of arbitrary instructions, a RISC design strives for a minimum set that is sufficient for all computation (e.g., thirty-two instructions). Instead of allowing a single instruction to compute an arbitrary function, each instruction performs a basic computation. To achieve the highest possible speed, RISC designs constrain instructions to be a fixed-size. Finally, as the next section explains, a RISC processor is designed to execute an instruction in one clock cycle‡. Motorola's MIPS processor is classified as RISC because the processor only has thirty-two instructions, and each instruction takes one clock cycle to execute.

---

†Instead of using the full name, most engineers use the acronyms, which are pronounced *sisk* and *risk*.
‡Recall from Chapter 2 that a clock, which pulses at regular intervals, is used to control digital logic.

We can summarize:

> *A processor is classified as CISC if the instruction set contains in-structions that perform complex computations that can require long times; a processor is classified as RISC if it contains a small number of instructions that can each execute in one clock cycle.*

5.12 RISC Design And The Execution Pipeline

We said that a RISC processor executes one instruction per clock cycle. In fact, a more accurate version of the statement is: a RISC processor is designed so the processor can complete one instruction on each clock cycle. To understand the subtle difference, it is important to know how the hardware works. We said that a processor performs a fetch-execute cycle by first fetching an instruction and then executing the instruction. In fact, the processor divides the fetch-execute cycle into several steps such as:

- Fetch the next instruction
- Examine the opcode to determine how many operands are needed
- Fetch each of the operands (e.g., extract values from registers)
- Perform the operation specified by the opcode
- Store the result in the location specified (e.g., a register)

To enable high speed, RISC processors contain parallel hardware units that each perform one step listed above. The hardware is arranged in a multistage *pipeline*, which means the results from one hardware unit are passed to the next hardware unit. Figure 5.3 illustrates a pipeline.

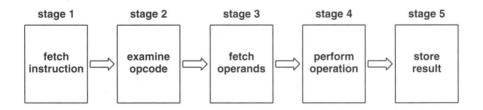

Figure 5.3 An example pipeline of five hardware stages that are used to per-form the fetch-execute cycle.

As the figure illustrates, an instruction moves left to right through the pipeline. The first stage fetches the instruction, the next stage examines the opcode, and so on. Whenever the clock ticks, all stages simultaneously pass the instruction to the right.

Thus, instructions move through the pipeline like an assembly line: at any time, the pipeline contains five instructions.

The speed of a pipeline arises because all stages can operate in parallel — while the fourth stage executes an instruction, the third stage fetches the operands for the next instruction. Thus, the fourth stage does not need to delay because an instruction is ready on each clock cycle. Figure 5.4 illustrates how instructions pass through a five-stage pipeline.

	clock	stage 1	stage 2	stage 3	stage 4	stage 5
Time	1	inst. 1	-	-	-	-
	2	inst. 2	inst. 1	-	-	-
	3	inst. 3	inst. 2	inst. 1	-	-
	4	inst. 4	inst. 3	inst. 2	inst. 1	-
	5	inst. 5	inst. 4	inst. 3	inst. 2	inst. 1
	6	inst. 6	inst. 5	inst. 4	inst. 3	inst. 2
	7	inst. 7	inst. 6	inst. 5	inst. 4	inst. 3
	8	inst. 8	inst. 7	inst. 6	inst. 5	inst. 4

Figure 5.4 Instructions passing through a five-stage pipeline. Once the pipeline is filled, each stage is busy on each clock cycle.

The figure clearly illustrates that although a RISC processor cannot perform all the steps needed to fetch and execute an instruction in one clock cycle, parallel hardware allows the processor to finish one instruction per clock cycle. We can summarize:

Although a RISC processor cannot perform all steps of the fetch-execute cycle in a single clock cycle, an instruction pipeline with parallel hardware provides approximately the same performance: once the pipeline is full, one instruction completes on every clock cycle.

5.13 Pipelines And Instruction Stalls

We say that the instruction pipeline is *transparent* to programmers because the instruction set does not contain any explicit references to the pipeline. That is, the hardware is constructed so the results of a program are the same whether or not a pipeline is present. Although transparency can be an advantage, it can also be a disadvantage because a programmer who does not understand the pipeline can inadvertently introduce inefficiencies.

To understand the effect of programming choices on a pipeline, consider a program that contains two successive instructions that perform an addition and subtraction on operands and results located in registers A, B, C, D, and E:

$$\text{Instruction K:} \qquad C \leftarrow \text{add A B}$$
$$\text{Instruction K+1:} \quad D \leftarrow \text{subtract E C}$$

Although instruction K can proceed through the pipeline from beginning to end, instruction K+1 encounters a problem because operand C is not available in time. That is, the hardware must wait for instruction K to finish before fetching the operands for instruction K+1. We say that a stage of the pipeline *stalls* to wait for the operand to become available. Figure 5.5 illustrates what happens during a pipeline stall.

	clock	stage 1	stage 2	stage 3	stage 4	stage 5
	1	inst. K	inst. K-1	inst. K-2	inst. K-3	inst. K-4
Time	2	inst. K+1	inst. K	inst. K-1	inst. K-2	inst. K-3
	3	inst. K+2	inst. K+1	inst. K	inst. K-1	inst. K-2
	4	inst. K+3	inst. K+2	(inst. K+1)	inst. K	inst. K-1
	5	-	-	(inst. K+1)	-	inst. K
	6	-	-	inst. K+1	-	-
	7	inst. K+4	inst. K+3	inst. K+2	inst. K+1	-
	8	inst. K+5	inst. K+4	inst. K+3	inst. K+2	inst. K+1

Figure 5.5 Illustration of a pipeline stall. Instruction K+1 cannot proceed until operand C becomes available.

The figure shows a normal pipeline running until clock cycle 4. Instruction K+1 has reached stage 3†. Because the value of C has not been computed, stage 3 cannot fetch the value. Thus, stages 1 through 3 stall during clock cycles 4 and 5. At clock cycle 6, stage 3 can fetch the value of C, and pipeline processing continues.

The rightmost column in Figure 5.5 shows the effect of a stall: the final stage of the pipeline does not produce any results during clock cycles 6 and 7. To describe the delay between the cause of a stall and the time at which output stops, we say that a *bubble* passes through the pipeline. Of course, the bubble is only apparent to an outsider — an instruction always passes directly to the next stage when the current stage completes.

---

†Recall that in our examples, stage 3 fetches the operands for an instruction.

5.14 Other Causes Of Pipeline Stalls

In addition to waiting for operands, a pipeline can stall when the processor executes any instruction that delays processing or disrupts the normal flow. For example, a stall can occur when a processor:

- Accesses external storage
- Invokes a coprocessor
- Branches to a new location
- Calls a subroutine

The most sophisticated processors contain additional hardware to avoid stalls. For example, some processors contain two copies of a pipeline, which allows the processor to start decoding the instruction that will be executed if a branch is taken as well as the instruction that will be executed if a branch is not taken. The two copies operate until a branch instruction can be executed. At that time, the hardware knows which copy of the pipeline to follow; the other copy is ignored.

5.15 Consequences For Programmers

To achieve maximum speed, a program must be written to accommodate an instruction pipeline. For example, a programmer should avoid introducing unnecessary branch instructions. Similarly, instead of referencing a result register immediately in the following instruction, the reference can be delayed. As an example, Figure 5.6 shows how code can be rearranged to run faster.

C ← add A B	C ← add A B
D ← subtract E C	F ← add G H
F ← add G H	M ← add K L
J ← subtract I F	D ← subtract E C
M ← add K L	J ← subtract I F
P ← subtract M N	P ← subtract M N
(a)	**(b)**

Figure 5.6 (a) A list of instructions, and (b) the instructions reordered to run faster. Reducing pipeline stalls increases speed.

In the figure, the optimized program separates references from computation. For example, in the original program, the second instruction references value C, which is produced by the previous instruction. Thus, a stall occurs between the first and second instructions. Moving the subtraction to a later point in the program allows the processor to continue to operate without a stall.

Of course, a programmer can choose to view a pipeline as an automatic optimization instead of a programming burden.

> *Although hardware that uses an instruction pipeline will not run at full speed unless programs are written to accommodate the pipeline, a programmer can choose to ignore pipelining and assume the hardware will automatically increase speed whenever possible.*

5.16 Programming, Stalls, And No-Op Instructions

In some cases, the instructions in a program cannot be rearranged to prevent a stall. In such cases, programmers usually document stalls so anyone reading the code will understand that a stall occurs. Such documentation is especially helpful if a program is modified because the programmer who performs the modification can reconsider the situation and attempt to reorder instructions to prevent a stall.

How should programmers document a stall? One technique is obvious: insert a comment that explains the reason for a stall. However, another technique is available: insert extra instructions in the code to show where instructions can be inserted to fill the pipeline. Of course, the extra instructions must be innocuous — they cannot change the values in registers or otherwise affect the program. In many cases, the hardware provides the answer: a *no-op*. That is, an instruction that does absolutely nothing except occupy time. The point is:

> *Most processors include a no-op instruction that does not reference data values, compute a result, or otherwise affect the state of the computer. A programmer can insert no-op instructions to document an instruction stall.*

5.17 Forwarding

One final hardware optimization further complicates an instruction pipeline: some hardware units are designed to detect and avoid stalls. In particular, an ALU can use a technique known as *forwarding* to solve the problem of successive arithmetic instructions passing results.

To understand how forwarding works, consider the example of two instructions where operands A, B, C, D, and E are in registers:

Instruction K: $C \leftarrow$ add A B

Instruction K+1: $D \leftarrow$ subtract E C

We said that such a sequence causes a stall on a pipelined processor. However, a processor that implements forwarding can avoid the stall by arranging for the hardware to detect the dependency and automatically pass the value for C from instruction K directly to instruction K+1. That is, a copy of the output from the ALU in instruction K is forwarded directly to the input of the ALU in instruction K+1. As a result, instructions continue to fill the pipeline, and no stall occurs.

5.18 Types Of Operations

When computer architects discuss instruction sets, they divide the instructions into a few basic categories. Figure 5.7 lists one possible division.

Arithmetic instructions (integer arithmetic)

Logical instructions (also called Boolean)

Data access and transfer instructions

Conditional and unconditional branch instructions

Floating point instructions

Processor control instructions

Figure 5.7 An example of categories used to classify instructions. A general-purpose processor includes instructions in all the categories.

5.19 Program Counter, Fetch-Execute, And Branching

Recall from Chapter 4 that every processor implements a basic fetch-execute cycle. During the cycle, control hardware in the processor automatically moves through instructions — once it finishes executing one instruction, the processor automatically moves to the next location in memory before fetching the next instruction. To implement the fetch-execute cycle, the processor uses a special-purpose internal register known as a *program counter*†.

When a fetch-execute cycle begins, the program counter contains the address of the next instruction to be executed. After an instruction has been fetched, the program counter is updated to the address of the next instruction. The update of the program counter during each fetch-execute cycle means the processor will automatically move through successive instructions in memory. Algorithm 5.1 specifies how the fetch-execute cycle moves through successive instructions.

---

†Some architects use the term *instruction pointer* instead of *program counter*; the two terms are equivalent.

Algorithm 5.1

Assign the program counter an initial program address. Repeat forever {

   Fetch: access the next step of the program from the location given by the program counter.

   Set an internal address register, A, to the address beyond the instruction that was just fetched.

   Execute: Perform the step of the program.

   Copy the contents of address register A to the program counter.

}

Algorithm 5.1

The algorithm allows us to understand how branch instructions work. There are two cases: absolute and relative. An *absolute branch* specifies the address of the next instruction to execute. Typically, an absolute branch instruction is known as a *jump*. During the execute step, a *jump* instruction loads the address given by the operand into internal register *A* that Algorithm 5.1 specifies. At the end of the fetch-execute cycle, the hardware copies the value into the program counter, which means the address will be used to fetch the next instruction. For example, the absolute branch instruction:

jump 0x05DE

causes the processor to load *0x05DE* into the internal address register, which is copied into the program counter before the next instruction is fetched. In other words, the next instruction fetch will occur at location *0x05DE*.

Unlike an absolute branch instruction, a *relative branch instruction* does not specify an exact memory address. Instead, a relative branch specifies a positive or negative increment for the program counter. For example, the instruction:

br +8

specifies branching to a location that is eight bytes beyond the current location (i.e., the current value of the program counter).

To implement relative branching, a processor adds the operand in the branch instruction to the program counter, and places the result in internal address register *A*. For example, if the branch operand is *-12*, the next instruction to be executed will be found at an address twelve bytes before the current instruction.

Most processors also provide an instruction to invoke a subroutine, typically *jsr*. In terms of the fetch-execute cycle, a *jsr* instruction operates like a branch instruction with one minor difference: before the branch occurs, the *jsr* instruction saves the value of the address register, *A*. When it finishes executing, a subroutine returns to the caller. To do so, the subroutine executes an absolute branch to the saved address. Thus, when the subroutine finishes, the fetch-execute cycle resumes at the instruction immediately following the *jsr*.

5.20 Subroutine Calls, Arguments, And Register Windows

A high-level language uses a subroutine call instruction, such as *jsr*, to implement a procedure or function call. The calling program supplies a set of *arguments* that the subroutine uses in its computation. For example, the function call *cos(3.14159)* has the floating point constant *3.14159* as an argument.

One of the principle differences among processors arises from the way the underlying hardware passes arguments to a subroutine. Some architectures use memory — the arguments are stored in memory before the call, and the subroutine extracts the values from memory, as needed. In other architectures, the processor uses either general-purpose or special-purpose registers to pass arguments.

Using either special-purpose or general-purpose registers to pass arguments is much faster than using memory because registers are part of the local storage in the processor itself. Because few processors provide special-purpose registers for argument passing, general-purpose registers are typically used. Unfortunately, general-purpose registers cannot be devoted exclusively to arguments because they are also needed for other computation (e.g., to hold operands for arithmetic operations). Thus, a programmer faces a tradeoff: using a general-purpose register to pass an argument can increase the speed of a subroutine call, but using the register to hold a data value can increase the speed of general computation. Thus, a programmer must choose which arguments to keep in registers and how many to store in memory.

Some modern processors include an optimization for argument passing known as a *register window*. Although a processor has a large set of general-purpose registers, the register hardware only exposes a subset of the registers at any time. The subset is known as a *window*. The window moves automatically each time a subroutine is invoked, and moves back when the subroutine returns. More important, the windows available to a program and subroutine overlap — some of the registers visible to the caller are visible to the subroutine. A caller places arguments in the registers that will overlap before calling a subroutine. Figure 5.8 illustrates the concept of a register window.

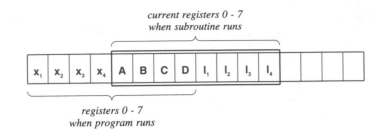

Figure 5.8 Illustration of a register window during a subroutine call. Values
A, *B*, *C*, and *D* correspond to arguments passed during a call.

As the figure shows, registers are always numbered from zero through the window
size minus one. However, the underlying register that corresponds to a given number
changes when a subroutine is called. Thus, the calling program places arguments *A*
through *D* in registers 4 through 7, and the subroutine finds the arguments in registers 0
through 3. Registers labeled x_i are only available to the calling program, and registers
labeled l_i are only available to the subroutine.

The illustration in Figure 5.8 uses a small window size (eight registers) to simplify
the diagram. In practice, processors that use a register window typically have larger
windows. For example, the Sparc architecture has one hundred twenty-eight or one
hundred forty-four physical registers and a window size of thirty-two registers; however, only eight of the registers in the window overlap (i.e., only eight registers can be
used to pass arguments).

5.21 An Example Instruction Set

An example instruction set will help clarify the concepts described above. We
have selected the MIPS processor as an example for two reasons. First, the MIPS processor is popular for use in embedded systems. Second, the MIPS instruction set is a
classic example of the instruction set offered by a RISC processor. Figure 5.9 lists the
instructions in the MIPS instruction set.

Instruction	Meaning
Arithmetic	
add	integer addition
subtract	integer subtraction
add immediate	integer addition (register + constant)
add unsigned	unsigned integer addition
subtract unsigned	unsigned integer subtraction
add immediate unsigned	unsigned addition with a constant
move from coprocessor	access coprocessor register
multiply	integer multiplication
multiply unsigned	unsigned integer multiplication
divide	integer division
divide unsigned	unsigned integer division
move from Hi	access high-order register
move from Lo	access low-order register
Logical (Boolean)	
and	logical *and* (two registers)
or	logical *or* (two registers)
and immediate	*and* of register and constant
or immediate	*or* of register and constant
shift left logical	shift register left N bits
shift right logical	shift register right N bits
Data Transfer	
load word	load register from memory
store word	store register into memory
load upper immediate	place constant in upper sixteen bits of register
move from coproc. register	obtain a value from a coprocessor
Conditional Branch	
branch equal	branch if two registers equal
branch not equal	branch if two registers unequal
set on less than	compare two registers
set less than immediate	compare register and constant
set less than unsigned	compare unsigned registers
set less than immediate	compare unsigned register and constant
Unconditional Branch	
jump	go to target address
jump register	go to address in register
jump and link	procedure call

Figure 5.9 An example instruction set. The table lists the instructions offered by the MIPS processor.

A MIPS processor contains thirty-two general-purpose registers, and most instructions require the operands and results to be in registers. For example, the *add* instruction takes three operands that are registers: the instruction adds the contents of the first two registers and places the result in the third.

In addition to the integer instructions that are listed in Figure 5.9, the MIPS architecture defines a set of floating point instructions for both single precision (i.e., thirty-two bit) and double precision (i.e., sixty-four bit) floating point values. The hardware provides a set of thirty-two floating point registers. Although they are numbered from zero to thirty-one, the floating point registers are completely independent of the general-purpose registers.

To handle double precision values, the floating point registers operate as pairs. That is, only an even numbered floating point register can be specified as an operand or target in a floating point instruction — the hardware uses the specified register plus the next odd numbered register as a combined storage unit to hold a double precision value. Figure 5.10 summarizes the MIPS floating point instruction set.

5.22 Minimalistic Instruction Set

It may seem that the instructions listed in Figure 5.9 are insufficient and that additional instructions are needed. For example, the MIPS architecture does not include an instruction that copies the contents of a register to another register, nor does the architecture include instructions that can add a value in memory to the contents of a register. Recall that the MIPS instruction set supports two principles: speed and minimalism. First, the basic instruction set has been designed carefully to ensure high speed (i.e., to ensure that one instruction can complete on every clock cycle). Second, the instruction set is *minimalistic* — it contains the fewest possible instructions necessary.

One feature of the MIPS architecture, which is also used in other RISC processors, helps achieve minimalism: fast access to a zero value. In the case of MIPS, register 0 provides the mechanism — the register is reserved and always contains the value zero. Thus, to test whether a register is zero, the value can be compared to register zero. Similarly, register zero can be used in any instruction. For example, to copy a value from one register to another, an *add* instruction can be used in which one of the two operands is register zero.

Instruction	**Meaning**
Arithmetic	
FP add	floating point addition
FP subtract	floating point subtraction
FP multiply	floating point multiplication
FP divide	floating point division
FP add double	double-precision addition
FP subtract double	double-precision subtraction
FP multiply double	double-precision multiplication
FP divide double	double-precision division
Data Transfer	
load word coprocessor	load value into FP register
store word coprocessor	store FP register to memory
Conditional Branch	
branch FP true	branch if FP condition is true
branch FP false	branch if FP condition is false
FP compare single	compare two FP registers
FP compare double	compare two double precision values

Figure 5.10 Floating point instructions defined by the MIPS architecture. Double precision values occupy two consecutive floating point registers.

5.23 The Principle Of Orthogonality

In addition to the technical aspects of instruction sets discussed above, an architect must consider the aesthetic aspects of a design. In particular, an architect strives for *elegance*. Elegance relates to human perception: how does the instruction set appear to a programmer? How do instructions combine to handle common programming tasks? Are the instructions balanced (if the set includes right-shift, does it also include left-shift)? Elegance calls for subjective judgment. However, experience with a few instruction sets often helps engineers and programmers recognize and appreciate elegance.

One particular aspect of elegance, known as *orthogonality*, concentrates on eliminating unnecessary duplication and overlap among instructions. We say that an instruction set is *orthogonal* if each instruction performs a unique task. An orthogonal instruction set has important advantages for programmers: orthogonal instructions can be understood more easily, and a programmer does not need to choose among multiple instructions that perform the same task. *Orthogonality* is so important that it has become a general principle of processor design. We can summarize:

> *The* principle of orthogonality *specifies that each instruction should perform a unique task without duplicating or overlapping the functionality of other instructions.*

5.24 Condition Codes And Conditional Branching

On many processors, each instruction produces a status, which the processor stores in an internal hardware mechanism. A later instruction can use the status to decide how to proceed. For example, when it executes an arithmetic instruction, the ALU sets a *condition code* that contains bits to record whether the result is positive, negative, zero, or an arithmetic overflow occurred. A *conditional branch* instruction that follows the arithmetic operation can test one or more of the condition code bits, and use the result to determine whether to branch.

An example will clarify how a condition code mechanism is used†. To understand the paradigm, consider a program that must place a zero in register 3 if the contents of register 4 are not equal to the contents of register 5. Figure 5.11 contains the code.

```
        cmp    r4, r5    # compare regs. 4 & 5, and set condition code
        be     lab1      # branch to lab1 if cond. code specifies equal
        mov    r3, 0     # place a zero in register 3
lab1: ...program continues at this point
```

Figure 5.11 An example of using a condition code. An ALU operation sets the condition code, and a later *conditional branch* instruction tests the condition code.

5.25 Summary

Each processor defines an instruction set that consists of operations the processor supports; the set is chosen as a compromise between programmer convenience and hardware costs. In some processors, each instruction is the same size, and in other processors size varies among instructions.

Most processors include a small set of general-purpose registers that are high-speed storage mechanisms. To program using registers, one loads values from memory into registers, performs a computation, and stores the result from a register into memory. To optimize performance, a programmer leaves values that will be used again in registers. On some architectures, registers are divided into banks, and a programmer must ensure that the operands for each instruction come from separate banks.

---

†Chapter 8 explains programming with condition codes and shows further examples.

Processors can be classified into two broad categories of CISC and RISC depending on whether they include many complex instructions or a minimal set of instructions. RISC architectures use an instruction pipeline to ensure that one instruction can complete on each clock cycle. Programmers can optimize performance by rearranging code to avoid pipeline stalls.

To implement conditional execution (e.g., an if-then-else), many processors rely on a condition code mechanism — an ALU instruction sets the condition code, and a later instruction (a conditional branch) tests the condition code.

EXERCISES

5.1   Classify the ARM architecture owned by ARM Limited and the SPARC architecture owned by Sun Microsystems Corporation as CISC or RISC.

5.2   Consider a pipeline of N stages in which stage i *takes time* t_i. Assuming no delay between stages, what is the total time (start to finish) that the pipeline will spend handling a single instruction?

5.3   In the previous exercise, how many instructions per second can the pipeline complete?

5.4   Given a pipeline, A, of 5 stages where each stage takes time t, produce a new pipeline, B, by dividing the third stage into two stages that each take time $t/2$. How many instructions per second does pipeline A complete per second? Pipeline B? Explain.

6

Operand Addressing And Instruction Representation

6.1 Introduction

The previous chapters discuss the variety of processor types and consider processor instruction sets. This chapter focuses on two details related to instructions: the way instructions are represented, and the ways that operands can be specified. We will see that the form of operands is especially relevant to programmers. We will also understand how the representation of instructions determines the possible operand forms.

The next chapter continues the discussion of processors by explaining how a Central Processing Unit (CPU) operates. We will see how a CPU combines many features we have discussed into a large, unified system.

6.2 Zero, One, Two, Or Three Address Designs

We said that an instruction is usually stored as an opcode followed by zero or more operands. How many operands are needed? The discussion in Chapter 5 assumes that the number of operands is determined by the operation being performed. Thus, an *add* instruction needs two operands because addition involves two quantities. Similarly, a Boolean *not* instruction needs one operand because logical inversion only involves one quantity. However, the example instruction set in Chapter 5 employs an additional operand on each instruction that specifies the location for the result. Thus, in the example instruction set, an *add* instruction requires three operands that specify the two values to be added and a location for the result.

Despite the intuitive appeal of a processor in which each instruction can have an arbitrary number of operands, many processors do not permit such a scheme. To understand why, we must consider the underlying hardware. First, because an arbitrary number of operands implies variable-length instructions, fetching and decoding instructions is less efficient than using fixed-length instructions. Second, because fetching an arbitrary number of operands takes time, the processor will run slower than a processor with a fixed number of operands.

It may seem that parallel hardware can solve some of the inefficiency. Imagine, for example, parallel hardware units that each fetch one operand of an instruction. If an instruction has two operands, two units operate simultaneously; if an instruction has four operands, four units operate simultaneously. However, parallel hardware uses more space on a chip and requires additional power. In addition, the number of pins on a chip limits the amount of data that can be accessed in parallel. Thus, parallel hardware is not an attractive option in many cases (e.g., a processor in a portable phone that operates on battery power).

Can an instruction set be designed without allowing arbitrary operands? If so, what is the smallest number of operands that can be useful for general computation? Early computers answered the question by using a scheme in which each instruction only has one operand. Later computers introduced instruction sets that limited each instruction to two operands. Surprisingly, computers also exist in which instructions have no operands. Finally, as we have seen in the previous chapter, some processors limit instructions to three operands.

6.3 Zero Operands Per Instruction

An architecture in which instructions have no operands is known as a *0-address* architecture. How can an architecture allow instructions that do not specify any operands? The answer is that operands must be *implicit*. That is, the location of the operands is already known. A 0-address architecture is also called a *stack architecture* because operands are kept on a stack. For example, an *add* instruction takes two values from the stack, adds them together, and places the result back on the stack. Of course, some of the instructions in a stack computer do allow a programmer to specify an operand: the *push* instruction places a new value on the top of the stack, and a *pop* instruction removes the top value from the stack and places the value in memory. Thus, to add seven to variable X on a stack machine, one might use a sequence of instructions similar to the example in Figure 6.1.

>   push X
>
>   push 7
>
>   add
>
>   pop X

Figure 6.1 An example of instructions used on a stack computer to add seven to a variable X. The architecture is known as a zero-address architecture because the operands for an instruction such as *add* are found on the stack.

6.4 One Operand Per Instruction

An architecture that limits each instruction to a single operand is classified as a *1-address* design. In essence, a 1-address design relies on an *implicit* operand for each instruction: a special register known as an *accumulator*†. The processor extracts the current value of the accumulator, performs the specified operation using the extracted value and the operand, and places the result back in the accumulator. We think of an instruction as operating on the value in the accumulator. For example, consider arithmetic operations. An addition instruction has only a single operand, X:

$$add   X$$

When it encounters such an instruction, the processor performs the following operation:

$$accumulator \leftarrow accumulator + X$$

Of course, the instruction set for a 1-address processor includes instructions that allow a programmer to load a constant or the value from a memory location into the accumulator or store the current value of the accumulator into a memory location.

6.5 Two Operands Per Instruction

Although it works well for arithmetic or logical operations, a 1-address design does not allow instructions to specify two values. For example, consider copying a value from one memory location to another. A 1-address design requires two instructions that load the value into the accumulator and then store the value in the new location. The design is especially inefficient for a system that moves graphics objects in display memory.

To overcome the limitations of 1-address systems, designers invented processors that allow each instruction to have two addresses. The approach is known as a *2-address* architecture. With a 2-address processor, an operation can be applied to a specified value instead of merely to the accumulator. Thus, in a 2-address processor,

---

†The general-purpose registers discussed in Chapter 5 can be considered an extension of the original accumulator concept.

$$\text{add} \quad X \quad Y$$

specifies that the value of X is to be added to the current value of Y:

$$Y \leftarrow Y + X$$

Because it allows an instruction to specify two operands, a 2-address processor can offer data movement instructions that treat the operands as a *source* and *destination*. For example, the instruction:

$$\text{move} \quad Q \quad R$$

copies data directly from Q to R†.

6.6 Three Operands Per Instruction

Although a 2-address design handles data movement, further optimization is possible, especially for processors that have multiple general-purpose registers: allow each instruction to specify three operands. Unlike a 2-address design, the key motivation for a *3-address* architecture does not arise from operations that require three input values. Instead, the point is that the third operand can specify a destination. For example, an addition operation can specify two values to be added as well as a destination for the result:

$$\text{add} \quad X \quad Y \quad Z$$

specifies an assignment of:

$$Z \leftarrow X + Y$$

6.7 Operand Sources And Immediate Values

The discussion above focuses on the number of operands that each instruction can have without specifying the exact details of an operand. Questions arise about the syntax and semantics of operands. How is a given operand represented in an instruction? Do all operands use the same representation? What meaning is given to a representation?

To understand the issue, observe that the data value used as an operand for an operation can be obtained in many ways. Figure 6.2 lists some of the possibilities for operands on a 3-address processor‡.

---

†Some architects reserve the term *2-address* to refer to an architecture in which both operands can specify a memory location, and use the term *1½-address* to refer to an architecture that allows one operand to be in memory but restricts the other operand to be in a register.

‡To increase performance, modern 3-address architectures often limit operands so that at most one of the operands in a given instruction refers to a value in memory; the other two operands must specify registers.

Operand that specifies a source

A signed constant
An unsigned constant
The contents of a register
The value in a memory location

Operand that specifies a destination

A single register
A pair of contiguous registers
A memory location

Figure 6.2 Examples of items an operand can reference in a 3-address processor. The operand can specify a value to be used in the instruction or a location into which the result should be placed.

Operands that contain an explicit constant are especially useful because programs use small constants (e.g., to increment a counter). That is, a constant to be used in a computation can be embedded in the instruction itself. Such a design improves programs by reducing the need for registers.

When a constant value appears in an operand, we say that the value is *immediate*. On some architectures, immediate values are interpreted as signed; on others, immediate values are interpreted as unsigned.

6.8 The Von Neumann Bottleneck

We said that conventional computers that store both programs and data in memory are known as Von Neumann computers. Operand addressing exposes the central weakness of a Von Neumann architecture: memory access can become a bottleneck. That is, because instructions are stored in memory, a processor must make at least one memory reference per instruction. If one or more operands specify items in memory, the processor must make additional memory references to fetch or store values. To optimize performance and avoid the bottleneck, operands must be taken from registers instead of memory.

The point is:

> *On a computer that follows the Von Neumann architecture, the time spent performing memory accesses can limit the overall performance. Architects use the term* Von Neumann bottleneck *to characterize the situation, and avoid the bottleneck with techniques such as restricting most operands to registers.*

6.9 Explicit And Implicit Operand Encoding

How should an operand be represented in an instruction? As Figure 6.2 shows, a string of bits is insufficient because we need to specify what the bits mean (e.g., whether they correspond to an immediate value, a register, or a memory location). There are two possibilities for specifying the interpretation of operands, as the next two sections describe.

6.9.1 Implicit Operand Encoding

An *implicit operand encoding* is easiest to understand: the opcode specifies the types of operands. That is, a processor that uses implicit encoding contains multiple opcodes for a given operation — each opcode corresponds to one possible combination of operands. For example, Figure 6.3 lists three instructions for addition that might be offered by a processor that uses implicit operand encoding.

Opcode	Operands		Meaning			
Add register	R1	R2	R1	←	R1	+ R2
Add immediate signed	R1	I	R1	←	R1	+ I
Add immediate unsigned	R1	UI	R1	←	R1	+ UI
Add memory	R1	M	R1	←	R1	+ memory[M]

Figure 6.3 An example of addition instructions for a processor that uses implicit operand encoding. The opcode tells the processor how to interpret each of the operands.

As the figure shows, not all operands need to have the same interpretation. For example, consider the *add immediate signed* instruction. The instruction takes two operands: the first operand is interpreted to be a register, and the second is interpreted to be a signed integer.

6.9.2 Explicit Operand Encoding

The chief disadvantage of implicit encoding is apparent from Figure 6.3: multiple opcodes are needed for a given operation. If the processor allows many types of operands, the list of opcodes can be large. As an alternative, an *explicit operand encoding* associates the type information with each operand. Figure 6.4 illustrates the format of two *add* instructions for an architecture that uses explicit operand encoding.

opcode	operand 1		operand 2	
add	register	1	register	2

	operand 1		operand 2	
add	register	1	signed integer	-93

Figure 6.4 Examples of operands on an architecture that uses explicit encoding. Each operand specifies a type as well as a value.

As the figure shows, each operand is represented by two fields: one field specifies the type of the operand and the other specifies a value. For example, an operand that references a register begins with a type field that specifies the remaining bits are to be interpreted as a register number†.

6.10 Operands That Combine Multiple Values

The discussion above implies that each operand consists of a single value extracted from a register, memory, or the instruction itself. Some processors do indeed restrict each operand to a single value. However, other processors provide hardware that can compute an operand value by extracting and combining values from multiple sources. Typically, the hardware computes a sum of several values.

An example will help clarify how hardware handles operands composed of multiple values. One approach is known as a *register-offset* mechanism. The idea is straightforward: instead of a type and value, each operand consists of three fields that specify a *type*, a *register*, and an *offset*. When it fetches an operand, the processor adds the contents of the offset field to the contents of the specified register to obtain a value that is then used as the operand. Figure 6.5 shows an example add instruction with register-offset operands.

opcode	operand 1			operand 2		
add	register-offset	2	-17	register-offset	4	76

Figure 6.5 An example of an instruction in which each operand consists of a register plus an offset. During operand fetch, the hardware adds the offset to the specified register to obtain the value of the operand.

---

†The SPARC architecture developed by Sun Microsystems, Inc. uses explicit operand encoding.

In the figure, the first operand consists of the current contents of register 2 minus the constant 17, and the second operand consists of the current contents of register 4 plus the constant 76. When we discuss memory, we will see that allowing an operand to specify a register plus an offset is especially useful when referencing a data aggregate such as a C language *struct*.

6.11 Tradeoffs In The Choice Of Operands

The discussion above is unsatisfying — it seems that we have listed many design possibilities without focusing on the design that is optimal. In fact, there is no best choice; each operand style we discussed has been used in practice. Why hasn't one particular style emerged as optimal? The answer is simple: each style represents a tradeoff between ease of programming, size of the code, speed of processing, and size of the hardware. The next paragraphs discuss several potential design goals, and explain how each relates to the choice of operands.

Ease Of Programming. Complex forms of operands make programming easier. For example, we said that allowing an operand to specify a register plus an offset makes data aggregate references straightforward. Similarly, a 3-address approach that provides an explicit target means a programmer does not need to code separate instructions to copy results into their final destination. Of course, to optimize ease of programming, an architect needs to trade off some of the other goals listed below.

Fewer Instructions. Increasing the expressive power of operands reduces the number of instructions in a program. For example, allowing an operand to specify both a register and an offset results in fewer instructions. Increasing the number of addresses per instruction also lowers the count of instructions (e.g., a 3-address processor requires fewer instructions than a 2-address processor). Unfortunately, fewer instructions produce a tradeoff in which each instruction is larger.

Smaller Instructions. Limiting the number of operands, the set of operands types, or the maximum size of an operand keeps instructions small because fewer bits are needed to identify the operand type or represent an operand value. In particular, an operand that specifies only a register will be smaller than an operand that specifies a register and an offset. As a result, some of the smallest, least powerful processors limit operands to registers — except for *load* and *store* operations, each value used in a program must come from a register. Unfortunately, making each instruction smaller decreases the expressive power, and therefore increases the number of instructions needed.

Larger Range Of Immediate Values. Recall from Chapter 3 that a string of k bits can hold 2^k possible values. Thus, the size of a field in the operand determines the numeric range of immediate values that can be specified. Increasing the size allows larger values, but results in larger instructions.

Faster Operand Fetch And Decode. Limiting the number of operands and the possible types of each operand allows hardware to operate faster. To maximize speed, for example, an architect avoids register-offset designs because hardware can fetch an operand from a register much faster than it can compute the value from a register plus an offset.

Decreased Hardware Size. The amount of space on an integrated circuit is limited, and an architect must decide how to use the space. Decoding complex forms of operands requires more hardware than decoding simpler forms. Thus, limiting the types and complexity of operands reduces the size of the circuitry required. Of course, the choice represents a tradeoff: programs are larger.

The point is:

> *Processor architects have created a variety of operand styles. No single form is optimal for all processors because the choice represents a compromise among functionality, program size, hardware required to fetch values, performance, and ease of programming.*

6.12 Values In Memory And Indirect Reference

We said that processors include at least one instruction that allows an operand to specify a value in memory. That is, the value in the operand is interpreted as a memory address†, which the processor uses to perform a memory lookup. The operand is fetched from memory.

We will see that memory lookup is significantly more expensive than accessing a register. Thus, although it helps ease programming, allowing arbitrary instructions to reference memory usually results in lower performance.

Some processors extend memory references by permitting various forms of *indirection*. For example, if an operand specifies *indirection through register 6*, the processor performs the two steps:

- Obtain A, the current value from register 6
- Interpret A as a memory address, and fetch the operand from memory.

One extreme form of indirection permits indirection through a memory address. That is, the operand contains a memory address, M, and specifies indirect reference. The processor performs the following steps:

- Obtain M, the value in the operand itself
- Interpret M as a memory address, and fetch the value A from memory.
- Interpret A as another memory address, and fetch the operand from memory.

---

†The third section of the text describes memory and memory addressing.

6.13 Operand Addressing Modes

A processor usually contains a special register, called an *instruction register*, that is used to hold an instruction that is being decoded. The possible types of operand addresses and the cost of each can be envisioned by considering the location of the operand and the references needed to fetch the value. An immediate value is the least expensive because the value can be found in the instruction register. A general-purpose register reference is the next most expensive, and an indirect memory reference is the most expensive. Figure 6.6 lists the possibilities, and illustrates the hardware units involved in resolving each.

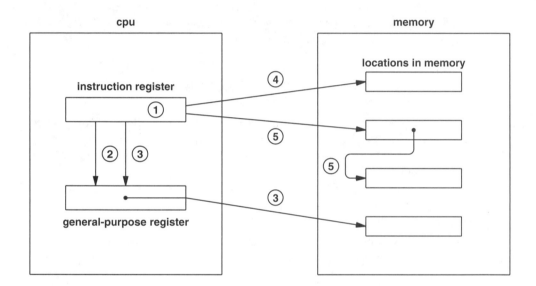

1 Immediate value (in the instruction)

2 Direct register reference

3 Indirect through a register

4 Direct memory reference

5 Indirect memory reference

Figure 6.6 Illustration of the hardware units accessed when fetching an operand in various addressing modes. Indirect references take longer than direct references.

6.14 Summary

When designing a processor, an architect chooses the number and possible types of operands for each instruction; to make operand handling efficient, many processors limit the number of operands to three or less.

An immediate operand specifies a constant value; other possibilities include an operand that specifies using the contents of a register or a value in memory. The type of the operand can be encoded implicitly (i.e., in the opcode) or explicitly.

Many variations exist because the choice of operand number and type represents a tradeoff among functionality, ease of programming, and engineering details such as the speed of processing.

EXERCISES

6.1 How many memory references are involved in executing an instruction that adds two registers and stores the result in memory?

6.2 Assume a stack machine keeps the stack in memory. How many *load* and *store* operations are required to increment a value by seven (assume the value is in memory, and the result must be returned to memory)?

6.3 How many memory operations are required to perform an operation on a 3-address architecture if each operand specifies an indirect memory reference?

6.4 Assume a memory reference takes twelve times as long as a register reference, and assume a program executes N instructions on a 2-address architecture. Compare the running time of the program if all operands are in registers to the running time if all operands are in memory. Hint: instruction fetch requires a memory operation.

7

CPUs: Microcode, Protection, And Processor Modes

7.1 Introduction

Previous chapters consider two key aspects of processors: instruction sets and operands. The chapters explain possible approaches, and discuss the advantages and disadvantages of each approach. This chapter considers a broad class of general-purpose processors, and shows how many of the concepts from previous chapters are applied. The next chapter considers low-level programming languages used with processors.

7.2 A Central Processor

Early in the history of computing, centralization emerged as an important architectural approach — as much functionality as possible was collected into a single processor. The processor, which became known as a *Central Processing Unit* (*CPU*), controlled the entire computer, including both calculations and I/O.

In contrast to early designs, a modern computer system follows a decentralized approach. The system contains multiple processors, many of which are dedicated to a specific function or a hardware subsystem. For example, we will see that an I/O device, such as a disk, can include a processor that handles disk transfers.

Despite the shift in paradigm, the term CPU has survived because one processor is still needed to coordinate and control other processors. In essence, the CPU manages the entire computer system by telling other processors when to start, when to stop, and exactly what to do. When we discuss I/O, we will see exactly how the CPU controls the operation of peripheral devices and processors.

7.3 CPU Complexity

Because it must handle a wide variety of control and processing tasks, a modern CPU is extremely complex. For example, one model of Intel's Pentium processor contains approximately fifty-four million transistors. Why is a CPU so complex? Why are so many transistors needed?

Multiple Roles. One aspect of CPU complexity arises because the CPU must fill several major roles: running application programs, running an operating system, handling external I/O devices, starting or stopping the computer, and managing memory. No single instruction set is optimal for all roles, so a CPU often includes multiple sets of instructions.

Protection And Privilege. Modern computer systems incorporate a system of protection that gives some subsystems higher privilege than others. For example, an application program can be prevented from directly interacting with I/O devices, and the operating system code can be protected from inadvertent or deliberate change.

Hardware Priorities. A CPU uses a priority scheme in which some computations are assigned higher priority than others. For example, we will see that I/O devices operate at higher priority than application programs — if the CPU is running an application program when an I/O device needs service, the CPU must stop running the application and handle the device.

Generality. A CPU is designed to work with as many applications as possible. Consequently, the CPU instruction set often contains many instructions and diverse types of instructions (i.e., a CISC design).

Data Size. To speed processing, a CPU is designed to handle large data values. Recall from Chapter 2 that digital logic gates each operate on a single bit of data and that gates must be replicated to handle integers. Thus, to operate on values composed of sixty-four bits, each digital circuit in the CPU must have sixty-four copies of each gate.

High Speed. The final, and perhaps most significant, source of CPU complexity arises from the desire for speed. Recall the important concept discussed earlier:

Parallelism is a fundamental technique used to create high-speed hardware.

That is, to achieve highest performance, the functional units in a CPU must be replicated, and the design must permit the replicated units to operate simultaneously. The large amount of parallel hardware needed to make a modern CPU operate at the highest rate also means that the CPU requires many transistors. We will see further details later in the chapter.

7.4 Modes Of Execution

The facilities listed above can be combined or used separately. For example, a processor can be granted increased memory access with or without higher priority. How can a CPU accommodate all the features in a way that allows programmers to understand and use them without becoming confused?

In most CPUs, the hardware uses a set of parameters to handle the complexity and control operation. We say that the hardware has multiple *modes of execution*. At any given time, the current execution mode determines how the CPU operates.

Figure 7.1 lists the features usually associated with a CPU mode of execution.

- The subset of instructions that are valid
- The size of data items
- The region of memory that can be accessed
- The functional units that are available
- The amount of privilege

Figure 7.1 Items typically controlled by a CPU mode of execution. The characteristics of a CPU can change dramatically when the mode changes.

7.5 Backward Compatibility

How much variation can execution modes introduce? In principle, the modes available on a CPU do not need to share much in common. As one extreme case, some CPUs have a mode that provides *backward compatibility* with a previous model. Backward compatibility allows a vendor to sell a CPU with new features, but also permits customers to use the CPU to run old software.

Intel's line of processors (i.e., 8086, 186, 286,...) exemplifies how backward compatibility can be used. When Intel first introduced a CPU that operated on thirty-two bit integers, the CPU included a *compatibility mode* that implemented the sixteen bit instruction set from Intel's previous CPU. In addition to using different sizes of integers, the two architectures have different numbers of registers and different instructions. The two architectures differ so significantly that it is easiest to think of the design as two separate pieces of hardware with the execution mode determining which of the two is used at any time.

We can summarize:

> *A CPU uses an* execution mode *to determine the current operational characteristics. In some CPUs, the characteristics of modes differ so widely that we think of the CPU as having separate hardware subsystems and the mode as determining which piece of hardware is used at the current time.*

7.6 Changing Modes

How does a CPU change modes? There are two ways:

- Automatic (initiated by hardware)
- Manual (under program control)

Automatic Mode Change. External hardware can change the mode of a CPU. For example, when an I/O device requests service, the hardware informs the CPU. Hardware in the CPU changes mode automatically before servicing the device. We will learn more when we consider how I/O works.

Manual Mode Change. In essence, manual changes occur under control of a running program. Most often, the program is the operating system, which changes mode before it executes an application. However, some CPUs also provide multiple modes that applications can use, and allow an application to switch among the modes.

Exactly how does a program change mode? Three mechanisms have been used. In the simplest case, the CPU includes an instruction to set the current mode. In other cases, the CPU contains a special-purpose *mode register* to control the mode. To change modes, a program stores a value into the mode register. Note that a mode register is not a storage unit in the normal sense. Instead, it consists of a hardware circuit that responds to the *store* command by changing the operating mode. Finally, a mode change can occur as the side-effect of another instruction. In most CPUs, for example, a mode change occurs automatically whenever an application invokes an operating system function.

To accommodate major changes in mode, additional facilities may be needed to prepare the new mode. For example, consider a case in which two modes of execution do not share general-purpose registers (e.g., in one mode the registers have sixteen bits and in another mode the registers contain thirty-two bits). It may be necessary to place values in alternate registers before changing mode to use the registers. In such cases, a CPU provides special instructions that allow software to create or modify values before changing the mode.

7.7 Privilege And Protection

The mode of execution is linked to CPU facilities for privilege and protection. That is, part of the current mode specifies the level of privilege for the CPU. For example, when it services an I/O device, a CPU must allow device driver software in the operating system to interact with the device and perform control functions. However, an arbitrary application program must be prevented from accidentally or maliciously issuing commands to the hardware or performing control functions. Thus, before it executes an application program, an operating system changes the mode to reduce privilege. When running in a less privileged mode, the CPU does not permit direct control of I/O devices (i.e., the CPU treats a privileged operation like an invalid instruction).

7.8 Multiple Levels Of Protection

How many levels of privilege are needed, and what operations should be allowed at each level? The subject has been discussed by hardware architects and operating system designers for many years. CPUs have been invented that offer no protection, and CPUs have been invented that offer eight levels, each with more privilege than the next. The idea of protection is to help prevent problems by using the minimum amount of privilege necessary at any time. We can summarize:

> *By using a protection scheme to limit the operations that are allowed, a CPU can detect attempts to perform unauthorized operations.*

Figure 7.2 illustrates the concept of two privilege levels.

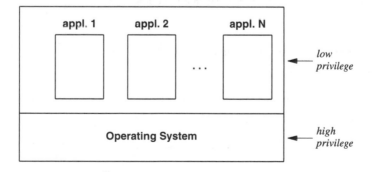

Figure 7.2 Illustration of a CPU that offers two levels of protection. The operating system executes with highest privilege, and application programs execute with less privilege.

Although no protection scheme suffices for all CPUs, designers generally agree on a minimum for a CPU that runs application programs:

A CPU that runs applications needs at least two levels of protection: the operating system must run with absolute privilege, but application programs can run with limited privilege.

When we discuss memory, we will see that the issues of protection and memory access are intertwined. More important, we will see how memory access mechanisms, which are part of the CPU mode, provide additional forms of protection.

7.9 Microcoded Instructions

How should a complex CPU be implemented? Interestingly, one of the key abstractions used to build a complex instruction set comes from software: complex instructions are programmed! That is, instead of implementing the instruction set directly with digital circuits, a CPU is built in two pieces. First, a hardware architect builds a fast, but small processor known as a *microcontroller†*. Second, to implement the CPU instruction set (called a *macro instruction set*), the architect writes software for the microcontroller. The software that runs on the microcontroller is known as *microcode*. Figure 7.3 illustrates the two-level organization, and shows how each level is implemented.

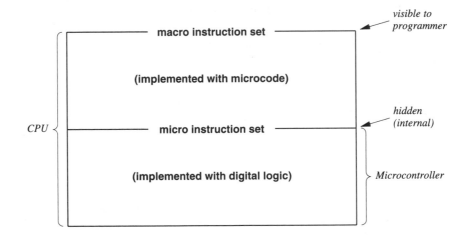

Figure 7.3 Illustration of a CPU implemented with a microcontroller. The macro instruction set that the CPU provides is implemented with microcode.

---

†The small processor is also called a *microprocessor*, but the term is somewhat ambiguous.

The easiest way to think about microcode is to imagine a set of procedures that each implement one of the CPU macro instructions. The CPU invokes the microcode during the fetch-execute cycle. That is, once it has obtained and decoded a macro instruction, the CPU invokes the microcode procedure that corresponds to the instruction.

The macro and micro architectures can differ. As an example, suppose that the CPU is designed to operate on data items that are thirty-two bits wide, and that the macro instruction set includes an *add32* instruction for integer addition. Further suppose that the microcontroller only offers sixteen bit arithmetic. To implement a thirty-two bit addition, the microcode must add sixteen bits at a time, and must add the carry from the low-order bits into the high-order bits. Figure 7.4 lists the microcode steps that are required.

```
/* Notes: the steps below assume that two 32-bit operands
      are located in registers labeled R5 and R6, and that the
      microcode must use 16-bit registers labeled r0 through r3
      to compute the results.
*/
add32:
      move low-order 16 bits from R5 into r2
      move low-order 16 bits from R6 into r3
      add r2 and r3, placing result in r1
      save value of the carry indicator
      move high-order 16 bits from R5 into r2
      move high-order 16 bits from R6 into r3
      add r2 and r3, placing result in r0
      copy the value in r0 to r2
      add r2 and the carry bit, placing the result in r0
      check for overflow and set the condition code
      move the thirty-two bit result from
          r0 and r1 to the desired destination
```

Figure 7.4 An example of the steps required to implement a thirty-two bit macro addition with a microcontroller that only has sixteen bit arithmetic. The macro and micro architectures can differ.

The exact details are unimportant; the figure is only meant to illustrate how the architecture of the microcontroller and the macro instruction set can differ dramatically. Also note that because each macro instruction is implemented by a microcode program, a macro instruction can perform arbitrary processing. For example, it is possible for a single macro instruction to implement a trigonometric function, such as *sine* or *cosine*, or to move large blocks of data in memory. Of course, to achieve higher performance, an architect can choose to limit the amount of microcode that corresponds to a given instruction.

7.10 Microcode Variations

Architects have invented many variations to the basic form of microcode. For example, we said that the CPU hardware implements the fetch-execute cycle and invokes a microcode procedure for each instruction. On some CPUs, microcode implements the entire fetch-execute cycle — the microcode interprets the opcode, fetches operands, and performs the specified operation. The advantage is greater flexibility: microcode defines all aspects of the macro system, including the format of macro instructions and the form and encoding of each operand. The chief disadvantage is lower performance: the CPU does not have an instruction pipeline implemented in hardware.

As another variation, a CPU can be designed that only uses microcode for extensions. That is, the CPU has a complete macro instruction set implemented directly with digital circuits. In addition, the CPU has a small set of additional opcodes that are implemented with microcode. Thus, a vendor can manufacture minor variations of the basic CPU (e.g., a version with a special encryption instruction intended for customers who implement security software or a version with a special pattern matching instruction intended for customers who implement text processing software). If some or all of the extra instructions are not used in a particular version of the CPU, the vendor can insert microcode that makes them undefined (i.e., the microcode raises an error if the instruction is executed).

7.11 The Advantage Of Microcode

Why is microcode used? There are three motivations. First, because microcode offers a higher level of abstraction, building microcode is less prone to errors than building hardware circuits. Second, building microcode takes less time than building circuits. Third, because changing microcode is easier than changing hardware circuits, new versions of a CPU can be created faster.

We can summarize:

> *A design that uses microcode is less prone to errors and can be updated faster than a design that does not use microcode.*

Of course, microcode does have some disadvantages that balance the advantages:

- Microcode has more overhead than a hardware implementation.
- Because it executes multiple micro instructions for each macro instruction, the microcontroller must run at much higher speed than the CPU.
- The cost of a macro instruction depends on the micro instruction set.

7.12 Making Microcode Visible To Programmers

Because a microcontroller is an internal mechanism intended to help designers, the micro instruction set is usually hidden in the final design. Typically, the microcontroller and microcode reside on the integrated circuit along with the rest of the CPU, and are only used internally. Thus, only the macro instruction set is available to programmers.

Interestingly, however, some CPUs have been designed that expose the microcontroller and the microcode to customers who purchase the CPU. That is, the CPU contains facilities that allow the microcode to be replaced (i.e., overwritten).

In most cases, replacing microcode is a time-consuming operation that may involve using special pins on the chip or may involve adding an external memory. More important, a change in the microcode changes the macro instructions. Thus, changes to microcode are performed once before macro execution begins, and the microcode does not change during execution. That is, a customer chooses a macro instruction set, creates microcode to implement each instruction, and then builds software to use the new instruction set.

Why provide access to the micro instruction set? The key ideas are flexibility and performance: allowing the microcode to be overwritten defers the final decision about a macro instruction set, and allows a CPU's owner to choose instructions that are optimal. For example, a company that sells video games might create macro instructions to manipulate graphics images, while a company that makes networking equipment might create macro instructions to process packet headers. Because microcode can access the internal hardware mechanisms, a single microcoded instruction can often execute faster than a sequence of macro instructions that perform the same function.

We can summarize:

> *Some CPUs provide a mechanism that allows microcode to be rewritten. The motivation for allowing such change arises from the desire for flexibility and optimization: the CPU's owner can create a macro instruction set that is optimized for a specific task.*

7.13 Vertical Microcode

The question arises, what architecture should be used for a microcontroller? From a programmer's point of view, the question becomes: what instructions should the microcontroller provide? We discussed the notion of microcode as if a microcontroller consists of a conventional processor (i.e., a processor that follows a conventional architecture). We will see shortly that other designs are possible.

In fact, a microcontroller cannot be exactly the same as a standard processor. Because it must interact with hardware units in the CPU, a microcontroller needs a few special hardware facilities. For example, a microcontroller must be able to access the ALU and store results in the general-purpose registers that the macro instruction set uses. Similarly, a microcontroller must be able to decode operand references and fetch values. Finally, the microcontroller must coordinate with the rest of the hardware, including memory.

Despite the requirements for special features, a microcontroller can follow the same general approach used for conventional processors. That is, the microcontroller's instruction set can contain conventional instructions such as *load*, *store*, *add*, *subtract*, *branch*, and so on. For example, the microcontroller used in a CISC processor can consist of a small, fast RISC processor. We say that such a microcontroller has a *vertical* architecture, and use the term *vertical microcode* to characterize the software that runs on the microcontroller.

Programmers are comfortable with vertical microcode because the programming interface is familiar. Most important, the semantics of vertical microcode are exactly what a programmer expects: one micro instruction is executed at a time. The next section discusses the alternative to vertical microcode.

7.14 Horizontal Microcode

From a hardware perspective, vertical microcode is unattractive. One of the primary disadvantages arises from the performance requirements. For example, most macro instructions require multiple micro instructions. Thus, to execute macro instructions at a rate of K per second, the microcontroller must execute micro instructions at a rate of $N \times K$ per second, where N is the average number of micro instructions per macro instruction. Furthermore, all aspects of the microcontroller hardware must be designed to operate at high speed (e.g., the memory used to hold microcode must be able to deliver micro instructions at a high rate).

Computer architects invented an alternative known as *horizontal microcode* to overcome the limitations of vertical microcode. Horizontal microcode has the advantage of working well with the hardware, but not providing a familiar interface for programmers. That is:

> *Horizontal microcode allows the hardware to run faster, but is more difficult to program.*

To understand horizontal microcode, we must know more about the underlying hardware. At the lowest level, CPU hardware consists of multiple functional units, with data paths connecting them. Operation of the units must be controlled, and each unit is controlled independently. Furthermore, moving data from one functional unit to another requires explicit control of the two units: one unit must be instructed to send data, and the other unit must be instructed to receive data.

An example will help clarify the concept. To make the example easy to understand, we will make a few simplifying assumptions and restrict the discussion to six
functional units. Figure 7.5 shows how the six functional units are interconnected.

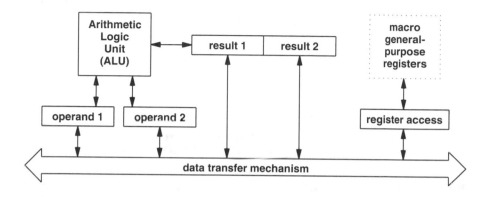

Figure 7.5 An illustration of the internal structure within a CPU. Solid arrows indicate a hardware path along which data can move.

The major item shown in the figure is an *Arithmetic Logic Unit (ALU)* that performs operations such as addition, subtraction, and bit shifting. The remaining functional units provide mechanisms that interface the ALU to the rest of the system. For
example, the hardware units labeled *operand 1* and *operand 2* denote operand storage
units. The ALU expects operands to be placed in the storage units before an operation
is performed, and places the result of an operation in the two hardware units labeled
result 1 and *result 2*†. Finally, the *register access* unit provides a hardware interface to
the general purpose registers.

In the figure, arrows indicate paths along which data can pass as it moves from one
functional unit to another. Most of the arrows connect to the *data transfer mechanism*,
which serves as a conduit between functional units‡.

7.15 Example Horizontal Microcode

Each functional unit is controlled by a set of wires that carry commands (i.e.,
binary values that the hardware interprets as a command). Although Figure 7.5 does
not show command wires, we can imagine that the number of command wires connected to a functional unit depends on the type of unit. For example, the unit labeled *result
1* only needs a single command wire because the unit can be controlled by a single
binary value: zero causes the unit to stop interacting with other units, and one causes
the unit to send the current contents of the result unit to the data transfer mechanism.

---

†Recall that an arithmetic operation, such as multiplication, can produce a result that is twice as large as
an operand.

‡A later chapter explains that the data transfer mechanism depicted here is called a *bus*.

Figure 7.6 summarizes the binary control values that can be passed to each functional unit, and gives the meaning of each.

Unit	Command	Meaning
ALU	0 0 0	No operation
	0 0 1	Add
	0 1 0	Subtract
	0 1 1	Multiply
	1 0 0	Divide
	1 0 1	Left shift
	1 1 0	Right shift
	1 1 1	Continue previous operation
operand 1 or 2	0	No operation
	1	Load value from data transfer mechanism
result 1 or 2	0	No operation
	1	Send value to data transfer mechanism
register interface	0 0 x x x x	No operation
	0 1 x x x x	Move register xxxx to data transfer mechanism
	1 0 x x x x	Move data transfer mechanism to register xxxx
	1 1 x x x x	No operation

Figure 7.6 Possible command values and the meaning of each for the example functional units in Figure 7.5. Commands are carried on parallel wires.

As the figure shows, the register access unit is a special case because each command has two parts: the first two bits specify an operation, and the last four bits specify a register to be used in the operation. Thus, the command 0 1 0 0 1 1 means that value in register three should be moved to the data transfer mechanism.

Now that we understand how hardware is organized, we can see how horizontal microcode works. Imagine that each microcode instruction consists of commands to functional units — when it executes an instruction, the hardware sends bits from the instruction to functional units. Figure 7.7 illustrates how bits of a microcode instruction correspond to commands in our example.

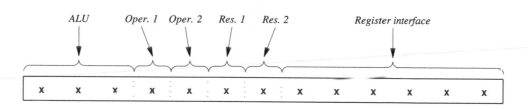

Figure 7.7 Illustration of thirteen bits in a horizontal microcode instruction that correspond to commands for six functional units.

7.16 A Horizontal Microcode Example

How can horizontal microcode be used to perform a sequence of operations? In essence, a programmer chooses which functional units should be active at any time, and encodes the information in bits of the microcode. For example, suppose a programmer needs to write microcode that adds the value in general-purpose register 4 to the value in general-purpose register 13 and places the result back in general-purpose register 4. Figure 7.8 lists the operations that must be performed.

- Move the value from register 4 to the hardware unit for operand 1

- Move the value from register 13 to the hardware unit for operand 2

- Arrange for the ALU to perform addition

- Move the value from the hardware unit for result 2 (the low-order bits of the result) to register 4

Figure 7.8 An example sequence of steps that the functional units must execute to add values from general-purpose registers 4 and 13, and place the result in general-purpose register 4.

Each of the steps can be expressed as a micro instruction. The instruction has bits set to specify which functional unit(s) operate when the instruction is executed. For example, Figure 7.9 shows a microcode program that corresponds to the four steps.

In the figure, each row corresponds to one instruction, which is divided into fields that each correspond to a functional unit. A field contains a command to be sent to the functional unit when the instruction is executed. Thus, commands determine which functional units operate at each step.

Instr.	ALU			OP$_1$	OP$_2$	RES$_1$	RES$_2$	REG. INTERFACE					
1	0	0	0	1	0	0	0	0	1	0	1	0	0
2	0	0	0	0	1	0	0	0	1	1	1	0	1
3	0	0	1	0	0	0	0	0	0	0	0	0	0
4	0	0	0	0	0	0	1	1	0	0	1	0	0

Figure 7.9 An example horizontal microcode program that consists of four instructions of thirteen bits per instruction. Each instruction corresponds to a step listed in Figure 7.8.

Consider the code in the figure carefully. The first instruction specifies that only two hardware units will operate: the unit for operand 1 and the register interface unit. The fields that corresponds to the other four units contain zero, which means that those units will not operate when the first instruction is executed. The first instruction also uses the data transfer mechanism — data is sent across the transfer mechanism from the register interface unit to the unit for operand 1†. That is, fields in the instruction cause the register interface to send a value across the transfer mechanism, and cause the operand 1 unit to capture the value.

7.17 Operations That Require Multiple Cycles

Timing is among the most important aspects of horizontal microcode. Some hardware units take longer to operate than others. For example, multiplication can take longer than addition. That is, when a functional unit is given a command, the results do not appear immediately. Instead, the program must delay before accessing the output from the functional unit.

A programmer who writes horizontal microcode must ensure that each hardware unit is given the correct amount of time to complete its task. For example, consider the code in Figure 7.9, which assumes that each step can be accomplished in one cycle. If the ALU requires two micro instruction cycles to complete an addition instead of one cycle, an extra instruction can be inserted following the third instruction. The extra instruction merely specifies that the ALU should continue the previous operation; no other units are affected. Figure 7.10 shows the microcode instruction that is used.

---

†For purposes of this example, we assume the data transfer mechanism always operates, and does not require any control.

ALU			OP$_1$	OP$_2$	RES$_1$	RES$_2$		REG. INTERFACE				
1	1	1	0	0	0	0	0	0	0	0	0	0

Figure 7.10 An instruction that can be inserted to add delay processing to wait for the ALU to complete an operation. Timing and delay are crucial aspects of horizontal microcode.

7.18 Horizontal Microcode And Parallel Execution

Now that we have a basic understanding of how hardware operates and a general idea about horizontal microcode, we can appreciate an important property: inherent parallelism. Parallelism is possible because the underlying hardware contains units that operate independently. A programmer can specify parallel operation because an instruction contains separate fields that each control one of the hardware units.

As an example, consider an architecture that has an ALU plus separate hardware units to hold operands. Assume the ALU requires multiple instruction cycles to complete an operation. Because the ALU accesses the operands during the first cycle, the hardware units used to hold operands remain unused during successive cycles. Thus, a programmer can insert an instruction that simultaneously moves a new value into an operand unit while an ALU operation continues. Figure 7.11 illustrates such an instruction.

ALU			OP$_1$	OP$_2$	RES$_1$	RES$_2$		REG. INTERFACE				
1	1	1	1	0	0	0	0	1	0	1	1	1

Figure 7.11 An example instruction that simultaneously continues an ALU operation and loads the value from register seven into operand hardware unit one. Horizontal microcode makes parallelism easy to specify.

The point is:

Because an instruction contains separate fields that each correspond to one hardware unit, horizontal microcode makes it easy to specify simultaneous, parallel operation of multiple hardware units.

7.19 Look-Ahead And High Performance Execution

In practice, CPU architecture and microcode are much more complex than the simplistic examples in this chapter. One of the most important sources of complexity arises from the desire to achieve high performance. Because silicon technology allows manufacturers to place millions of transistors on a single chip, it is possible for a CPU to include many functional units that all operate simultaneously.

A later chapter considers architectures that make parallel hardware visible to a programmer. For now, we will consider an architectural question: can multiple functional units be used to improve performance without changing the macro instruction set? In particular, can the internal organization of a CPU be arranged to automatically detect and exploit situations in which parallel execution will produce higher performance?

We have already seen a trivial example of an optimization: Figure 7.11 shows that horizontal microcode can allow an ALU operation to continue at the same time a data value is transferred to a hardware unit that holds an operand. However, our example requires the architect to explicitly code the parallel behavior when creating the microcode.

To understand how a CPU exploits parallelism, imagine a system that includes an intelligent microcontroller and multiple functional units. Instead of working on one macro instruction at a time, the intelligent controller is given access to many macro instructions. The controller looks ahead at the instructions, finds values that will be needed, and directs functional units to start fetching or computing the values. For example, suppose the intelligent controller finds the following four instructions on a 3-address architecture:

```
add     R1, R3, R7
sub     R4, R4, R6
add     R9, R1, R2
shift   R12, 5
```

We say that an intelligent controller *schedules* the instructions by assigning the necessary work to functional units. For example, the controller can assign each operand to a functional unit that fetches and prepares operand values. Once the operand values are available for an instruction, the controller assigns the instruction to a functional unit that performs the operation. For example, the instructions listed above can each be assigned to an ALU. Finally, when the operation completes, the controller can assign a functional unit the task of moving the result to the appropriate destination register. The point is: if the CPU contains enough functional units, an intelligent controller can schedule all four macro instructions to be executed at the same time.

7.20 Parallelism And Execution Order

Our above description of an intelligent microcontroller overlooks an important detail: the semantics of the macro instruction set. In essence, the controller must ensure that computing values in parallel does not change the meaning of the program. For example, consider the following sequence of instructions:

div	R1, R3, R7
sub	R4, R4, R6
add	R7, R1, R2
shift	R12, 5

Unlike the previous example, the operands overlap. In particular, the first instruction specifies register seven as a destination, and the third instruction specifies register seven as an operand. The macro instruction set specifies sequential processing of instructions, which means that the first instruction will place a value in register seven before the third instruction references the value. To preserve sequential semantics, an intelligent controller must understand and accommodate such overlap. In essence, the controller must balance between two goals: maximize the amount of parallel evaluation, while preserving the original (i.e., sequential) semantics.

7.21 Out-Of-Order Instruction Execution

How can a controller that schedules parallel activities handle the case where an operand in one instruction depends on the results of a previous instruction? The controller uses a mechanism known as a *scoreboard* that tracks the status of each instruction being executed. In particular, a scoreboard maintains information about dependencies among instructions and the original macro instruction sequence execution. Thus, the controller can use the scoreboard to decide when to fetch operands, when execution can proceed, and when an instruction is finished. In short, the scoreboard approach allows the controller to execute instructions out of order, but then reorders the results to reflect the order specified by the code.

> *To achieve highest speed, a modern CPU contains multiple copies of functional units that permit multiple instructions to be executed simultaneously. An intelligent controller schedules execution in an order that preserves the appearance of sequential processing.*

7.22 Conditional Branches And Branch Prediction

Conditional branches pose another problem for parallel execution. For example, consider the following computation:

$$Y \leftarrow f(X)$$
$$if\,(Y > Z)\,\{$$
$$Q$$
$$\}\,else\,\{$$
$$R$$
$$\}$$

When translated into machine instructions, the computation contains a conditional branch which directs execution either to the code that corresponds to Q or the code that corresponds to R. The condition depends on the value of Y, which is computed in the first step. Now consider running the code on a CPU that uses parallel execution of instructions. In theory, once it reaches the conditional branch, the CPU must wait for the results of the comparison — the CPU cannot start to schedule code for R or Q until it knows which one will be selected.

In practice, there are two approaches used to handle conditional branches. The first, which is known as *branch prediction*, is based on measurements which show that in most code, the branch is taken approximately sixty percent of the time. Thus, building hardware that schedules instructions along the branch path provides more optimization than hardware that schedules instructions along the non-branch path. Of course, assuming the branch may be incorrect — if the CPU eventually determines that the branch should not be taken, the results from the branch path must be discarded, and the CPU must return to the other path. The second approach simply follows both paths in parallel. That is, the CPU schedules instructions for both outcomes of the conditional branch. As with branch prediction, the CPU must eventually decide which result is valid. That is, the CPU continues to execute instructions, but holds the results internally. Once the value of the condition is known, the CPU discards the results from the path that is not valid, and proceeds to move the other results into the appropriate destinations. Of course, a second conditional branch can occur in either Q or R; the scoreboard mechanism handles all the details.

The point is:

A CPU that offers parallel instruction execution can handle conditional branches by proceeding to precompute values on one or both branches, and choosing which values to use at a later time when the computation of the branch condition completes.

It may seem wasteful for a CPU to compute values that will be discarded later. However, the goal is higher performance, not elegance. We can also observe that if a CPU is designed to wait until a conditional branch value is known, nothing is saved — hardware will merely sit idle. Therefore, high speed CPUs, such as Intel's Pentium, are designed with parallel functional units and sophisticated scoreboard mechanisms.

7.23 Consequences For Programmers

Can understanding how a CPU is structured help programmers write faster code? In some cases, yes. For example, suppose a CPU is designed to use branch prediction and that the CPU assumes the branch is taken. A programmer can optimize performance by arranging code so that the most common cases take the branch. For example, instead of testing whether $Y > Z$, a programmer can rewrite the code to test whether $Y \leq Z$.

7.24 Summary

A modern CPU is a complex processor that uses multiple modes of execution to handle some of the complexity. An execution mode determines operational parameters such as the operations that are allowed and the current privilege level. Most CPUs offer at least two levels of privilege and protection: one for the operating system and one for application programs.

To reduce the internal complexity, a CPU is often built with two levels of abstraction: a microcontroller is implemented with digital circuits, and a macro instruction set is created by adding microcode.

There are two broad classes of microcode. A microcontroller that uses vertical microcode resembles a conventional RISC processor. Typically, vertical microcode consists of a set of procedures that each correspond to one macro instruction; the CPU runs the appropriate microcode during the fetch-execute cycle. Horizontal microcode, which allows a programmer to schedule functional units to operate on each cycle, consists of instructions in which each bit field corresponds to a functional unit.

Advanced CPUs extend parallel execution by scheduling a set of instructions across multiple functional units. The CPU uses a scoreboard mechanism to handle cases where the results of one instruction are used by a successive instruction. The idea can be extended to conditional branches by allowing parallel evaluation of each path to proceed, and then, once the condition is known, discarding the values along the path that is not taken.

EXERCISES

7.1   Investigate the effects of backward compatibility on elegance. Can you find an example of a processor where backward compatibility impacts elegance?

7.2   Find an example of a commercial processor that uses horizontal microcode, and document the meaning of bits for an instruction similar to the diagram in Figure 7.7.

8

Assembly Languages And Programming Paradigm

8.1 Introduction

Previous chapters in this section describe processor instruction sets and operand addressing. This chapter discusses programming languages that allow programmers to specify all the details of instructions and operand addresses. The chapter is not a tutorial about a language for a particular processor. Instead, it provides a general assessment of features commonly found in low-level languages. The chapter examines programming paradigms, and explains how programming in a low-level language differs from programming in a conventional language. Finally, the chapter describes software that translates a low-level language into binary instructions.

Low-level programming and low-level programming languages are not strictly part of computer architecture. We consider them here, however, because such languages are so closely related to the underlying hardware that the two cannot be separated easily. Later chapters return to the focus on hardware by examining memory and I/O facilities.

8.2 Characteristics Of A High-level Programming Language

Programming languages can be divided into two broad categories:

- High-level languages
- Low-level languages

A conventional programming language, such as Java or C, is classified as *high-level* because the language exhibits the following characteristics:

- Many-to-one translation
- Hardware independence
- Application orientation
- General-purpose
- Powerful abstractions

Many-To-One Translation. The fundamental characteristic used to classify a programming language as high-level concerns the relationship between statements in the language and instructions on a typical processor: each statement corresponds to many machine instructions. That is, when a compiler translates the language into equivalent machine instructions, a statement usually translates into multiple instructions.

Hardware Independence. Because they are intended for use with many computers, high-level languages do not specify any details of the underlying hardware. Instead, a programmer can create a program without knowing exactly which processor will be used to execute the program. For example, a high-level language allows a programmer to specify floating point operations, such as addition and subtraction, without knowing whether the ALU implements floating point arithmetic directly or uses a separate floating point coprocessor.

Application Orientation. A high-level language, such as C or Java, is designed to allow a programmer to create application programs. Thus, a high-level language usually includes I/O facilities as well as facilities that permit a programmer to define arbitrarily complex data objects.

General-Purpose. A high-level language, like C or Java, is not restricted to a specific task or a specific problem domain. Instead, the language contains features that allow a programmer to create a program for an arbitrary task.

Powerful Abstractions. A high-level language provides abstractions, such as procedures, that allow a programmer to express complex tasks succinctly.

8.3 Characteristics Of A Low-Level Programming Language

The alternative to a high-level language is known as a *low-level language* and has the following characteristics:

- One-to-one translation
- Hardware dependence
- Systems programming orientation
- Special-purpose
- Few abstractions

One-To-One Translation. The fundamental characteristic used to classify a programming language as low-level concerns the relationship between statements in the language and instructions on a typical processor: each statement corresponds to a single instruction. Thus, when the language is translated into machine code, each statement generates a single machine instruction.

Hardware Dependence. We have seen that each processor defines an instruction set. Thus, if a programming language is created in which each statement corresponds to a machine instruction, the resulting language will correspond directly to the processor that was chosen; a low-level language created for one type of processor cannot be used with another type of processor.

Systems Programming Orientation. Unlike a high-level language, a low-level language is optimized for systems programming — the language has facilities that allow a programmer to create an operating system or other software that directly controls the hardware.

Special-Purpose. Because they focus on the underlying hardware, low-level languages are only used in cases where extreme control or efficiency is needed. For example, a low-level language provides a programmer explicit control over which values are stored in registers and the exact order of instructions. Such control is only needed in special cases.

Few Abstractions. Unlike a high-level language, a low-level language does not have complex data structures (e.g., strings or objects), and does not usually have control statements for tasks such as conditional execution (an *if-then-else* statement), iteration (a *while* or *for* statement), or procedure invocation. Instead, the language forces a programmer to construct abstractions from low-level mechanisms†.

8.4 Assembly Language

The most widely used form of low-level programming language is known as *assembly language*, and the software that translates an assembly language program into a binary image that the hardware understands is known as an *assembler*.

It is important to understand that the phrase *assembly language* differs from phrases such as *Java language* or *C language* because *assembly* does not refer to a single language. Instead, a given assembly language uses the instruction set and operands from a single processor. Thus, many assembly languages exist, one for each processor. To summarize:

> *Because an assembly language is a low-level language that incorporates specific characteristics of a processor, such as the instruction set, operand addressing, and registers, many assembly languages exist.*

---

†Computer scientist Alan Perlis once said that a programming language is low-level if programming requires attention to irrelevant details. His point is that because most applications do not need direct control of the underlying hardware, a low-level language increases programming complexity without providing benefits.

The consequence for programmers should be obvious: when moving from one processor to another, an assembly language programmer must learn a language. Fortunately, most assembly languages tend to follow a basic pattern. Thus, a programmer who learns one assembly language can learn others quickly. More important, once a programmer understands the basic assembly language paradigm, moving to a new architecture usually involves learning new details, not learning a new programming style. The point is:

> *Despite differences, many assembly languages share the same fundamental structure. Consequently, a programmer who understands the assembly programming paradigm can learn a new assembly language quickly.*

To help programmers understand the concept of assembly language, the next sections focus on general features and programming paradigms that apply to most assembly languages. In addition to specific language details, we will discuss concepts such as macros.

8.5 Assembly Language Syntax And Opcodes

8.5.1 Statement Format

Because assembly language is low-level, a single assembly language statement corresponds to a single machine instruction. To make the correspondence between language statements and machine instructions clear, most assemblers require a program to contain a single statement per line of input. The general format is:

$$\text{label:} \quad \text{opcode} \quad \text{operand}_1, \text{operand}_2, \ ...$$

where *label* gives an optional label for the statement, *opcode* specifies one of the possible instructions, each *operand* specifies an operand for the instruction, and whitespace separates the opcode from other items.

8.5.2 Opcode Names

The assembly language for a given processor defines a symbolic name for each instruction that the processor provides. Although the symbolic names are intended to help a programmer remember the purpose of the instruction, most assembly languages use extremely short abbreviations instead of long names. Thus, if a processor has an instruction for addition, the assembly language might use the opcode *add*. However, if the processor has an instruction that branches to a new location, the opcode for the instruction typically consists of a single letter, *b*, or the two-letter opcode *br*. Similarly, if the processor has an instruction that jumps to a subroutine, the opcode is often *jsr*.

Unfortunately, there is no global agreement on opcode names even for basic operations. For example, most architectures include an instruction that copies the contents of one register to another. To denote such an operation, some assembly languages use the opcode *mov* (an abbreviation for *move*), and others use the opcode *ld* (an abbreviation for *load*).

8.5.3 Commenting Conventions

Short opcodes tend to make assembly language easy to write but difficult to read. Furthermore, because it is low-level, assembly language tends to require many instructions to achieve a straightforward task. Thus, to ensure that assembly language programs remain readable, programmers add two types of comments: block comments that explain the purpose of each major section of code, and a detailed comment on each individual line to explain the purpose of the line.

To make it easy for programmers to add comments, assembly languages often allow comments to extend until the end of a line. That is, the language only defines a character (or sequence of characters) that starts a comment. As an example, one assembly language defines the pound sign character (#) as the start of a comment†. A block comment can be created in which each line begins with a pound sign, or a detailed comment can be created by placing a pound sign and a comment at the end of a statement. Programmers often add additional characters to surround a block comment. For example, the block comment below explains that a section of code searches a list to find a memory block of a given size:

```
###############################################################
#                                                             #
#    Search linked list of free memory blocks to find a block #
#    of size N bytes or greater.  Pointer to list must be in  #
#    register 3, and N must be in register 4.  The code also  #
#    destroys the contents of register 5, which is used to    #
#    walk the list.                                           #
#                                                             #
###############################################################
```

A comment on each line in the section of code is used to explain how the instruction fits into the algorithm. For example, the code to search for a memory block might begin:

```
        ld      r5,r3    # load the address of list into r5
loop_1: cmp     r5,r0    # test to see if at end of list
        bz      notfnd   # if reached end of list go to notfnd
```

Although details in the example above may seem obscure, the point is relatively straightforward: the comment on a line explains how the instruction fits the overall algorithm.

---

†At least one assembly language uses a semicolon to denote the start of a comment, and another assembly language adopts the C++ comment style and uses two adjacent slash characters.

8.6 Operand Order

One minor difference among assembly languages can cause subtle problems for programmers: the order of operands. To help programmers, an assembly language usually chooses a consistent operand order. For example, consider a load instruction (*ld* in the example code) that copies the contents of one register to another register. In the code above, the first operand represents the *target* register (i.e., the register into which the value will be placed), and the second operand represents the *source* register (i.e., the register from which the value will be copied). Thus, in such an interpretation, the statement:

```
ld      r5,r3     # load the address of list into r5
```

moves the contents of register 3 into register 5. To help them remember the right-to-left interpretation, programmers are told to think of an assignment statement in which the expression is on the right and the target of the assignment is on the left.

As an alternative to the example code, some assembly languages specify the opposite order — the source register is on the left and the target register is on the right. In such assembly languages, the code above is written:

```
ld      r3,r5     # load the address of list into r5
```

To help them remember the left-to-right interpretation, programmers are told to think of a computer reading the instruction. Because text is read left to right, we can imagine the computer reading the opcode, picking up the first operand, and depositing the value in the second operand. Thus, in the alternate interpretation, the value is left in the last operand that the computer reads.

Operand ordering is further complicated by several factors. First, unlike a *load* operation, many assembly language instructions do not have source and destination operands. For example, an instruction that performs bitwise complement only needs one operand. Furthermore, an instruction that performs a comparison specifies two operands, but neither can be classified as a target. Thus, a programmer who is unfamiliar with a given assembly language may need to consult a manual to find the order of operands for a given opcode.

Of course, the notion of reading the text of an instruction from left-to-right is a fiction: the textual representation that a programmer creates is replaced by a binary representation before the processor executes the program. Interestingly, the translation from assembly language to binary code means that the operand order that a programmer uses does not need to correspond to the operand order used by the underlying hardware. Instead, operands can be reordered during translation. For example, the author once worked on a computer that had two assembly languages, one produced by the computer's vendor and another produced by researchers at Bell Labs. Although both languages were used to produce code for the same underlying computer, one language used a left-to-right interpretation of the operands, and the other used a right-to-left interpretation.

8.7 Register Names

Because a typical instruction includes a reference to at least one register, most assembly languages include a special way to denote registers. For example, in many assembly languages, names that consist of the letter *r* followed by one or more digits are reserved to refer to registers. Thus, a reference to *r10* refers to register 10.

However, there is no universal standard for register references. In one assembly language, all register references begin with a dollar sign followed by digits; thus, $10 refers to register 10. Other assemblers are more flexible: the assembler allows a programmer to choose register names. That is, a programmer can insert a series of declarations that define a specific name to refer to a register. Thus, one might find declarations such as:

```
#
#  Define register names used in the program
#
r1      register 1        # define name r1 to be register 1
r2      register 2        #    and so on for r2, r3, and r4
r3      register 3
r4      register 4
```

The chief advantage of allowing programmers to define register names arises from increased readability: a programmer can choose meaningful names. For example, suppose a program manages a linked list. Instead of using numbers or names like *r6*, a programmer can give meaningful names to the registers:

```
#
#  Define register names for a linked list program
#
listhd   register 6        # holds starting address of list
listptr  register 7        # moves along the list
```

Of course, allowing programmers to choose names for registers can also lead to unexpected results that make the code difficult to understand. For example, consider reading a program in which a programmer has used the following declaration:

```
r3      register 8         # define name r3 to be register 8!
```

The points can be summarized:

> *Because registers are fundamental to assembly language program-*
> *ming, each assembly language provides a way to identify registers. In*
> *some languages, special names are reserved; in others, a programmer*
> *can assign a name to a register.*

8.8 Operand Types

As Chapter 6 explains, most processors provide multiple types of operands. The assembly language for each processor must accommodate all operand types. As an example, suppose a processor allows each operand to specify a register, an immediate value (i.e. a constant), a memory address specified by a register or a group of registers, or a memory address specified as an offset beyond a register. The assembly language for the processor needs a syntactic form for each possible operand type.

We said that assembly languages often use special characters or names to distinguish registers from other values. In many assembly languages, for example, *10* refers to the constant ten, and *r10* refers to register ten. However, some assembly languages require a special symbol before a constant (e.g., *#10* to refer to the constant ten).

Each assembly language must provide syntactic forms for each possible operand type. Consider, for example, copying a value from a source to a target. If the processor allows the instruction to specify either a register (direct) or a memory location (indirect) as the source, the assembly language must provide a way for a programmer to distinguish the two. One assembly language uses parentheses to distinguish the two possibilities:

```
        mov     r2,r1       # copy contents of reg. 1 into reg. 2
        mov     r2,(r1)     # treat r1 as a pointer to memory and
                            # copy from the mem. location to reg. 2
```

The point is:

> *An assembly language provides a syntactic form for each possible*
> *operand type that the processor supports, including a reference to a*
> *register, an immediate value, and an indirect reference to memory.*

8.9 Assembly Language Programming Paradigm And Idioms

Because a programming language provides facilities that programmers use to structure data and code, a language can impact the programming process and the resulting code. Assembly language is especially significant because the language does not provide high-level constructs nor does the language enforce a particular style. Instead, assembly language gives a programmer complete freedom to code arbitrary sequences of instructions and store data in arbitrary memory locations.

Experienced programmers understand that consistency and clarity are usually more important than clever tricks or optimizations. Thus, experienced programmers develop idioms: patterns that they use consistently. The next sections use basic control structures to illustrate the concept of assembly language idioms.

8.10 Assembly Code For Conditional Execution

We use the term *condition execution* to refer to code that may or may not be executed, depending on a certain condition. Because conditional execution is a fundamental part of programming, high-level languages usually include one or more statements that allow a programmer to express conditional execution. The basic form of conditional execution is known as an *if* statement.

In assembly language, a programmer must code a sequence of statements to perform conditional execution. Figure 8.1 illustrates the form used for conditional execution in a typical high-level language and the equivalent form used in a typical assembly language.

```
    if (condition) {                code to test condition and
          body                          set condition code
    }                               branch not true to label
    next statement                  code to perform body
                            label:  code for next statement

        (a)                             (b)
```

Figure 8.1 (a) Conditional execution as specified in a high-level language, and (b) the equivalent assembly language code.

As the figure indicates, some processors use a *condition code* as the fundamental mechanism for conditional execution: when it performs an arithmetic operation or a comparison, the ALU sets the condition code. A conditional branch instruction is then used. Note that the branch must test the opposite of the condition (i.e., the branch is taken if the condition is not met). For example, consider the statement:

$$if \ (a == b) \ \{ \ x \ \}$$

If we assume *a* and *b* are stored in registers five and six, the equivalent assembly language is:

```
          cmp    r5, r6        # compare the values of a and b and set cc
          bne    lab1          # branch if previous comparison not equal
          code for x
lab1:     code for next statement
```

8.11 Assembly Code For A Conditional Alternative

High-level languages usually extend condition execution with an *if-then-else* statement that specifies code to be executed for the case when a condition is false as well as code to be executed when a condition is true. Figure 8.2 shows the assembly language equivalent of an *if-then-else* statement.

if (condition) {	code to test condition and
then_part	set condition code
} *else* {	branch not true to label1
else_part	code to perform then_part
}	branch to label2
next statement	label1: code for else_part
	label2: code for next statement
(a)	**(b)**

Figure 8.2 (a) An *if-then-else* statement used in a high-level language, and (b) the equivalent assembly language code.

8.12 Assembly Code For Definite Iteration

The term *definite iteration* refers to a programming language construct that causes a piece of code to be executed a fixed number of times. A typical high-level language uses a *for* statement to implement definite iteration. Figure 8.3 shows the assembly language equivalent of a *for* statement.

Definite iteration illustrates an interesting difference between a high-level language and assembly language: location of code. In assembly language, the code to implement a control structure can be divided into separate locations. In particular, although a programmer thinks of the initialization, continuation test, and increment as being specified in the header of a *for* statement, the equivalent assembly code places the increment after the code for the body.

```
for  (i= ; i<10; i++) {              sct r4 to zero
        body                  label1: compare r4 to 10
}                                     branch to label2 if >=
next statement                        code to perform body
                                      increment r4
                                      branch to label1
                              label2: code for next statement
```

        (a)   **(b)**

Figure 8.3 (a) A *for* statement used in a high-level language, and (b) the equivalent assembly language code using register 4 as an index.

8.13 Assembly Code For Indefinite Iteration

In programming language terminology, *indefinite iteration* refers to a loop that executes zero or more times. Typically, a high-level language uses the keyword *while* to indicate indefinite iteration. Figure 8.4 shows the assembly language equivalent of a *while* statement.

```
while  (condition) {           label1: code to compute condition
        body                           branch to label2 if not true
}                                      code to perform body
next statement                         branch to label1
                               label2: code for next statement
```

        (a)   **(b)**

Figure 8.4 (a) A *while* statement used in a high-level language, and (b) the equivalent assembly language code.

8.14 Assembly Code For Procedure Invocation

Architects use the term *procedure* or *subroutine* to refer to a piece of code that can be invoked, and the terms *procedure call* or *subroutine call* to refer to the invocation. The key idea is that when a subroutine is invoked, the processor records the location from which the call occurred, and resumes execution at that point once the subroutine completes. Thus, a given subroutine can be invoked from multiple points in a program because control always passes back to the location from which the invocation occurred.

Many processors provide two basic assembly instructions for procedure invocation. A *jump to subroutine* (*jsr*) instruction saves the current location and branches to a subroutine at a specified location, and a *return from subroutine* (*ret*) instruction causes the processor to return to the previously saved location. Figure 8.5 shows how the two assembly instructions can be used to code a procedure declaration and two invocations.

```
x( ) {                                x:    code for body of x
        body of function x                  ret

}


x( );                                       jsr  x
other statement;                            code for other statement
x( );                                       jsr  x
next statement                              code for next statement
```

            (a)   **(b)**

Figure 8.5 (a) A declaration for procedure *x* and two invocations in a high-level language, and (b) the assembly language equivalent.

8.15 Assembly Code For Parameterized Procedure Invocation

In a high-level language, procedure calls are *parameterized*. The procedure body is written with references to parameters, and the caller passes a set of values to the procedure that are known as *arguments*. When the procedure refers to a parameter, the value is obtained from the corresponding argument. The question arises: how are arguments passed to a procedure in assembly code?

Unfortunately, the details of argument passing vary widely among processors. For example, each of following three schemes has been used in at least one processor†:

- The processor uses a stack in memory for arguments
- The processor uses register windows to pass arguments
- The processor uses special-purpose argument registers

As an example, consider a processor in which registers *r1* through *r8* are used to pass arguments during a procedure call. Figure 8.6 shows the assembly language code for a procedure call on such an architecture.

---

†The storage used for a *return address* (i.e., the location to which a *ret* instruction should branch) is often related to the storage used for arguments.

x (a, b) {
 	
        body of function x
 	
}
	x: code for body of x that assumes
	            register 1 contains parameter *a*
	            and register 2 contains *b*
	    ret

x (-4, 17); other statement; x (71, 27); next statement	load -4 into register 1 load 17 into register 2 jsr x code for other statement load 71 into register 1 load 27 into register 2 jsr x code for next statement
(a)	**(b)**

Figure 8.6 (a) A declaration for parameterized procedure *x* and two invocations in a high-level language, and (b) the assembly language
equivalent for a processor that passes arguments in registers.

8.16 Consequence For Programmers

The consequence of a variety of argument passing schemes should be clear: the assembly language code needed to pass and reference arguments varies significantly from
one processor to another. More important, programmers are free to invent new mechanisms for argument passing that optimize performance. For example, even if the
hardware is designed to use a stack in memory, a programmer might choose to increase
performance by passing some arguments in general-purpose registers rather than
memory.

The point is:

No single argument passing paradigm is used in assembly languages
because a variety of hardware mechanisms exist for argument pass-
ing. In addition, programmers sometimes use alternatives to the basic
mechanism to optimize performance (e.g., passing values in registers).

8.17 Assembly Code For Function Invocation

The term *function* refers to a procedure that returns a single-value result. For example, an arithmetic function can be created to compute *sine(x)* — the argument specifies an angle, and the function returns the sine of the angle. Like a procedure, a function can have arguments, and a function can be invoked from an arbitrary point in the program. Thus, for a given processor, function invocation uses the same basic mechanisms as procedure invocation.

Despite the similarities between functions and procedures, function invocation requires one additional detail: an agreement that specifies exactly how the function result is returned. As with argument passing, many alternative implementations exist. Processors have been built that provide a separate, special-purpose hardware register for a return value. Other processors assume that the program will use one of the general-purpose registers. In any case, before executing a *ret* instruction, a function must load the return value into the location that the processor uses. After the return occurs, the calling program extracts and uses the return value.

8.18 Interaction Between Assembly And High-Level Languages

Interaction is possible in either direction between code written in an assembly language and code written in a high-level language. That is, a program written in a high-level language can call a procedure or function that has been written in assembly language, and a program written in assembly language can call a procedure or function that has been written in a high-level language. Of course, because a programmer can only control the assembly language code and not the high-level language code, the assembly program must follow the *calling conventions* that the high-level language uses. That is, the assembly code must use exactly the same mechanisms as the high-level language uses to store a return address, invoke a procedure, pass arguments, and return a function value.

Why would a programmer mix code written in assembly language with code written in a high-level language? In some cases, assembly code is needed because a high-level language does not allow direct interaction with the underlying hardware. For example, a computer that has special graphics hardware may need assembly code to use the graphics functions. In most cases, however, assembly language is only used to optimize performance — once a programmer identifies a particular piece of code as a bottleneck, the programmer writes an optimized version of the code in assembly language. Typically, optimized assembly language code is placed into a procedure or function; the rest of the program remains written in a high-level language. As a result, the most common case of interaction between code written in a high-level language and code written in assembly language consists of a program written in a high-level language calling a procedure or function that is written in an assembly language.

The point is:

> *Because writing application programs in assembly language is diffi-*
> *cult, assembly language is reserved for situations where a high level*
> *language has insufficient functionality or results in poor performance.*

8.19 Assembly Code For Variables And Storage

In addition to statements that generate instructions, most assembly languages permit a programmer to define data items. Both initialized and uninitialized variables can
be declared. For example, some assembly languages use the directive *.word* to declare
storage for a sixteen bit item, and the directive *.long* to declare storage for a thirty-two
bit item. Figure 8.7 shows declarations in a high-level language and equivalent assembly code.

```
int    x, y, z;              x:   .long
                             y:   .long
                             z:   .long
short  w, q;                 w:   .word
                             q:   .word
statement                         code for statement
```

            (a)   **(b)**

Figure 8.7 (a) Declaration of variables in a high-level language, and (b)
equivalent variable declarations in assembly language.

The keywords *.word* and *.long* are known as assembly language *directives*.
Although it appears in the same location that an opcode appears, a directive does not
correspond to an instruction. Instead, a directive controls the translation. The directives
in the figure specify that storage locations should be reserved to hold variables. In most
assembly languages, a directive that reserves storage also allows a programmer to specify an initial value. Thus, the directive:

```
x:   .word   949
```

reserves a sixteen bit memory location, assigns the location the integer value 949, and
defines *x* to be a *label* (i.e., a name) that the programmer can use to refer to the location.

8.20 Two-Pass Assembler

We use the term *assembler* for a piece of software that translates assembly language programs into binary code for the processor to execute. Conceptually, an assembler is similar to a compiler because each takes a source program as input and produces equivalent binary code as output. An assembler differs from a compiler, however, because a compiler has significantly more responsibility. For example, a compiler can choose how to allocate variables to memory, which sequence of instructions to use for each statement, and which values to keep in general-purpose registers. An assembler cannot make such choices because the programmer specifies the exact details.

The difference between an assembler and compiler can be summarized:

> *Although both a compiler and an assembler translate a source program into equivalent binary code, a compiler has more freedom to choose which values are kept in registers, the instructions used to implement each statement, and the allocation of variables to memory. An assembler merely provides a one-to-one translation of each statement in the source program to the equivalent binary form.*

Conceptually, an assembler follows a *two-pass algorithm*, which means the assembler scans through the source programs two times†. To understand why two passes are needed, observe that many branch instructions contain *forward references* (i.e., the label referenced in the branch is defined later in the program). Thus, to generate code for a branch instruction, the assembler needs to know the address that will be associated with each label. For example, Figure 8.8 shows a snippet of assembly language code and the relative location of statements.

locations			assembly code		
0x00	–	0x03	x:	.word	
0x04	–	0x07	label1:	cmp	r1, r2
0x08	–	0x0B		bne	label2
0x0C	–	0x0F		jsr	label3
0x10	–	0x13	label2:	ld	r3, 0
0x14	–	0x17		br	label4
0x18	–	0x1B	label3:	add	r5, 1
0x1C	–	0x1F		ret	
0x20	–	0x23	label4:	ld	r1, 1
0x24	–	0x27		ret	

Figure 8.8 A snippet of assembly language code and the locations assigned to each statement for a hypothetical processor. Locations are determined in the assembler's first pass.

---

†Assembly can be performed in a single pass if an assembler can return and update locations that were generated previously.

Once the assembler has completed its first pass, a location has been assigned to each statement. Consequently, the assembler knows the value for each label in the program. In the figure, for example, the assembler knows that *label4* starts at location 32 (0x20). Thus, when the second pass of the assembler encounters the statement:

br   label4

the assembler can generate a branch to location 32. Similarly, code can be generated for each of the other instructions during the second pass because the location of each label is known.

It is not important to understand the details of an assembler, but merely to know that:

> *Conceptually, an assembler makes two passes over an assembly language program. During the first pass, the assembler assigns a location to each statement. During the second pass, the assembler uses the assigned locations to generate code.*

Now that we understand how an assembler works, we can discuss one of the chief advantages of using an assembler: automatic recalculation of branch addresses. To see how automatic recalculation helps, consider a programmer working on a program. If the programmer inserts a statement in the program, the location of each successive statement changes. As a result, every branch instruction that refers to a label beyond the insertion point must be changed.

Without an assembler, changing branch labels can be tedious and prone to errors. Furthermore, programmers often make a series of changes while debugging a program. An assembler allows a programmer to make a change easily — the programmer merely reruns the assembler to produce a binary image with all branch addresses corrected.

8.21 Assembly Language Macros

Because assembly language is low-level, even trivial operations can require many instructions. More important, an assembly language programmer often finds that sequences of code are repeated with only minor changes between instances. Repeated sequences of code make programming tedious, and can lead to errors if a programmer uses a cut-and-paste approach.

To help programmers avoid repetitive coding, many assembly languages include a *parameterized macro* facility. To use a macro facility, a programmer adds two types of items to the source program: one or more macro *definitions* and one or more macro *expansions*.

In essence, a macro facility adds an extra pass to the assembler. That is, the assembler makes an initial pass in which macros are expanded. The important concept is that the macro expansion pass does not begin the translation to binary. Instead, macro expansion produces an assembly language source program which becomes the input to the usual two-pass assembly process. In fact, many assemblers allow a programmer to obtain a copy of the expanded source code for use in debugging (i.e., to see if macro expansion is proceeding as planned).

Although the details of assembly language macros vary across assembly languages, the concept is straightforward. A macro definition is usually bracketed by keywords (e.g., *macro* and *endmacro*), and contains a sequence of code. For example, Figure 8.9 illustrates a definition for a macro named *addmem* that adds the contents of two memory locations and places the result in a third location.

```
macro   addmem(a, b, c)
load    r1, a    # load 1st arg into register 1
load    r2, b    # load 2nd arg into register 2
add     r1, r2   # add register 2 to register 1
store   r3, c    # store the result in 3rd arg
endmacro
```

Figure 8.9 An example macro definition using the keywords *macro* and *endmacro*. Items in the macro can refer to parameters *a*, *b*, and *c*.

Once a macro has been defined, the macro can be expanded by supplying arguments in place of the parameters. The assembler replaces the macro call with a copy of the body of the macro. For example, Figure 8.10 shows the assembly code generated by an expansion of the *addmem* macro defined in Figure 8.9.

```
#
# note: code below results from addmem(xxx, YY, zqz)
#
load    r1, xxx  # load 1st arg into register 1
load    r2, YY   # load 2nd arg into register 2
add     r1, r2   # add register 2 to register 1
store   r3, zqz  # store the result in 3rd arg
```

Figure 8.10 An example of the assembly code that results from an expansion of macro *addmem*.

It is important to understand that although the macro definition in Figure 8.9 resembles a procedure declaration, a macro does not operate like a procedure. First, there is no code associated with the declaration of a macro. Second, when a macro is expanded, a complete copy of the code is inserted in the program. Third, macro argu-

ments are treated as strings that replace the corresponding parameter. The literal substitution of arguments is especially important to understand because it can yield unexpected results. For example, consider Figure 8.11 which illustrates how an illegal assembly
program can result from a macro expansion.

```
#
# note: code below results from addmem(1+, %*J , +)
#
load    r1, 1+    # load 1st arg into register 1
load    r2, %*J   # load 2nd arg into register 2
add     r1, r2    # add register 2 to register 1
store   r3, +     # store the result in 3rd arg
```

Figure 8.11 An example of an illegal program that can result from an expansion of macro *addmem*. The assembler substitutes arguments
without checking validity.

As the figure shows, an arbitrary string can be used as an argument to the macro,
which means a programmer can make a mistake without any warning until the assembler processes the expanded source program. For example, the first argument in the example consists of the string *1+*, which is an error. The assembler substitutes the string
which results in:

load r1, 1+

Similarly, substitution of the second argument, *%*J*, results in:

load r2, %*J

which make no sense. However, the errors will not be detected until after the macro expander has run and the assembler attempts to assemble the program. More important,
because macro expansion produces a source program, error messages that refer to line
numbers will reference lines in the expanded program, not in the original source code
that a programmer submits.

The point is:

> *A macro expansion facility preprocesses an assembly language source program to produce another source program in which each macro invocation is replaced by the text of the macro with parameters substituted. Because a macro processor uses textual substitution, errors in the source program are not detected by the macro processor; errors are only detected by the assembler after the macro processor completes.*

8.22 Summary

Assembly languages are low-level languages that incorporate characteristics of a processor, such as the instruction set, operand addressing, and registers. Many assembly languages exist, one or more for each type of processor. Despite differences, most assembly languages follow the same basic structure.

Each statement in an assembly language corresponds to a single instruction on the underlying hardware; the statement consists of an optional label, opcode, and operands. The assembly language for a processor defines a syntactic form for each type of operand the processor accepts.

Although assembly languages differ, most follow the same basic paradigm. Thus, we can specify typical assembly language sequences for conditional execution, conditional execution with alternate paths, definite iteration, and indefinite iteration. Although most processors include instructions used to invoke a subroutine and return to the caller, the details of argument passing, return address storage, and return of a function value differ. Some processors place arguments in memory, and others pass arguments in registers.

An assembler is a piece of software that translates an assembly language source program into binary code that the processor can execute. Conceptually, an assembler makes two passes over the source program: one to assign addresses and one to generate code. Many assemblers include a macro facility to help programmers avoid tedious coding repetition; the macro expander generates a source program which is then assembled. Because it uses textual substitution, macro expansion can result in illegal code that is reported by the assembler.

Memories

Program And Data
Storage Technologies

9

Memory And Storage

9.1 Introduction

Previous chapters examine one of the major components used in computer systems: processors. The chapters review processor architectures, including instruction sets, operands, and the structure of complex CPUs.

This chapter introduces the second major component used in computer systems: memories. Successive chapters explore the basic forms of memory: physical memory, virtual memory, and caches. Later chapters examine I/O, and show how I/O devices use memory.

9.2 Definition

When programmers think of memory, they usually focus on the main memory found in a conventional computer. From the programmer's point of view, the main memory holds running programs as well as the data the programs use. As we will see, however, memory has a much broader meaning that includes a variety of special-purpose memory devices such as the memory in a cell phone that holds an address book of phone numbers, the memory that holds the program for an embedded processor, or the memory in a digital camera that holds a set of images.

An architect views a *memory* as a solid-state digital device that provides storage for data values. The next sections clarify the concept by examining the variety of possibilities.

9.3 The Key Aspects Of Memory

When an architect begins to design a memory, two key choices arise:

- Technology
- Organization

Technology refers to the properties of the underlying hardware mechanisms used to construct the memory system. We will learn that many technologies are available, and see examples of properties. We will also learn how basic technologies operate, and understand when each technology is appropriate.

Organization refers to the way the underlying technology is used to form a working system. We will see that there are many choices about how to combine individual bits into larger units and how to address the units.

In essence, technology refers to the lowest-level pieces (i.e., individual chips), and organization refers to how those chips are used to create meaningful storage systems. We will see that both aspects contribute to a memory system.

9.4 Characteristics Of Memory Technologies

Memory technology is not easy to define because a wide range of technologies has been invented. To help clarify the broad purpose and intent of a given type of memory, engineers use several characteristics:

- Volatile or nonvolatile
- Random or sequential access
- Read-write or read-only
- Primary or secondary

9.4.1 Memory Volatility

Memory is classified as *volatile* if the contents of the memory disappear when power is removed. The main memory used in most computers is volatile — when the computer is shut down, the running applications vanish.

In contrast, memory is known as *nonvolatile* if the contents survive even after power is removed. For example, memory used in most digital cameras is nonvolatile — the images remain even if the memory is removed from the camera and plugged into a computer or printer.

9.4.2 Memory Access Paradigm

The most common forms of memory are classified as *random access*, which means that any value in the memory can be accessed at any time. The alternative to random access is *sequential access* in which values must be read from memory in the same order they were inserted. Hardware engineers use the term *FIFO*† for a sequential access memory.

9.4.3 Permanence Of Values

Memory is characterized by whether values can be extracted, updated, or both. The primary form of memory used in a conventional computer system permits an arbitrary value in memory to be accessed (read) or updated (written) at any time. However, other forms of memory provide more permanence. For example, some memory is characterized as *Read Only Memory* (*ROM*) because the memory contains data values that can be accessed, but cannot be changed.

A form of ROM, *Programmable Read Only Memory* (*PROM*), allows data values to be entered once, and then accessed many times. Typically, values are initially placed in PROM by using high voltage to alter the physical circuits on the chip (e.g., to destroy the electrical path that corresponds to a zero bit). Informally, we say that values are burned into the memory.

Intermediate forms of permanence also exist. For example, an *Electrically Erasable Programmable Read Only Memory* (*EEPROM*) is a form of nonvolatile memory that permits values to change. However, storing a value in EEPROM memory requires activation of special circuits, and takes much longer than reading a value. Thus, EEPROMs are used in situations where nonvolatility is desired, but values change infrequently.

A popular variant of EEPROM technology known as *Flash memory* or *Flash ROM* is commonly used in digital cameras — although it takes longer to store an image in Flash, the delay is not critical because it happens in less time than is required for a human to aim and focus the camera.

9.4.4 Primary And Secondary Memory

The terms *primary* and *secondary* are qualitative. Originally, they were used to distinguish between the fast, volatile, internal main memory of a computer and the slower, nonvolatile storage provided by an external electromechanical device such as a hard disk. However, architects can also create systems in which two distinct solid-state memory technologies are used for primary and secondary storage. For example, small, portable devices known as *microdrives* are available commercially that use solid-state memory to store files.

---

†FIFO abbreviates *First-In-First-Out*.

9.5 The Important Concept Of A Memory Hierarchy

The notions of primary and secondary memory arise as part of the *memory hierarchy* in a computer system. To understand the hierarchy, we must consider both performance and cost: memory that has the highest performance characteristics is also the most expensive. Thus, an architect must choose memory that satisfies cost constraints.

Research on memory use has led to an interesting principle: for a given cost, optimal performance is not achieved by using one type of memory throughout a computer. Instead, a set of technologies should be arranged in a conceptual *memory hierarchy*. The hierarchy has a small amount of the highest performance memory, a slightly larger amount of slightly slower memory, and so on. For example, an architect selects a small number of general-purpose registers, a larger amount of primary memory, and an even larger amount of secondary memory. We can summarize the principle:

> *To optimize memory performance for a given cost, a set of technologies are arranged in a hierarchy that contains a relatively small amount of fast memory and larger amounts of less expensive, but slower memory.*

Chapter 12 returns to the concept of memory hierarchy. The chapter presents the scientific principle behind a hierarchical structure, and explains how a memory mechanism known as a *cache* uses the principle to achieve higher performance without high cost.

9.6 Instruction And Data Store

Some of the earliest computer systems used separate memories for programs and data. Later, most architects adopted a *Von Neumann architecture†* in which a single memory holds both programs and data.

Interestingly, the advent of specialized solid state memory technologies has reintroduced the separation of program and data memory — special-purpose systems sometimes use separate memories. Memory used to hold a program is known as *instruction store*, and memory used to hold data is known as *data store*.

One of the motivations for a separate instruction store comes from the notion of memory hierarchy: on many systems, an instruction store needs higher performance than a data store. To understand why, observe that high-speed instructions are designed to operate on values in general-purpose registers rather than values in memory. Thus, many instructions do not use the data store. Furthermore, an instruction is accessed on each iteration of the fetch-execute cycle. Thus, the instruction store experiences more activity than the data store. We can summarize:

---

†The architectures are named for John Von Neumann, a mathematician and computer pioneer.

Although most modern computer systems place programs and data in a single memory, it is possible to separate the instruction store from the data store. Doing so allows an architect to select memory performance appropriate for each activity.

9.7 The Fetch-Store Paradigm

As we will see, all memory technologies use a single paradigm that is known as *fetch-store*. For now, it is only important to understand that there are two basic operations associated with the paradigm: fetching a value from the memory or storing a value into the memory. The fetch operation is sometimes called *read* or *load*, and the store operation is sometimes called *write*. When we discuss I/O, we will understand how the fetch-store paradigm is implemented and how memory access is related to I/O.

9.8 Summary

The two key aspects of memory are the underlying technology and the organization. A variety of technologies exist; they can be characterized as volatile or nonvolatile, random or sequential access, permanent or nonpermanent (read-only or read-write), and primary or secondary.

To achieve maximal performance at a given cost, an architect organizes memory into a conceptual hierarchy. The hierarchy contains a small amount of high performance memory and a large amount of lower performance memory.

Memory systems use a fetch-store paradigm in which the memory supports two operations: one that retrieves a value from memory and another that stores a value into memory.

10

Physical Memory And Physical Addressing

10.1 Introduction

The previous chapter introduces the topic of memory, lists characteristics of memory systems, and explains the concept of a memory hierarchy. This chapter explains how a basic memory system operates. The chapter considers both the underlying technologies used to construct a computer memory, and the organization of the memory into bytes and words. The next chapter expands the discussion to consider virtual memory.

10.2 Characteristics Of Computer Memory

Engineers use the term *Random Access Memory* (*RAM*) to denote the type of memory used as the primary memory system in most computers. As the name implies, RAM provides random access. In addition, RAM offers read-write capability that allows either access or update. Finally, most RAM is volatile; values do not persist after the computer is powered down.

10.3 Static And Dynamic RAM Technologies

The technologies used to implement Random Access Memory can be divided into two broad categories. *Static RAM (SRAM†)* is the easiest type for programmers to understand because it is a straightforward extension of digital logic. Conceptually, SRAM stores each data bit in a miniature digital circuit composed of multiple transistors similar to the *flip-flop* discussed in Chapter 2. Although the details are beyond the scope of this text, Figure 10.1 illustrates the circuit connections.

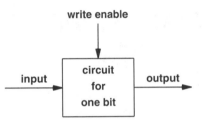

Figure 10.1 Illustration of a miniature Static RAM circuit that stores one data bit. The circuit contains multiple transistors.

In the figure, the circuit has two inputs and one output. Whenever the *write enable* input is on (i.e., a positive voltage), the circuit sets the output value equal to the input (zero or one). Whenever the *write enable* input is off (i.e., zero volts), the circuit ignores the input and keeps the output at the last setting. Thus, to write a value, the hardware places the desired value on the input, turns on the write enable line and then turns it off again. While the enable line is on, the circuit records the input value. When the enable line is turned off, the circuit holds the output value.

Although it performs at high speed, SRAM has a significant disadvantage: power consumption and heat. The miniature circuit contains many transistors that operate continuously. Each transistor consumes a small amount of power and generates heat.

The alternative to Static RAM, which is known as *Dynamic RAM (DRAM‡)*, consumes less power. However, the internal working of Dynamic RAM is surprising and can be confusing. At the lowest level, to store information, DRAM uses a circuit that acts like a *capacitor*, a device that stores electrical charge. When a value is written to DRAM, the hardware charges or discharges the capacitor to reflect the digital value. Later, when a value is read from DRAM, the hardware examines the charge on the capacitor and generates the appropriate digital value.

The conceptual difficulty surrounding DRAM arises from the way a capacitor works: because physical systems are imperfect, a capacitor gradually loses its charge. In essence, a DRAM chip is an imperfect memory device — if a value is left long enough, the charge dissipates and the bit becomes zero. More important, DRAM loses its charge in a short time (e.g., in some cases, under a second).

---

†SRAM is pronounced ''ess-ram''.
‡DRAM is pronounced ''dee-ram''.

How can DRAM be used as a computer memory if values quickly become zero? The answer lies in a simple technique: devise a way to read a bit out of memory before the charge has time to dissipate, and then write the same value back again. Writing a value causes the capacitor to start again with a full charge. So, reading and then writing a bit will reset the capacitor without changing the value of the bit.

In practice, computers that use DRAM contain an extra hardware circuit, known as a *refresh circuit*, that performs the task of reading and then writing a bit. Figure 10.2 illustrates the concept.

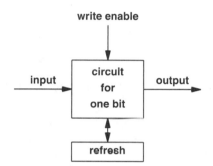

Figure 10.2 Illustration of a bit in Dynamic RAM. An external refresh circuit must periodically read the data value and write it back again or the charge will dissipate, and the value will be lost.

The refresh hardware is more complex than the figure implies. To keep the refresh circuit small, architects do not build one refresh circuit for each bit. Instead, a single, small refresh mechanism is designed that can cycle through the entire memory. As it reaches a bit, the refresh circuit reads the bit, writes the value back, and then moves on.

Complexity also arises because a refresh circuit must coordinate with normal memory operations. In addition to avoiding delay, the hardware must ensure that the value of a bit does not change between the time the refresh circuit reads the bit and the time the refresh circuit writes the same value back. Despite the need for a refresh circuit, the cost and power consumption advantages of DRAM are so great that most computer memory is composed of DRAM rather than SRAM.

10.4 Measures Of Memory Technology

Architects use several quantitative measures to assess memory technology; two stand out:

- Density
- Latency and cycle times

10.5 Density

In a strict sense, the term *density* refers to the number of memory cells per square area of silicon. In practice, however, density often refers to the number of bits that can be represented on a standard size chip. Thus, an engineer might refer to a "1 meg chip", meaning a standard size chip that holds one megabit of memory. Higher density is usually desirable because it means more memory can be held in the same physical space. However, higher density has the disadvantages of increased power utilization and, because more electric current generates more heat, increased heat generation.

The density of memory chips is related to the size of transistors in the underlying silicon technology, which has followed Moore's Law. Thus, memory density tends to double approximately every eighteen months.

10.6 Separation Of Read And Write Performance

A second measure of a memory technology focuses on speed: how fast can the memory respond to requests. It may seem that speed should be easy to measure, but it is not. For example, as the previous chapter discusses, some memory technologies take much longer to write values than to read them. To choose an appropriate memory technology, an architect needs to understand both the cost of access and the cost of update. Thus, a principle arises:

> *In many memory technologies, the time required to fetch information from memory differs from the time required to store information in memory, and the difference can be dramatic. Therefore, any measure of memory performance must give two values: the performance of* read *operations and the performance of* write *operations.*

10.7 Latency And Memory Controllers

In addition to separating *read* and *write* operations, we must decide exactly what to measure. It may seem that the most important measure is *latency* (i.e., the time that elapses between the start of an operation and the completion of the operation). However, latency is a simplistic measure that does not provide complete information.

To see why latency does not suffice as a measure of memory performance, we need to understand how the hardware works. In addition to the memory chips themselves, additional hardware known as a *memory controller* provides an interface†. Figure 10.3 illustrates the organization.

---

†We will learn more about the memory controller later in the chapter.

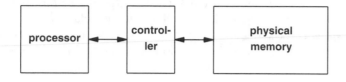

Figure 10.3 Illustration of the hardware used for memory access. A controller sits between the processor and physical memory.

To access memory, a device (typically a processor) presents a *read* or *write* request to the controller. The controller translates the memory address and request into signals appropriate for the underlying memory, and passes the signals to the memory chips. To minimize latency, the controller returns an answer as quickly as possible (i.e., as soon as the memory responds). However, after it responds to the device, a controller may need additional clock cycle(s) to reset hardware circuits and prepare for the next operation.

A second principle of memory performance arises:

> *Because a memory system may need extra time between operations, latency is an insufficient measure of performance; a performance measure needs to measure the time required for successive operations.*

That is, to assess the performance of a memory system, we need to measure how fast the system can perform a sequence of operations. Engineers use the term *memory cycle time* to capture the idea. Specifically, they use two separate measures: the *read cycle time* (abbreviated *tRC*) and the *write cycle time* (abbreviated *tWC*).

We can summarize:

> *The* read cycle time *and* write cycle time *are used as measures of memory system performance because they measure how quickly the memory system can handle successive requests.*

10.8 Synchronized Memory Technologies

Like most other digital circuits in a computer, memory systems use a *clock* that controls exactly when a *read* or *write* operation begins. As Figure 10.3 shows, however, a memory system is linked to a device such as a processor. What happens if the processor's clock differs from the clock used for memory? The system still works because the controller holds a request from the processor or a response from the memory until the other side is ready.

Unfortunately, the difference in clock rates does affect performance — although the delay is small, it can be nontrivial. To eliminate the delay, some memory systems use a *synchronized* clock system. That is, the clock pulses used with the memory system are aligned with the clock pulses used to run the processor, which helps eliminate further delays. Synchronization can be used with DRAM or SRAM, which results in two technologies:

SDRAM– Synchronized Dynamic Random Access Memory

SSRAM– Synchronized Static Random Access Memory

In practice, synchronization has been effective; many computers now use SDRAM as the primary memory technology.

10.9 Multiple Data Rate Memory Technologies

In many computer systems, memory is the bottleneck — speeding the memory system improves overall performance. As a result, engineers have concentrated on memory technologies with lower cycle times. One approach uses a technique that runs the memory system at a multiple of the normal clock rate (e.g., double). Because the clock runs faster, the memory can deliver data faster. Therefore, the technologies are known as *fast data rate* memories, typically *double data rate* or *quadruple data rate*.

10.10 Examples Of Memory Technologies

Although we have covered the highlights, our discussion of memory technology does not begin to illustrate the range of choices available to an architect or the detailed differences among them. For example, Figure 10.4 lists a few commercially available RAM technologies

10.11 Memory Organization

We said that there are two key aspects of memory: the technology used and the way memory is organized. As we have seen, an architect can choose from a variety of memory technologies; we will now consider the second aspect. Memory organization refers to both the internal structure of the hardware and the external addressing structure that the memory presents to a processor. We will see that the two are related.

Technology	Description
DDR-DRAM	Double Data Rate Dynamic RAM
DDR-SDRAM	Double Data Rate Synchronized Dynamic RAM
FCRAM	Fast Cycle RAM
FPM-DRAM	Fast Page Mode Dynamic RAM
QDR-DRAM	Quad Data Rate Dynamic RAM
QDR-SRAM	Quad Data Rate Static RAM
SDRAM	Synchronized Dynamic RAM
SSRAM	Synchronized Static RAM
ZBT-SRAM	Zero Bus Turnaround Static RAM
RDRAM	Rambus Dynamic RAM
RLDRAM	Reduced Latency Dynamic RAM

Figure 10.4 Examples of commercially available RAM technologies. Many other technologies exist.

10.12 Memory Access And Memory Bus

To understand how memory is organized, we need to examine the access paradigm. Recall from Figure 10.3 that a *memory controller* provides the interface between a physical memory and a processor that uses the memory†. Several questions arise. What is the structure of the connection between a processor and memory? What values pass across the connection? How does the processor view the memory system?

To achieve high performance, memory systems use parallelism: the connection between the processor and controller consists of many wires that are used simultaneously. Each wire can transfer one data bit at any time. Figure 10.5 illustrates the concept.

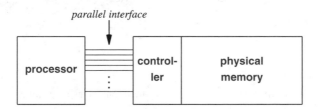

Figure 10.5 The parallel connection between a processor and memory. A connection that contains N wires, allows N bits of data to be transferred simultaneously.

The technical name for the hardware connection between a processor and memory is *bus* (more specifically, *memory bus*). We will learn about buses in the chapters on I/O; for now, it is sufficient to understand that a bus provides parallel connections.

---

†In later chapters, we will learn that I/O devices also access memory through the memory controller; for now, we will use a processor in the examples.

10.13 Memory Transfer Size

The parallel connections of a memory bus are important to both programmers and computer architects. From an architectural standpoint, the parallel connections improve performance. From a programming point of view, the parallel connections define a *memory transfer size* (i.e., the amount of data that can be read or written to memory in a single operation).

In the next section, we will see that transfer size is a crucial aspect of memory organization. A later section considers how transfer size affects programming.

10.14 Physical Addresses And Words

The bits that comprise physical memory are divided into blocks of N bits per block, where N is the memory transfer size. A block of N bits is sometimes called a *word*, and the transfer size is called the *word size* or the *width* of a word.

Each word of physical memory is assigned a unique number known as a *physical memory address*; the approach is known as *word addressing*. As Figure 10.6 illustrates, we can think of physical memory as an array of words, with addresses starting at zero.

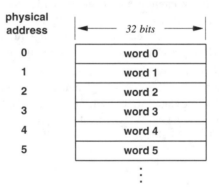

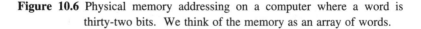

Figure 10.6 Physical memory addressing on a computer where a word is thirty-two bits. We think of the memory as an array of words.

10.15 Physical Memory Operations

The controller for physical memory supports two operations: *read* and *write*. In the case of a *read* operation, the processor specifies an address; in the case of a *write* operation, the processor specifies an address as well as data to be written. The crucial idea is that the controller always accepts or delivers an entire word; physical memory hardware does not provide a way to read or write less than a complete word (i.e., the hardware does not allow the processor to access or alter part of a word).

The point is:

> *Physical memory is organized into words, where a word is equal to the memory transfer size. Each read or write operation applies to an entire word.*

10.16 Word Size And Other Data Types

We said that because simultaneous transfer is possible, a memory with many wires has high performance. More important: an interface that has more wires will transfer data at a higher rate. That is, a memory system that uses a word size of K will have higher performance than a memory system that uses a word size less than K. Of course, increasing the word size increases the cost of the hardware.

What word size should an architect choose? The question is complicated by several factors. First, because memory is used to store data, the word size should accommodate common data values (e.g., the word should be large enough to hold an integer). Second, because memory is used to store programs, the word size should accommodate frequently used instructions. Third, because parallel hardware takes space and adds to the economic cost, the word size is chosen as a compromise between performance and various costs. For example, some architects have chosen a word size of thirty-two bits; others have selected sixty-four.

In most cases, an architect designs all parts of a computer system to work together. Thus, if an architect chooses a memory word size equal to thirty-two bits, the architect will make a standard integer and a single-precision floating point value each occupy thirty-two bits. As a result, a computer system is often characterized by stating the word size (e.g., a thirty-two bit processor).

10.17 An Extreme Case: Byte Addressing

Programmers who have used a conventional computer are usually surprised to learn that physical memory is organized into words because most programmers are familiar with an alternate form of addressing known as *byte addressing*. Byte addressing is especially convenient for programming because it gives a programmer an easy way to access small data items such as characters.

When byte addressing is used, memory is organized as an array of bytes rather than an array of words. The choice of byte addressing has two important consequences. First, because each byte of memory is assigned an address, byte addressing requires more addresses than word addressing. Second, because byte addressing allows a program to read or write a single byte, the memory controller must support byte transfer.

10.18 Byte Addressing With Word Transfers

We said that because a parallel interface supports simultaneous transfer, a memory interface with many wires has higher performance than a memory interface with fewer wires. Because a byte is smaller than a typical word, a memory system that offers byte addressing will have lower performance than a memory system that offers word addressing.

Can we devise a memory system that combines the higher speed of word addressing with the programming convenience of byte addressing? Yes. To do so, we need an intelligent memory controller that can translate between the two addressing schemes. The controller accepts byte addresses from the processor, and uses word addresses for the underlying memory — when the processor requests a byte, the controller reads the appropriate word of memory and extracts the specified byte. Figure 10.7 illustrates a mapping between the two addressing schemes.

physical address	32 bits			
0	0	1	2	3
1	4	5	6	7
2	8	9	10	11
3	12	13	14	15
4	16	17	18	19
5	20	21	22	23

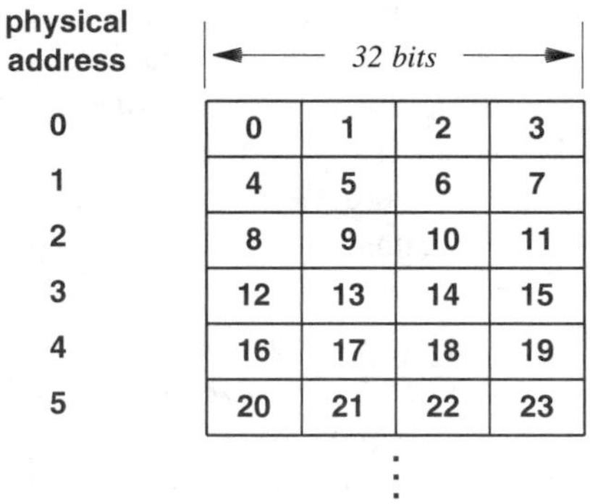

Figure 10.7 Illustration of one possible mapping between byte addresses used by a processor and word addresses used by the underlying hardware.

To implement the mapping shown in the figure, a controller must convert byte addresses issued by the processor to word addresses. For example, if the processor requests a *read* operation for byte address 17, the controller must issue a *read* request for word 4, and then extract the second byte from the word.

Because the memory can only transfer an entire word at a time, a byte *write* operation is expensive. For example, if a processor writes byte 11, the controller must read word 2 from memory, replace the rightmost byte, and then write the entire word back to memory.

Mathematically, the translation of addresses is straightforward. To translate a byte address, B, to the corresponding word address, W, the controller divides B by N, the number of bytes per word, and ignores the remainder. Similarly, to compute a byte offset within a word, the controller computes the remainder of B divided by N. That is, the word address is given by:

$$W = \left\lfloor \frac{B}{N} \right\rfloor$$

and the offest is given by:

$$O = B \bmod N$$

As an example, consider the values in Figure 10.7, where $N=4$. A byte address of 11 translates to a word address of 2 and an offset of 3, which means that byte 11 is found in word 2 at byte offset 3†.

10.19 Using Powers Of Two

Performing a division or computing a remainder is time consuming and requires extra hardware (e.g., an Arithmetic Logic Unit). To avoid computation, architects organize memory using powers of two. Doing so means that hardware can perform the two computations above simply by extracting bits. In Figure 10.7, for example, $N = 2^2$, which means that the offset can be computed by extracting the two low-order bits, and the word address can be computed by extracting everything except the two low-order bits. Figure 10.8 illustrates the idea:

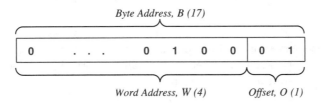

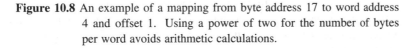

Figure 10.8 An example of a mapping from byte address 17 to word address 4 and offset 1. Using a power of two for the number of bytes per word avoids arithmetic calculations.

We can summarize:

> *To avoid arithmetic calculations, such as division or remainder, physical memory is organized such that the number of bytes per word is a power of two, which means the translation from a byte address to a word address and offset can be performed by extracting bits.*

---

†The offset is measured from zero.

10.20 Byte Alignment And Programming

Knowing how the underlying hardware works helps explain a concept that programmers encounter: *byte alignment*. We say that an integer value is *aligned* if the bytes of the integer correspond to a word in the underlying physical memory. In Figure 10.7, for example, an integer composed of bytes 12, 13, 14, and 15 is aligned, but an integer composed of bytes 6, 7, 8, and 9 is not.

On some architectures, byte alignment is required — the processor raises an error if a program attempts an integer access using an unaligned address. On other processors, arbitrary alignment is allowed, but unaligned accesses result in lower performance than aligned accesses. We can now understand why an unaligned address requires more accesses of physical memory: the memory controller must convert each processor request into operations on the underlying memory. If an integer spans two words, the controller must perform two *read* operations to obtain the requested bytes. Thus, even if the processor permits unaligned access, programmers are strongly encouraged to align data values.

We can summarize:

> *The organization of physical memory affects programming: even if a processor allows unaligned memory access, aligning data on boundaries that correspond to the physical word size can improve program performance.*

10.21 Memory Size And Address Space

How large can a memory be? It may seem that memory size is only an economic issue — more memory simply costs more money. However, size turns out be an essential aspect of memory architecture because overall memory size is inherently linked to other choices such as the addressing scheme.

The most significant limitation on size arises because a processor imposes a fixed bound on the size of an address that can be generated. Typically, the processor limits an address to be the same size as an integer. For example, a system that uses thirty-two bit integers typically uses thirty-two bit addresses. As Chapter 3 points out, a string of k bits can represent 2^k values. Thus, a thirty-two bit value can represent:

$$2^{32} = 4,294,967,296$$

unique addresses (i.e., addresses 0 through 4,294,967,295). We use the term *address space* to denote the set of possible addresses.

The tradeoff between byte addressing and word addressing is now clear: given a fixed address size, the amount of memory that can be addressed depends on whether the processor uses byte addressing or word addressing. Furthermore, if word addressing is used, the amount of memory that can be addressed depends on the word size. For example, on a computer that uses word addressing with four bytes per word, a thirty-two bit value can hold enough addresses for 17,179,869,184 bytes (i.e., four times as much as when byte addressing is used).

10.22 Programming With Word Addressing

Many processors use byte addressing because byte addressing provides the most convenient interface for programmers. However, byte addressing does not maximize memory size. Therefore, some systems use word addressing, which provides access to the maximum amount of memory for a given address size†.

On a processor that uses word addressing, software must handle the details of byte manipulation. In essence, software performs the controller functions. For example, to extract a byte, software must locate and read the appropriate word, and extract the desired byte. Similarly, to write a byte, software locates the appropriate word, reads the word, updates the specified byte, and writes the modified word back to memory. To optimize software performance, logical shifts and bit masking are used to manipulate an address rather than division or remainder computation. Similarly, shifts and logical operations are used to extract bytes from a word. For example, to extract the leftmost byte from a thirty-two bit word, w, a programmer can code a C statement:

$$(w \ >> \ 24 \ ) \ \& \ 0xff$$

10.23 Measures Of Memory Size

We can characterize physical memory architecture as follows:

Physical memory is organized into a set of M *words that each contain* N *bytes; to make controller hardware efficient,* M *and* N *are each chosen to be powers of two.*

The use of powers of two for word and address space size has an interesting consequence: the maximum amount of memory is always a power of two rather than a power of ten. As a result, memory size is measured in powers of two. For example, a *Kilobyte (Kbyte)* is defined to consist of 2^{10} bytes, and a *Megabyte (MB)* is defined to consist of 2^{20} bytes. The terminology is confusing because it is an exception. In computer networking, for example, a measure of *Megabits per second* refers to base ten. Thus one must be careful when mixing memory size with other measures (e.g., although there are eight bits per byte, one Kilobyte of data in memory is not eight times larger than one Kilobit of data sent across a network).

---

†Systems, such as supercomputers, that are designed to manipulate numeric values often use word addressing because applications running on such systems seldom manipulate individual bytes.

10.24 Pointers And Data Structures

Memory addresses are important because they form the basis for commonly used data abstractions, such as linked lists or trees. Consequently, programming languages often provide facilities that allow a programmer to declare a *pointer* variable that holds a memory address, assign a value to a pointer, or dereference a pointer to obtain an item.

In the C programming language, for example, the declaration:

char   *cptr;

declares variable *cptr* to be a pointer to a character (a byte in memory). That is, the compiler allocates storage for variable *cptr* equal to the size of a memory address, and allows the variable to be assigned the address of an arbitrary byte in memory.

The C programming language has a heritage of both byte and word addressing: when performing arithmetic on pointers, for example, C accommodates the size of the underlying item. As an example, the declaration:

int   *iptr;

declares variable *iptr* to be a pointer to an integer (i.e., a pointer to a word). If each integer contains four bytes, the *autoincrement* statement:

iptr++;

increases the value of *iptr* by four. That is, if *iptr* is declared to be the address of a word in memory, autoincrement moves to the next word.

10.25 A Memory Dump

A trivial example will help us understand the relationship between pointers and memory addresses. Consider a linked list as Figure 10.9 illustrates.

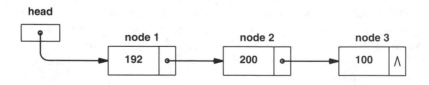

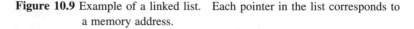

Figure 10.9 Example of a linked list. Each pointer in the list corresponds to a memory address.

To create such a list, a programmer must write a declaration that specifies the contents of a node, and then must allocate memory to hold the list. In our trivial example, each node in the list will contain two items: an integer count and a pointer to the next node on the list. In C, a *struct* declaration is used to define the contents of a node:

```
struct node {
    int count;
    struct node *next;
}
```

Similarly, a variable named *head* that serves as the head of the list is defined as:

```
struct node *head;
```

To understand how the list appears in memory, consider a *memory dump* as Figure 10.10 illustrates†.

Address	Contents Of Memory			
0001bde0	00000000	0001bdf8	deadbeef	4420436f
0001bdf0	6d657200	0001be18	000000c0	0001be14
0001be00	00000064	00000000	00000000	00000002
0001be10	00000000	000000c8	0001be00	00000006

Figure 10.10 Illustration of a small portion of a memory dump that shows the contents of memory. The address column gives the memory address of the left-most byte on the line, and all values are shown in hexadecimal.

The example in the figure is taken from a processor that uses byte addressing. Each line of the figure corresponds to sixteen contiguous bytes of memory that are divided into four groups of four bytes. Each group contains eight hexadecimal digits to represent the values of four bytes. The address at the beginning of a line specifies the memory address of the first byte on that line. Therefore, the address on each line is sixteen greater than the address on the previous line.

Assume the head of a linked list is found at address 0x0001bde4, which is located on the first line of the dump. The first node of the list starts at address 0x0001bdf8, which is located on the second line of the dump, and contains the integer 192 (hexadecimal constant 000000c0).

Although the processor uses byte addressing, spacing has been inserted to divide the output into groups of bytes. In the example, grouping output into four-byte units implies that the underlying word size is four bytes (i.e., thirty-two bits).

---

†As the figure shows, a programmer can initialize memory to a hexadecimal value that makes it easy to identify items in a memory dump. In the example, a programmer has used the value *deadbeef*.

10.26 Indirection And Indirect Operands

When we discussed operands and addressing modes in Chapter 6, the topic of indirection arose. Now that we understand memory organization, we can understand how a processor evaluates an indirect operand. As an example, suppose a processor executes an instruction in which an operand specifies an immediate value of 0x1be1f, and specifies indirection. Further suppose that the processor has been designed to use thirty-two bit values. Because the operand specifies an immediate value, the processor first loads the immediate value (hexadecimal 1be1f). Because the operand specifies indirection, the processor treats the resulting value as an address in memory, and fetches the word from the address. If the values in memory correspond to the values shown in Figure 10.10, the processor will load the value from the rightmost word in the last line of the figure, and the final operand value will be 6.

10.27 Memory Banks And Interleaving

Our discussion of physical memory has assumed a single memory and a single memory controller. In practice, however, some architectures use parallelism to provide higher memory performance. Instead of a single memory and a single controller, the processor connects to multiple *memory banks*† that each has its own controller. Higher performance results from simultaneous operation — the controller hardware is designed to permit all banks to operate simultaneously.

How do memory banks appear to a programmer? In some architectures, memory banks are transparent — memory hardware automatically finds and exploits parallelism. For example, a CPU that uses horizontal microcode and parallel functional units can schedule access to multiple memory banks as independent operations. In other architectures, the programmer is responsible for organizing data into separate memory banks; in such cases, placing data items in separate banks can produce higher performance.

Another optimization used with physical memory systems is known as *interleaving*. In essence, interleaving spreads consecutive bytes of memory across separate physical memory modules. Like memory banks, interleaving achieves higher performance through hardware parallelism (i.e., by allowing hardware to simultaneously access multiple memory items). Unlike memory banks, interleaving is often hidden from programmers — a programmer accesses contiguous bytes of memory (e.g., to fetch an integer), and the memory hardware automatically divides the request into the underlying memory modules.

We use the terminology *N-way interleaving* to describe the number of underlying memory modules. For example, Figure 10.11 illustrates how bytes are assigned to memory modules in a four-way interleaving scheme.

---

†The concept of a memory bank is analogous to the concept of a register bank described in Chapter 5.

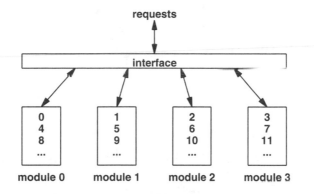

Figure 10.11 Illustration of 4-way interleaving with numbers showing the bytes assigned to each module. Successive bytes are placed in separate memory banks to optimize performance.

10.28 Content Addressable Memory

An unusual form of memory exists that blends the two key aspects we discussed: technology and memory organization. The form is known as a *Content Addressable Memory (CAM)*. As we will see, a CAM does much more than merely store data items — it includes hardware for high-speed searching.

The easiest way to think about a CAM is to view it as memory that has been organized as a two-dimensional array. Each row, which is used to store an item, is called a *slot*. In addition to allowing a processor to place a value in each slot, a CAM allows a processor to specify a *search key* and request the hardware to perform a search. Figure 10.12 illustrates the organization of a CAM.

As the figure shows, a search key is the same size as a slot in the CAM. For the most basic form of a CAM, the search mechanism performs an *exact match*. That is, the CAM hardware compares the key against each slot, and reports whether a match was found. Unlike a search performed by a conventional processor, however, a CAM reports results instantly. In essence, each slot in a CAM contains hardware that performs the comparison — because all slots operate in parallel, the time required to perform the search does not depend on the number of slots.

Of course, parallel search hardware makes CAM extremely expensive. Thus, an architect only uses a CAM when lookup speed is more important than cost. For example, in a high speed Internet router, the system must check each incoming packet to determine whether other packets have arrived previously from the same source. To handle high speed connections, some designs use a CAM to store a list of source identifiers.

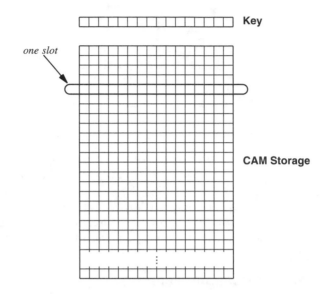

Figure 10.12 Illustration of a Content Addressable Memory (CAM). CAM provides both a memory technology and a memory organization.

10.29 Ternary CAM

An alternative form of CAM, known as *Ternary CAM* (*T-CAM*), extends the idea of CAM to provide *partial match searches*. In essence, each bit in a slot can have three values: zero, one, or "don't care". Like a standard CAM, a T-CAM performs the search operation in parallel by examining all slots simultaneously. Unlike a standard CAM, however, a T-CAM only performs the match on bits that have the value zero or one. Partial matching allows a T-CAM to be used in cases where two or more entries in the CAM overlap — a T-CAM can find the best match (e.g., the *longest prefix* match).

10.30 Summary

We examined two aspects of physical memory: the underlying technology and the memory organization. Many memory technologies exist. Differences among them include permanence (RAM or ROM), clock synchronization, and the read and write cycle times.

Physical memory is organized into words and accessed through a controller. Although programmers find byte addressing convenient, most underlying memory systems use word addressing. An intelligent memory controller can translate from byte addressing to word addressing. To avoid arithmetic computation in a controller, memory is organized so the address space and bytes per word are powers of two.

Programming languages, such as C, provide pointer variables and pointer arithmetic that allow a programmer to obtain and manipulate memory addresses. A memory dump, which shows the contents of memory along with the memory address of each location, can be used to relate data structures in a program to values in memory at runtime.

Content Addressable Memory (CAM) combines memory technology and memory organization. A CAM organizes memory as an array of slots, and provides a high-speed search mechanism.

EXERCISES

10.1   Compute the number of memory operations required for a 2-address instruction if the instruction and both operands are unaligned.

10.2   Write a C function that declares a static integer array, *M*, and implements *fetch* and *store* operations that use shift and Boolean operations to access individual bytes.

10.3   Find the memory in a PC, identify the type of chips used, and look up the vendor's specification of the chips to determine the memory type and speed.

11

Virtual Memory
Technologies And Virtual
Addressing

11.1 Introduction

The previous chapter discusses physical memory. The chapter considers the hardware technologies used to create memory systems, the organization of physical memory into words, and the physical addressing scheme used to access memory.

This chapter considers the important concept of virtual memory. It examines the motivation, the technologies used to create virtual address spaces, and the mapping between virtual and physical memory. Although our focus is primarily on the hardware systems, we will learn how an operating system uses virtual memory facilities.

The next chapter completes the discussion of memory by examining the topic of caching. We will see how caching relates to both physical and virtual memory systems.

11.2 Definition

We use the term *virtual memory* (*VM*) to refer to a mechanism that hides the details of the underlying physical memory to provide a more convenient memory environment. In essence, a virtual memory system creates an illusion — an address space and a memory access scheme that overcome limitations of the physical memory and physical addressing scheme. The definition may seem vague, but we need to encompass a wide variety of technologies and uses. The next sections will define the concept more precisely by giving examples of virtual memory systems that have been created and the technologies used to implement each. We will learn that the variety in virtual memory schemes arises because no single scheme is optimal in all cases.

11.3 A Virtual Example: Byte Addressing

We have already seen an example of a technology that fits our definition of virtual memory in Chapter 10: an intelligent memory controller that provides byte addressing with an underlying physical memory that uses word addressing. The implementation consists of a controller that allows a processor to specify requests using byte addressing. We further saw that choosing sizes to be powers of two avoids arithmetic computation and makes the translation of byte addresses to word addresses trivial.

11.4 Virtual Memory Terminology

Architects use the term *Memory Management Unit* (*MMU*) to describe an intelligent memory controller. The MMU creates a *virtual address space* for the processor; the addresses the processor generates are *virtual addresses*. Most important, we classify the entire mechanism as a *virtual memory system* because it is not part of the underlying physical memory.

Informally, to help distinguish virtual memory from physical memory, architects use the term *real* to refer to parts of a physical memory. For example, they might use the term *real address* to refer to a physical address, or the term *real address space* to refer to the set of addresses recognized by the physical memory.

11.5 An Interface To Multiple Physical Memory Systems

An MMU that can map from byte addresses to underlying word addresses can be extended to create more complex memory organizations. For example, Intel Corporation makes a network processor that uses two types of physical memory: SRAM and DRAM. Interestingly, the number of bytes per word in the two underlying physical memories differ: SRAM memory uses four bytes per word, and DRAM uses eight. Intel's network processor contains an embedded RISC processor that has access to both memories, and the RISC processor uses byte addressing. Rather than using separate instructions to access the two memories, the Intel design follows a standard approach: it integrates both physical memories into a single virtual address space.

To implement a uniform virtual address space out of two dissimilar physical memory systems, we use hardware to perform the necessary translations. Figure 11.1 illustrates an architecture.

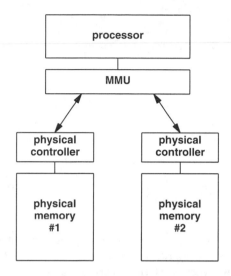

Figure 11.1 Illustration of an architecture in which two dissimilar memories connect to a processor. The processor can use either memory.

In the figure, the processor connects to a Memory Management Unit. The MMU receives memory requests from the processor, translates each request, and forwards the request to the controller for physical memory 1 or the controller for physical memory 2. The controllers for the two physical memories operate as described in Chapter 10 — a controller accepts a request that specifies byte addressing, and translates the request into operations that use word addressing.

How can the hardware in Figure 11.1 provide a virtual address space? Conceptually, the MMU divides the address space into two parts, which the MMU associates with physical memory 1 and physical memory 2. For example, if each physical memory contains 1000 bytes of RAM, the MMU can create a virtual address space that associates the first 1000 byte addresses with memory 1 (i.e., addresses 0 through 999) and the next 1000 addresses with memory 2 (i.e., addresses 1000 through 1999). Figure 11.2 illustrates the resulting virtual memory system.

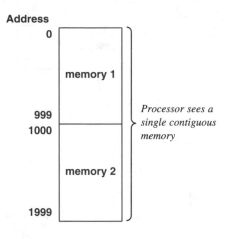

Address

0

memory 1

999
1000

Processor sees a single contiguous memory

memory 2

1999

Figure 11.2 Illustration of a virtual memory system that divides an address space among two physical memories. The MMU uses an address to decide which memory to access.

11.6 Address Translation Or Address Mapping

Each of the underlying memory systems in Figure 11.2 operates like the physical memory systems discussed in Chapter 10: the hardware expects requests to reference addresses beginning at zero. Thus, each of the two memories recognizes the same set of addresses. For memory 1, the virtual addresses associated with the memory cover the same range as the hardware expects, which means the MMU can pass a request from the processor to memory 1 with no changes. For memory 2, however, the processor generates addresses starting at 1000, so the MMU must *map* an address to the lower range (i.e., real addresses 0 through 999) before passing a request to memory 2. We say that the MMU *translates* the address.

Mathematically, address mapping for memory 2 is straightforward: the MMU merely subtracts 1000 from an address. Figure 11.3 explains the concept.

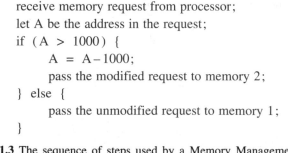

```
receive memory request from processor;
let A be the address in the request;
if ( A > 1000 ) {
      A = A − 1000;
      pass the modified request to memory 2;
} else {
      pass the unmodified request to memory 1;
}
```

Figure 11.3 The sequence of steps used by a Memory Management Unit to create the virtual memory depicted in Figure 11.2. The MMU maps the virtual address space onto two physical memories.

The point is:

> *An MMU can combine multiple underlying physical memory systems to create a virtual address space that provides a processor with the illusion of a single, uniform memory system. Because each underlying memory uses addresses that start at zero, the MMU must translate between the addresses generated by the processor and the addresses used by each memory.*

11.7 Avoiding Arithmetic Calculation

In practice, an MMU cannot use subtraction to implement address translation because subtraction requires substantial hardware (e.g., an ALU) and takes too much time to perform for each memory reference. The solution consists of dividing the address space along boundaries that correspond to powers of two. Doing so makes it possible for the MMU to choose an underlying memory and perform the necessary address translation without using subtraction.

For example, reconsider the memory address mapping illustrated in Figure 11.2. Suppose that instead of exactly one thousand bytes, each memory contains $2^{10}=1024$ bytes. In terms of the virtual address space, the MMU will map addresses 0 through 1023 onto memory 1, and addresses 1024 through 2047 onto memory 2. In decimal, the values do not seem similar. When expressed in binary, however, values in the two ranges differ only in the high-order bit. Figure 11.4 shows the binary values:

Addresses	Values In Binary
0	0 0 0 0 0 0 0 0 0 0 0
to	to
1023	0 1 1 1 1 1 1 1 1 1 1
1024	1 0 0 0 0 0 0 0 0 0 0
to	to
2047	1 1 1 1 1 1 1 1 1 1 1

Figure 11.4 The binary values for addresses in the range 0 through 2047. Values above 1023 are the same as those below except for the high-order bit.

As the example shows, choosing a power of two can eliminate the need for subtraction because low-order bits can be used as a physical address. In the example, when mapping an address to one of the underlying physical memories, an MMU merely extracts the low-order eleven bits of the virtual address. Similarly, instead of an arithmetic comparison to determine which physical memory to use, the controller can test the high-order bit of an address.

To summarize:

Dividing a virtual address space on a boundary that corresponds to a power of two allows the MMU to choose a physical memory and perform the necessary address translation without requiring arithmetic operations.

11.8 Discontiguous Address Spaces

Figure 11.2 shows an example of a *contiguous virtual address space*, an address space in which all addresses are mapped onto an underlying physical memory. That is, the processor can reference any address from zero to the highest address because each address corresponds to a location in one of the physical memories. Interestingly, most computers are designed to be flexible — the physical memory is designed to allow the computer's owner to determine how much memory to install. The computer contains physical slots for memory, and the owner can choose to populate all the slots with memory chips or leave some of the slots empty.

Consider the consequence of allowing an owner to install an arbitrary amount of memory. Because it is defined when the computer is created, the virtual address space includes an address for each possible physical memory location (i.e., addresses for the maximum amount of memory that can be installed in the computer). If an owner decides to omit some of the memory, part of the virtual space becomes unusable — if the processor references an address that does not correspond to physical memory, an error results. More important, the virtual address space will not be contiguous because regions of valid addresses are separated by invalid addresses. For example, Figure 11.5 shows how a virtual address space might appear if the virtual space is mapped onto two physical memories, and part of each physical memory is omitted.

When part of a virtual space does not map onto physical memory, we say that the address space contains a *hole*. In Figure 11.5, for example, the virtual space contains two holes†.

We can summarize:

A virtual address space can be contiguous, in which case every address maps to a location of an underlying physical memory, or noncontiguous, in which case the address space contains one or more holes. If a processor attempts to read or write any address that does not correspond to physical memory, an error results.

---

†We will see further examples of address spaces that contain holes when we discuss I/O.

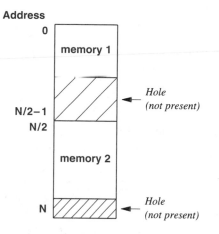

Figure 11.5 Illustration of a virtual address space of N bytes mapped onto two physical memories. The space is not contiguous because only part of each memory is present.

11.9 Other Memory Organizations

Many other possibilities exist for mapping a virtual address space onto physical memories. For example, the two low-order bits of an address can be used to interleave memory among four separate physical memory modules (i.e., banks), and the remaining bits of the address can be used to select a byte within a module. One of the chief advantages of interleaving bytes among a set of modules arises from the ability of underlying hardware to access separate physical memories simultaneously. Using low-order bits to select a module means that successive bytes of memory come from different modules. In particular, if a processor accesses a data item composed of thirty-two bits, the underlying memory system can fetch all four bytes simultaneously.

11.10 Motivation For Virtual Memory

The trivial examples above show that a memory system can present a processor with a virtual address space that differs from the underlying physical memory. The rest of the chapter explores more complex virtual memory schemes. In most cases, the schemes incorporate and extend the concepts discussed above. We will learn that there are four main motivations for the use of complex virtual memory:

- Homogeneous integration of hardware
- Programming convenience
- Support for multiprogramming
- Protection of programs and data

Homogeneous Integration Of Hardware. Our examples explain how a virtual memory system can provide a homogeneous interface to a set of physical memories. More important, the scheme allows *heterogeneity* in the underlying memories. For example, some of the underlying physical memories can use a word size of thirty-two bits, while others use a word size of sixty-four bits. Some of the memories can have a much faster cycle time than others, or some of the memories can consist of RAM while others consist of ROM. The MMU hides the differences by allowing the processor to access all memories from a single address space.

Programming Convenience. One of the chief advantages of a virtual memory system arises from the ease of programming. If separate physical memories are not integrated into a uniform address space, a processor needs special instructions (or special operand formats) for each memory. Programming memory accesses becomes painful. More important, if a programmer decides to move an item from one memory to another, the program must be rewritten, which means that the decision cannot be made at run time.

Support For Multiprogramming. Modern computer systems allow multiple applications to run at the same time. For example, a user who is editing a document can leave a word processor open, and temporarily launch a web browser to check a reference. The terms *multiprogramming* and *multiprocessing* each characterize a computer system that allows multiple programs to run at the same time. We will see that a virtual memory system is needed to support multiprogramming.

Protection Of Programs And Data. We said that a CPU uses *modes of execution* to determine which instructions are allowed at any time. We will see that virtual memory is inherently linked to a computer's protection scheme.

11.11 Multiple Virtual Spaces And Multiprogramming

Early computer designers thought that multiprogramming was impractical. To understand why, consider how an instruction set works. The operands that specify indirection each reference a memory address. If two programs are loaded into a single memory and run at the same time, a conflict can occur if the programs attempt to use the same memory location for two different purposes. Thus, programs can only run together if they are written to avoid using the same memory addresses.

The most common technology for multiprogramming uses virtual memory to establish a separate virtual address space for each program. To understand how a virtual memory system can be used, consider an example. Figure 11.6 illustrates a straightforward mapping.

The mechanism in the figure divides the physical memory into equal-size areas that are known as *partitions*. Partitioned memory systems were used on mainframe computers in the 1960s and 1970s, but have since been replaced. One of the main drawbacks of partitioned memory is that the memory available to a given program is a fraction of total physical memory on the computer. As Figure 11.6 illustrates, systems that used partitioned memory typically divided memory into four partitions, which meant that one-fourth of the total memory was dedicated to each program.

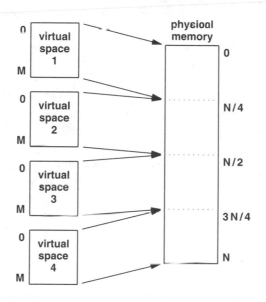

Figure 11.6 Illustration of four partitions mapped onto a single physical memory. Each virtual space starts at address zero.

11.12 Multiple Levels Of Virtualization

The diagram in Figure 11.6 implies that an MMU translates multiple virtual address spaces onto a single physical memory. In practice, however, MMU hardware can perform additional mappings that translate the physical address space in Figure 11.6 onto one or more underlying physical memories or translate from byte addresses to word addresses.

11.13 Creating Virtual Spaces Dynamically

How should a virtual memory system be created? In the simplistic examples above, we implied that an architect chooses a mapping from virtual address space(s) to physical memories, and then designs memory management hardware to perform the mapping. Although some small, special-purpose systems have the mappings designed into hardware, general-purpose computer systems usually do not. Instead, the MMU in a general-purpose system can be changed dynamically at run time. That is, a processor tells the MMU exactly how the virtual address space maps onto the physical address space.

How can a program running on a processor change the address space and continue to run? In general, the address space to be used is part of the *processor mode*, which means a processor can first specify an address mapping, and then decide to use the mapping. The processor begins running in *real mode*, which means that the processor passes all memory references directly to the physical memory without using the MMU. While operating in real mode, the processor interacts with the MMU to establish a mapping. Finally, after the new mapping has been specified, the processor executes an instruction that changes the mode, enables the MMU, and branches to a specified location. The processor interprets the location as an address in the virtual memory space.

The next sections examine technologies that have been used to create dynamic virtual memory systems. We will consider three examples:

- Base-Bound Registers
- Segmentation
- Demand Paging

11.14 Base-Bound Registers

A mechanism known by the name *base-bound* is the easiest dynamic virtual memory scheme to understand. In essence, the *base-bound* scheme creates a single virtual address space and maps the space onto a region of physical memory. The name refers to a pair of registers that are part of the MMU; both must be loaded before the MMU is enabled. The base register holds an address in physical memory that specifies where to map the virtual space, and the bound register holds an integer that specifies the size of the address space. Figure 11.7 illustrates the mapping.

11.15 Changing The Virtual Space

It may seem that a base-bound mechanism is uninteresting because it only provides a single virtual address space. We must remember, however, that a base-bound mechanism is dynamic (i.e., easy to change). The idea is that an operating system can use the base-bound mechanism to move among multiple virtual spaces. For example, suppose the operating system has loaded two application programs at different locations in memory. The operating system, which runs in real mode, controls the MMU. When an application, A, is ready to run, the operating system changes the virtual memory mapping to correspond to A's memory, and then executes an instruction that enables the MMU and branches to the application. Later, when control returns to the operating system, the operating system selects another application to run, B, configures the MMU so the virtual memory corresponds to B's memory, and then executes an instruction that enables the MMU and branches to the code for B.

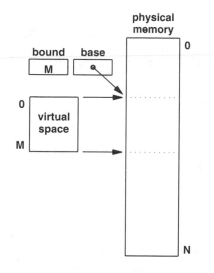

Figure 11.7 Illustration of a virtual memory that uses a base-bound mechanism. The base register specifies the location of the virtual space, and the bound register specifies the size.

The point is that an operating system can use a base-bound mechanism to provide as much functionality as the static virtual memory mechanisms considered earlier. We can summarize:

> *A base-bound mechanism uses two values in the MMU to specify how a virtual address space maps onto the physical address space. The base-bound mechanism is powerful because an operating system can change the mapping dynamically.*

11.16 Virtual Memory, Base-Bound, And Protection

Why is a bound register used in the base-bound approach? The answer is *protection*: although a base register is sufficient to establish the mapping from virtual address to physical address, the mapping does not prevent a program from accidentally or maliciously referencing arbitrarily large memory locations. In Figure 11.7, for example, addresses higher than M lie beyond the region allocated to the program.

The base-bound scheme uses the bound register to guarantee that a program will not exceed its allocated space. To implement protection, the MMU must check each memory reference, and raise an error if the program generates an address greater than M. The protection offered by a base-bound mechanism provides an example of an important concept:

> *A virtual memory system that supports multiprogramming must also provide protection that prevents one program from reading or altering memory that has been allocated to another program.*

11.17 Segmentation

The memory mappings described above are intended to map a complete address space (i.e., all memory that is needed for an application to run, including the compiled program and the data the program uses). We say that a virtual memory technology that maps an entire address space is a *coarse granularity mapping*. The alternative, which consists of mapping parts of an address space, is known as a *fine granularity mapping*.

To understand the motivation for a fine granularity mapping, consider a typical application program. The program consists of a set of procedures, and flow passes from one procedure to another through a procedure call. Early computer architects observed that although memory was a scarce resource, an entire program occupied memory. Most of the memory was unused because only one procedure was actively executing at any time.

To reduce the amount of memory needed, the architects proposed that each program be divided into variable-size blocks, and only the blocks of the program that are needed at any time be loaded in memory. That is, pieces of program are kept on an external storage device, typically a disk, until one of them is needed. At that time, the operating system finds an unused region of memory that is large enough, and loads the piece into memory. The operating system then configures the MMU to establish the mapping between the virtual addresses that the piece uses and the physical addresses used to hold the piece. When a piece is no longer used, the operating system moves the piece back to disk, thereby making the memory available for another piece.

The scheme is known as *segmentation*, and the pieces of programs are known as *segments*. Segmentation was the subject of research. What hardware support would be needed to make segmentation efficient? Should the hardware dictate an upper bound on the size of a segment?

After much research and a few hardware experiments, segmentation faded. The central problem with segmentation arises after an operating system begins to move blocks in and out of memory. Because segments are variable size, the memory tends toward a situation in which the unused memory is divided into many small blocks. Computer scientists use the term *fragmentation* to describe the situation, and say that the memory is *fragmented*†. We can summarize:

> *Segmentation refers to a virtual memory scheme in which programs are divided into variable-size blocks, and only the blocks currently needed are kept in memory. Because it leads to a problem known as memory fragmentation, segmentation is seldom used.*

---

†To avoid memory fragmentation, some architects experimented with fixed-size segments (e.g., 64 Kbytes per segment). However, fixed-size segments can be considered a variation of paging.

11.18 Demand Paging

An alternative to segmentation was invented that is extremely successful. Known as *demand paging*, the technique follows the same general scheme as segmentation: divide a program into pieces, keep the pieces on external storage until they are needed, and load an individual piece when the piece is referenced.

The most significant difference between demand paging and segmentation lies in how the program is divided. Instead of variable-size segments that are large enough to hold a complete procedure, demand paging uses fixed-size blocks called *pages*.

Initially, when memories and application programs were much smaller, architects chose a page size of 512 bytes or 1 Kbyte; current architectures use larger page sizes (e.g., a Pentium uses 4 Kbyte pages).

11.19 Hardware And Software For Demand Paging

Two technologies are needed for a virtual memory system that supports demand paging:

- Hardware that handles address mapping and detects missing pages
- Software that moves pages between external store and physical memory

Paging Hardware. Technically, the hardware architecture provides a *paging system*, and allows software to handle the demand aspect. That is, software (usually an operating system) configures the MMU to specify which pages from a virtual address space are present in memory and where each page is located, and runs an application that uses the virtual address space. The MMU translates each memory address until the application references an address that is not available (i.e., an address on one of the pages that is not present in memory).

A reference to a missing page is called a *page fault*, and is treated as an error condition (e.g., like a division by zero). That is, instead of fetching the missing page from external storage, the hardware merely informs the operating system that a fault has occurred and allows the software to handle the problem.

Demand Paging Software. Software is responsible for management of the memory: software must decide which page or pages to keep in memory and which to keep on external storage. More important, the software acts to fill demand whenever a page is needed. That is, once the hardware reports a page fault, paging software takes over. The software identifies the page that is needed, locates the page on secondary storage, locates a slot in memory, reads the page into memory, and reconfigures the MMU. Once the page has been loaded, the software resumes executing the application, and the fetch-execute cycle continues until another page fault occurs.

Of course, the paging hardware and software must work together. For example, when a page fault occurs, the hardware must save the state of the computation (e.g., registers in the processor) in such a way that the values can be reloaded later. Similarly, the software must understand exactly how to configure the MMU.

11.20 Page Replacement

To understand paging, we must consider what happens after a set of applications has been running a long time. As applications reference pages, the virtual memory system moves the pages into memory. Eventually, the memory becomes full. The system always knows when a page is needed because the application references the page. The difficult decision, however, involves selecting one of the existing pages to evict to make space for an incoming page. Moving a page between external storage and memory takes time, so performance is optimized by choosing to move a page that will not be needed in the near future. The process is known as *page replacement*.

Because page replacement is handled by software, the discussion of algorithms and heuristics is beyond the scope of this text. We will see, however, that the hardware provides mechanisms that assist the operating system in making a decision.

11.21 Paging Terminology And Data Structures

The term *page* refers to a block of a program's address space, and the term *frame* refers to a slot in physical memory that can hold a page. Thus, we say that software *loads* a page into a frame of memory. When a page is in memory, the page is *resident*, and the set of all pages from an address space that are currently in memory is called the *resident set*.

The primary data structure used for demand paging is known as a *page table*. The easiest way to envision a page table is to imagine a one-dimensional array that is indexed by a page number. That is, entries in the table have index zero, one, and so on. Each entry in the page table either contains a null value (if the page is not resident) or the address of the frame in physical memory that currently holds the page. Figure 11.8 illustrates a page table.

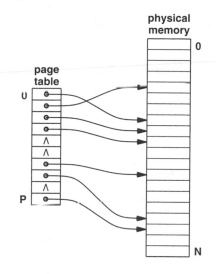

Figure 11.8 Illustration of an active page table with some entries pointing to frames in memory. A null pointer (Λ) in a page table entry means the page is not currently resident.

11.22 Address Translation In A Paging System

To understand paging hardware, imagine an address space divided into fixed-size pages as Figure 11.9 shows.

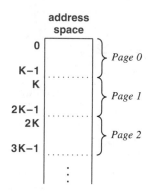

Figure 11.9 Illustration of a virtual address space divided into pages of K bytes per page.

We will see that the addresses associated with each page are important. As the figure shows, if each page contains K bytes, bytes on page zero have addresses zero through K−1, bytes on page 1 have addresses K through 2K−1, and so on.

Conceptually, translation of a virtual address, V, to a corresponding physical address, P, requires three steps:

1. Determine the number of the page on which address V lies.
2. Use the page number as an index into the page table to find the location in memory that corresponds to the first byte of the page.
3. Determine how far into the page V lies, and move that far into the frame in memory.

We saw from Figure 11.9 how addresses are associated with pages. Mathematically, the page number on which an address lies, N, can be computed by dividing the address by the number of bytes per page, K:

$$N = \left\lfloor \frac{V}{K} \right\rfloor$$

Similarly, the offset of the address within the page, O, can be computed as the remainder of the division†.

$$O = V \; modulo \; K$$

Thus, a virtual address, V, is translated to a corresponding physical address, P, by using the page number and offset, N and O, as follows:

$$P = pagetable\,[N] + O$$

11.23 Using Powers Of Two

As Chapter 10 discusses, an arithmetic operation, such as division, is too expensive to perform on each memory reference. Therefore, like other parts of a memory system, a paging system is designed to avoid arithmetic computation. The number of bytes per page is chosen to be a power of two, 2^q, which means that the address of the first byte in each frame has q low-order bits equal to zero. Thus, the page table does not need to store a full address, and no addition is needed. The consequence of using a power of two is that the division and addition operations specified in the mathematical equations can be replaced by extracting bits. Thus, the MMU performs the following computation to translate a virtual address, V, into a physical address, P:

$$P \; = \; pagetable\,[\,high\_order\_bits\,(V)\,] \; or \; low\_order\_bits\,(V)$$

---

†Note that the computation of a byte address within a page is similar to the computation of a byte address within a word discussed on page 153.

Figure 11.10 illustrates how MMU hardware operates. When considering the figure, remember that hardware can move bits in parallel. Thus, the arrow that points from the low-order bits in the virtual address to the low-order bits in the physical address represents a parallel data path — the hardware sends all the bits at the same time.

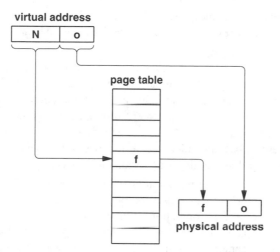

Figure 11.10 Illustration of how an MMU performs address translation on a paging system. Making the page size a power of two eliminates the need for division and remainder computation.

11.24 Presence, Use, And Modified Bits

Our description of paging hardware omits several details. For example, in addition to a value that specifies the frame in which a page is located, each page table entry contains control bits that the hardware and software use to coordinate. Figure 11.11 lists three control bits found in most paging hardware.

Control Bit	Meaning
Presence bit	Tested by hardware to determine whether page is currently present in memory
Use bit	Set by hardware whenever page is referenced
Modified bit	Set by hardware whenever page is changed

Figure 11.11 Examples of control bits found in each page table entry and the actions hardware takes with each. The bits are intended to assist the page replacement software in the operating system.

Presence Bit. The most straightforward control bit is called a *presence bit*, which specifies whether the page is currently in memory. The bit is set by software and tested by the hardware. Once it has loaded a page and filled in other values in the page table entry, the operating system sets the presence bit to one; when it evicts a page, the operating system sets the presence bit to zero. When it translates an address, the MMU examines the presence bit in the page table entry — if the presence bit is one, translation proceeds, and if the presence bit is zero, the hardware declares a page fault has occurred.

Use Bit. The *use bit*, which provides information needed for page replacement, is initialized and later tested by software, and is set by hardware. The hardware mechanism is straightforward: whenever it accesses a page table entry, the MMU sets the use bit. The operating system periodically sweeps through the page table, testing the use bit to determine whether the page has been referenced since the last sweep. A page that has not been referenced becomes a candidate for eviction; otherwise, the operating system clears the use bit and leaves the page for the next sweep.

Modified Bit. The *modified bit* is initialized and later tested by software, and is set by hardware. The paging software clears the bit when a page is loaded. The MMU sets the bit to one whenever a *write* operation occurs to the page. Thus, the modified bit is one if any byte on the page has been written since the page was loaded. The value is used during page replacement — if a page is selected for eviction, the value of the modified bit tells the operating system whether the page must be written back to external storage or can be discarded (i.e., whether the page is identical to the copy on external storage).

11.25 Page Table Storage

Where do page tables reside? Some systems store page tables in a special MMU chip that is external from the processor. Of course, because memory references play an essential role in processing, the MMU must be designed to work efficiently. In particular, to ensure that memory references do not become a bottleneck, some processors use a special-purpose, high-speed hardware interface to access an MMU. The interface contains parallel wires that allow the processor and MMU to send many bits at the same time.

Surprisingly, some processors are designed to store page tables in memory! That is, the processor contains an instruction that allows the operating system to specify the location of the current page table. Of course, the location of the page table is specified by giving a physical address. Typically, such systems are designed to divide memory into regions as Figure 11.12 illustrates.

The design in the figure illustrates one of the motivations for a memory system composed of heterogeneous technologies: because page tables are used frequently, the memory used to store page tables needs high performance (e.g., SRAM). However, because high performance memory is expensive, overall cost can be reduced by using a lower-cost memory (e.g., DRAM). Thus, an architect can design a system that uses SRAM to hold page tables and DRAM for frame storage.

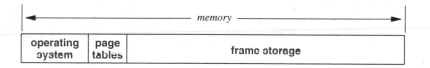

Figure 11.12 Illustration of how physical memory is divided in an architecture that stores page tables in memory. A large area of physical memory is reserved for frames.

11.26 Paging Efficiency And A Translation Lookaside Buffer

A central question underlies all virtual memory architectures: how efficient is the resulting system? Because memory is among the most heavily used resources in a computer system, the mechanisms used to implement virtual memory must be efficient enough to avoid becoming a bottleneck. Architects are primarily concerned with the amount of time the MMU uses to translate a virtual address to a physical address; they are less concerned with the amount of time it takes for the operating system to configure page tables.

One technique used to optimize the performance of a demand paging system stands out as especially important. The technique uses special, high-speed hardware known as a *Translation Lookaside Buffer* (*TLB*) to achieve faster page table lookups. A TLB is a form of Content Addressable Memory that stores recently used values from a page table. When it first translates an address, the MMU places a copy of the page table entry in the TLB. On successive lookups, the hardware performs two operations in parallel: the standard address translation steps depicted in Figure 11.10 and a high-speed search of the TLB. If the requested information is found in the TLB, the MMU aborts the standard translation and uses the information from the TLB. Otherwise, the standard translation proceeds.

To understand why a TLB improves performance, consider the fetch-execute cycle. A processor tends to fetch instructions from successive locations in memory. Furthermore, if the program contains a branch, probability is extremely high that the destination will be nearby, probably on the same page. Thus, rather than randomly accessing pages, a processor tends to fetch successive instructions from the same page. A TLB improves performance because it optimizes successive lookups by avoiding indexing into a page table. The difference in performance is especially dramatic for architectures that store page tables in memory; without a TLB, such systems are too slow to be useful. We can summarize:

> *A special high-speed hardware device, called a Translation Lookaside Buffer (TLB), is used to optimize performance of a paging system. A virtual memory that does not have a TLB can be unacceptably slow.*

11.27 Consequences For Programmers

Experience has shown that demand paging works well for most computer programs. The code that programmers produce tends to be organized into procedures that each fit onto a page. Similarly, data objects, such as character strings, are designed so the data occupies consecutive memory locations, which means that once a page has been loaded, the page tends to remain resident for multiple references. Finally, some compilers understand paging, and optimize performance by placing data items onto pages.

One way that programmers can affect virtual memory performance arises from array access. Consider a two-dimensional array in memory. Many programming systems allocate an array in *row-major order*, which means that rows of an array are placed in contiguous memory as Figure 11.13 illustrates.

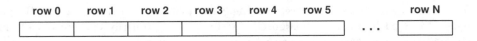

Figure 11.13 An illustration of a two-dimensional array stored in row-major order. A row is contiguous in memory.

As the figure shows, rows of the matrix occupy successive locations in memory. Thus, if A is a two-dimensional array of bytes, the location of A[i, j] is given by:

$$location(A) \ + \ i \times Q \ + \ j$$

where Q is the number of bytes per row.

The chief alternative to row-major order is known as *column-major order*. When an array is stored in column-major order, the elements of a column occupy contiguous memory locations. The choice between row-major or column-major order is usually determined by the programming language and compiler, not by a programmer.

A programmer can control how a program iterates through an array, and a good choice can optimize virtual memory performance. For example, if a large array of characters, A[N,M], is stored in row-major order, the nested loops shown here:

```
for i = 1 to N {
        for j = 1 to M {
                A [ i, j ] = 0;
        }
}
```

will require less time to execute than a loop that varies the indices in the opposite order:

```
for j = 1 to M {
       for i = 1 to N {
               A [ i, j ] = 0;
       }
}
```

because varying the row index may force the virtual memory system to move from one page of memory to another for each reference, but varying the column index means many successive references stay on the same page.

11.28 Summary

Virtual memory systems present an abstract address space to a processor and to each application program running on the processor. A virtual memory system hides details of the underlying physical memory.

Several virtual memory architectures are possible. The virtual memory system can hide details of word addressing or can present a uniform address space that incorporates multiple, possibly heterogeneous, memory technologies.

Virtual memory offers convenience for programmers, support for multiprogramming, and protection. When multiple programs run concurrently, virtual memory can be used to provide each program with an address space that begins at zero.

Virtual memory technologies include base-bound, segmentation, and demand paging; demand paging is the most popular. A demand paging system uses page tables to map from a virtual address to a physical address; a high-speed search mechanism known as a TLB makes page table lookup efficient.

To avoid arithmetic computation, virtual memory systems make physical memory and page sizes a power of two. Doing so allows the hardware to translate addresses without using arithmetic or logical operations.

EXERCISES

11.1   Compute the amount of memory needed to hold page tables. Assume that each page table entry occupies thirty-two bits, the page size is 4 Kbytes, and a memory address occupies thirty-two bits.

11.2   Consider a two-level page table in which the high-order ten bits of an address are used as an index into a *directory table* to select among 1K page tables, the next ten bits of the address select a page table entry, and the final twelve bits of the address select a byte on the page. How much memory is required for the directory table and page tables?

12

Caches And Caching

12.1 Introduction

The previous chapters discuss physical and virtual memory systems, focusing on the underlying technologies used to build memory systems and the organization of address spaces. The chapters also discuss mechanisms used for address translation.

This chapter takes a different view of the problem: instead of concentrating on technologies used to construct memory systems, the chapter discusses the fundamental concept of caching, and then shows how caching is used in memory systems. The chapter explains why caching is essential, and how caching achieves high performance with low cost. More important, the chapter presents caching as a key concept in computing that transcends memory systems.

12.2 Definition

The term *caching* refers to an important optimization technique used to reduce the Von Neumann bottleneck† and improve the performance of any hardware or software system that retrieves information. A *cache* acts as an intermediary. That is, a cache is placed on the path between a mechanism that makes requests and a mechanism that answers requests, and the cache is configured to intercept and handle all requests.

The central idea in caching is high-speed, temporary storage: the cache keeps a local copy of selected data, and answers requests from the local copy whenever possible. Performance improvement arises because the cache is designed to return answers faster than the mechanism that normally fulfills requests. Figure 12.1 illustrates how a cache is positioned between a mechanism that makes requests and a mechanism that answers requests.

---

†The Von Neumann bottleneck is defined on page 87.

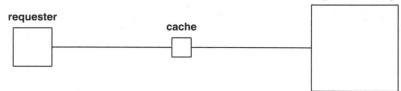

Figure 12.1 Illustration of the cache concept. A cache, which is positioned
on the path between a mechanism that makes requests and a
storage mechanism that holds items, can answer requests faster
than the data store.

12.3 Characteristics Of A Cache

The above description is purposefully vague because caching is a broad concept
that appears in many forms in computer and communication systems. This section clar-
ifies the definition by explaining the concept in more detail; later sections give examples of how caching can be used.

Although a variety of caching mechanisms exist, they share the following general
characteristics:

- Small
- Active
- Transparent
- Automatic

Small. To keep economic cost low, the amount of storage associated with a cache
is much smaller than the amount of storage needed to hold the entire set of data items.
Most cache sizes are less than ten percent of the main storage size; in many cases, a
cache holds less than one percent as much as the data store. Thus, one of the central
design issues revolves around the selection of data items to keep in the cache.

Active. A cache contains an active mechanism that examines each request and decides how to respond. Activities include: checking to see if a requested item is available in the cache, retrieving a copy of an item from the data store if the item is not
available locally, and deciding which items to keep in the cache.

Transparent. We say that a cache is *transparent*, which means that a cache can be
inserted without making changes to the requester or data store. That is: the interface the
cache presents to the requester is exactly the same as the interface a data store presents,
and the interface the cache presents to the data store is exactly the same as the interface
a requester presents†.

---

†The notion of transparency explains the terminology — the term *cache* generally refers to a secret hiding
place.

Automatic. In most cases, a cache mechanism does not receive instructions on how to act or which data items to store in the cache storage. Instead, a cache implements an algorithm that examines the sequence of requests, and uses the requests to determine how to manage the cache.

12.4 The Importance Of Caching

We said that caching occurs in a variety of forms, but variety does not capture the importance or pervasiveness of caching. In fact, caching is one of the most fundamental optimization techniques available; most computer systems contain one or more instances of a cache.

Caching's importance arises from its flexibility: caching can be used with:

- Hardware, software, and combinations of both
- Small data items (e.g., a byte or word of memory)
- Medium-size data items (e.g., a segment or page of memory)
- Large data items (e.g., a complete program)
- Generic data items (e.g., a file or a disk block)
- Data items that are specific to an application (e.g., a web page, a document from a word processor, or an entry in a database)
- Textual data (e.g., an email message)
- Nontextual data (e.g., an image, an audio file, or a video clip)
- A single computer system (e.g., between a processor and a memory)
- Many computer systems (e.g., between a set of desktop computers and a database server)
- Systems that are designed to retrieve data (e.g., the World Wide Web)
- Systems that store as well as retrieve data (e.g., a physical memory)

It should be obvious from the above list that the items in a cache can all have the same size (e.g., the cache holds a set of disk blocks that are identical size), or can vary in size (e.g., the cache holds a set of web pages).

We can summarize the importance of caching:

Caching is a fundamental optimization technique used throughout most hardware and software systems that retrieve information. Caching is a broad concept; data items kept in a cache are not limited to a specific type, form, or size.

12.5 Examples Of Caching

A few examples will illustrate some of the ways caching is used. Most operating systems cache disk blocks in memory, which is much faster than a disk. Whenever an application accesses a file, the operating system checks the cache to determine whether the block is available in memory. If so, the operating system uses the copy in memory; if not, the operating system retrieves the data from disk.

Most web browsers maintain a cache of web pages on the local disk. When it first fetches a page, the browser stores a copy in the local cache. If the user requests the same page again, the browser retrieves a copy from the disk cache, which is much faster than using the Internet to retrieve a copy of the page.

Many ISPs use a web cache that handles multiple customers. The ISP sends all web requests from customers through the cache. If a customer downloads a web page, the ISP's cache stores a copy. If another customer requests the same page, the ISP cache will return a copy, without sending the request over the Internet.

12.6 Cache Terminology

Because caching appears in so many places, no set of terminology suffices for all cases. In particular, the terminology used for a data store depends on the type of cache. For example, in memory systems, the storage mechanism is sometimes called a *backing store*. In a system designed to cache web pages, we use the term *browser* to refer to a program that requests web pages, and *origin server* to refer to a server that handles such requests. A system that caches database lookups uses the term *client* to refer to a program that makes requests, and *database server* to refer to a system that handles such requests.

Some terms related to caching seem to have universal acceptance across all caching systems. A *cache hit* (abbreviated *hit*) is defined as a request that can be satisfied by the cache, without any need to access the underlying data store. Conversely, a *cache miss* (abbreviated *miss*) is defined as a request that cannot be satisfied by the cache.

Another term that has universal acceptance refers to a property of references. We say that a sequence of references exhibits *high locality of reference* if the sequence contains repetitions of the same requests; otherwise, we say that the sequence has *low locality of reference*†. We will see that high locality of reference leads to higher performance.

---

†If a cache stores large data items (e.g., pages of memory), repeated requests do not need to be identical as long as they reference the same item in the cache (e.g., memory references to items on the same page).

12.7 Best And Worst Case Cache Performance

We said that if a data item is stored in the cache, the cache mechanism can return the item faster than the data store. As Figure 12.2 shows, we represent the costs of retrieval from the requester's view.

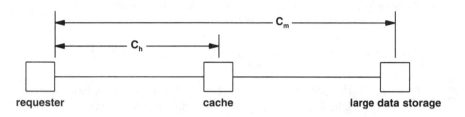

Figure 12.2 Illustration of access costs when using a cache. Costs are measured with respect to the requester

In the figure, C_h is the cost if an item is found in the cache (i.e., a hit), and C_m is the cost if an item is not found in the cache (i.e., a miss). Interestingly, individual costs do not reveal much. Observe that because a cache uses the contents of requests to determine which items to keep, the performance depends on the sequence of requests. Thus, to understand caching, we must examine the performance on a sequence of requests. For example, we can easily analyze the best and worst possible behavior for a sequence of N requests. At one extreme, if each request references a new item, caching does not improve performance at all — the cache must forward each request to the data store. Thus, in the worst case, the cost is†:

$$C_{worst} = N \ C_m$$

If we divide by N to compute the average cost per request, the result is C_m.

At the other extreme, if all requests in the sequence specify the same data item (i.e., the highest possible locality of reference), the cache can indeed improve performance. When it receives the first request, the cache fetches the item from the data store and saves a copy; subsequent requests can be satisfied by using the copy in the cache. Thus, in the best case. the cost is:

$$C_{best} = C_m + (N - 1) \ C_h$$

Dividing by N produces the cost per request:

$$\frac{C_m + (N - 1) \ C_h}{N} \ = \ \frac{C_m}{N} - \frac{C_h}{N} + C_h$$

†Our analysis ignores administrative overhead required to maintain the cache.

As $N \rightarrow \infty$, the first two terms approach zero, which means that the cost per request in the best case becomes C_h. We can see why caching is such a powerful tool:

> *If we ignore overhead, in the worst case, the performance of caching is no worse than if the cache were not present. In the best case, the cost per request is approximately equal to the cost of accessing the cache, which is lower than the cost of accessing the data store.*

12.8 Cache Performance On A Typical Sequence

To estimate performance of a cache on a typical sequence of requests, we need to consider how the cache handles a sequence that contains both hits and misses. Cache designers use the term *hit ratio* to refer to the percentage of requests in the sequence that are satisfied from the cache. Specifically, the hit ratio is defined to be:

$$hit \ ratio \ = \ \frac{number \ of \ requests \ that \ are \ hits}{total \ number \ of \ requests}$$

The hit ratio is a value between zero and one. We can also define a *miss ratio* to be one minus the hit ratio.

Of course, the actual hit ratio depends on a specific sequence of requests. However, experience has shown that for many caches, the hit ratio tends to be nearly the same across the requests encountered in practice. In such cases, we can write an equation for the cost of access in terms of the cost of a miss and the cost of a hit:

$$Cost \ = \ rC_h \ + \ (1 - r)C_m$$

where r is the hit ratio.

The cost of accessing the data store, given by C_m in the equation, is fixed. Thus, there are two ways a cache designer can improve the performance of a cache: increase the hit ratio or decrease the cost of a hit.

12.9 Cache Replacement Policy

How can a cache designer increase the hit ratio? Recall that a cache is usually small compared to a large data store. When it begins to operate, a cache keeps a copy of each response. Once the cache storage is full, however, the cache must use a *replacement policy* to decide how to handle further items†. The replacement policy is invoked whenever the cache is full and a new response arrives. The replacement policy can specify ignoring the new item, or can specify which of the old items to evict to make space for the new item.

---

†Although it may be possible to increase the size of the cache, most caches are so small that an increase in size does not help in the long run.

12.10 LRU Replacement

What replacement policy should be used? There are two issues. First, to increase the hit ratio, the replacement policy should retain those items that will be referenced most frequently. Second, the replacement policy should be inexpensive to implement.

One replacement policy is extremely popular. Known as *Least Recently Used (LRU)*, the policy specifies replacing the item that was referenced the longest time in the past†.

LRU is extremely easy to implement. The cache mechanism keeps a list of data items that are currently in the cache. When an item is referenced, the item moves to the front of the list; when replacement is needed, the item at the back of the list is removed.

LRU works well in many situations. In cases where the set of requests has a high locality of reference (i.e., the cases where a cache can improve performance), a few items will be referenced again and again. LRU tends to keep those items in the cache, which means the cost of access is kept low.

We can summarize:

> *When its storage is full and a new item arrives, a cache must choose whether to retain the current set of items or replace one of the current items with the new item. The Least Recently Used policy is a popular choice for replacement because it is trivial to implement and tends to keep items that will be requested again.*

12.11 Multi-level Cache Hierarchy

One of the most unexpected and astonishing aspects of caching arises from an optimization that uses caching to improve the performance of a cache! To understand how such an optimization is possible, recall that the insertion of a cache lowers the cost of retrieving items by placing some of the items closer to the requester. Now imagine an additional cache placed between the requester and the existing cache as Figure 12.3 illustrates.

Figure 12.3 The organization of a system with an additional cache inserted.

Can a second cache improve performance? Yes, provided the cost to access the new cache is lower than the cost to access the original cache (e.g., the new cache is closer to the requester). In essence, the cost equation becomes:

$$Cost = r_1 C_{h1} + r_2 C_{h2} + (1 - r_1 - r_{2)} C_m$$

---

†Note that "least recently" refers to how long ago the item was last referenced, not to the number of accesses.

where r_1 denotes the fraction of hits for the new cache, r_2 denotes the fraction of hits for the original cache, C_{h1} denotes the cost of accessing the new cache, and C_{h2} denotes the cost of accessing the original cache.

When more than one cache is used along the path from requester to data store, we say that the system implements a *multi-level cache hierarchy*. In fact, we have already discussed an example of a multi-level hierarchy: web caches. The path between a browser running on a user's computer can pass through a cache at the user's ISP as well as the local cache mechanism used by the browser.

The point is:

> *Adding an additional cache can be used to improve the performance of a system that uses caching. Conceptually, the caches are arranged in a multi-level hierarchy.*

12.12 Preloading Caches

How can cache performance be improved further? Cache designers observe that although many cache systems perform well in the steady state (i.e., after the system has run for awhile), the system exhibits higher cost during startup. That is, the initial hit ratio is extremely low because the cache must fetch items from the data store. In some cases, the startup period can be eliminated by *preloading* the cache. Of course, preloading only works in cases where the cache can anticipate requests. For example, an ISP's web cache can be preloaded with so-called *hot* pages (i.e., pages that have been accessed frequently in the past day or pages for which the owner expects frequent access). As an alternative, some caches use an automated method of preloading. In one form, the cache periodically places a copy of its contents on nonvolatile storage, allowing recent values to be preloaded at startup. In another form, the cache uses a reference to *prefetch* related data. For example, if a processor accesses a byte of memory, the cache fetches sixty-four bytes. Thus, if the processor accesses the next byte, the value will come from the cache.

12.13 Caches Used With Memory

Now that we understand the basic idea of caching, we can consider some of the ways caches are used in memory systems. The concept of caching originated with computer memory systems†. Because memory was both expensive and slow, architects looked for ways to improve performance without the cost of higher-speed memory. The architects discovered that a small amount of high-speed cache improved performance dramatically. By the 1980s, many computer systems had a single cache located

---

†In addition to introducing the use of microcode, Maurice Wilkes is credited with inventing memory cache in 1965.

between the processor and memory. Physically, the cache occupied a separate board, which allowed owners to change the memory or the cache independently.

As we have seen, however, caching is a general optimization technique that can be used in many ways. Thus, a modern computer memory system employs multiple caches. Caching is used with both virtual and physical memory as well as with secondary storage. The next sections present a few examples.

12.14 TLB As A Cache

We have already seen a key example of how caching improves performance: a TLB used in a demand paging memory system. Recall that a TLB consists of a small, high-speed hardware mechanism that improves the performance of a demand paging system dramatically. In fact, a TLB is nothing more than a cache: whenever it looks up a page table entry, the MMU stores the entry in the TLB. A successive lookup for the same page will receive an answer from the TLB.

Like many cache systems, a TLB uses the Least Recently Used replacement strategy. That is, when an entry is referenced, the TLB moves the entry to the front of the list; when a new reference occurs, the TLB discards the page table entry on the back of the list to make space for the new entry. Of course, the TLB cannot afford to keep a linked list in memory. Instead, the TLB contains digital circuits that move values into a Content Addressable Memory (CAM) at high speed.

12.15 Demand Paging As A Form Of Caching

Conceptually, demand paging can be viewed as a form of caching. The cache corresponds to main memory, and the data store corresponds to the external storage where pages are kept until needed. Furthermore, the page replacement policy corresponds to the cache replacement policy (even the terminology is the same).

Interestingly, thinking of demand paging as a cache can help us understand an important idea: a virtual address space can be much larger than physical memory. Like a cache, physical memory only holds a fraction of the total pages. From our analysis of caching, we know that the performance of a demand-paged virtual memory can approach the performance of physical memory. In other words:

> *The cache analysis shows that using demand paging on a computer system with a small physical memory can perform almost as well as if the computer had a physical memory large enough for the entire virtual address space.*

12.16 Physical Memory Cache

We said that caching became popular as a way to achieve higher memory performance without significantly higher cost. Early computers used a physical memory system. That is, when it generated a request, the processor specified a physical address, and the memory system responded to the physical address. Thus, to be inserted on the path between a processor and the memory, a cache had to understand and use physical addresses.

It may seem that a physical memory cache is trivial. We can imagine the memory cache receiving a *read* request, checking to see if the request can be answered from cache, and then, if the item is not present, passing the request to the underlying memory. Furthermore, we can imagine that once an item has been retrieved from the underlying memory, the cache saves a copy locally, and then returns the value to the processor.

In fact, our imagined scenario is misleading — a physical memory cache is much more complex than the above. To understand why, we must remember that hardware achieves high speed through parallelism. For example, when it encounters a *read* request, a memory cache performs two tasks at the same time: the cache simultaneously passes the request to the physical memory and searches for an answer locally. If it finds an answer locally, the cache must cancel the memory operation. If it does not find an answer locally, the cache must wait for the underlying memory operation to complete. Furthermore, when an answer does arrive from memory, the cache uses parallelism again by simultaneously saving a local copy of the answer and transferring the answer back to the processor. Parallel activities make the hardware complex. The point is:

> *To achieve high performance, a physical memory cache is designed to simultaneously search the local cache and access the underlying memory. Parallelism complicates the hardware.*

12.17 Write Through And Write Back

In addition to parallelism, memory caches are also complicated by *write* operations. There are two issues: performance and coherence. Performance is easiest to understand: caching improves the performance for retrieval requests, but not for storage requests. That is, a *write* operation must change the value in the underlying memory. More important, in addition to forwarding the request to the memory, a cache must also check to see whether the item is in the cache. If so, the cache must update its copy as well†.

Initial implementations of memory caches handled *write* operations as described above: the cache kept a copy, and forwarded the *write* operation to the underlying memory. We use the term *write-through cache* to describe the approach. As an alter-

---

†Experience has shown that a memory cache should keep a local copy of every value that is written because programs tend to read the same value again.

native, a cache can use a *write-back* scheme in which the cache keeps the data item locally, and only writes the value to memory, if necessary. In particular, a *write-back cache* writes a value to memory only if the value reaches the end of the LRU list and must be replaced. To determine whether a value should be written the cache keeps an extra bit known as the *dirty bit*.

To understand why write-back improves performance, imagine a loop in a program that increments a value in memory. A write-back cache places the item in the cache. Thus, all *write* operations are performed by updating the cached copy. After the loop ends, the program stops referencing the item, and eventually generates enough references so the item reaches the end of the list. Before it can reclaim the slot, the cache must write the item to the underlying physical memory.

12.18 Cache Coherence

Memory caches are especially complex in a multiprocessor system. We said that a write-back cache achieves higher performance than a write-through cache. In a multiprocessor environment, performance is also optimized by giving each processor its own cache. Unfortunately, the two optimizations conflict. To understand why, look at the architecture in Figure 12.4, which shows two processors that each has a private cache.

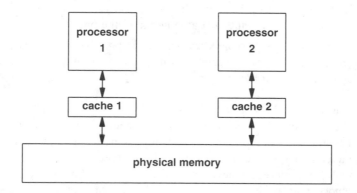

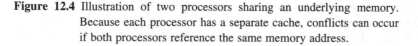

Figure 12.4 Illustration of two processors sharing an underlying memory. Because each processor has a separate cache, conflicts can occur if both processors reference the same memory address.

Now consider what happens if the two caches use a write-back approach. When processor 1 writes to a memory location, cache 1 holds the value. Eventually, when it needs space, cache 1 writes the value to the memory. Similarly, if processor 2 writes to a memory location, cache 2 holds the value temporarily. Unfortunately, without an additional mechanism, incorrect results can occur if both processors issue a sequence of *read* and *write* operations for the same address.

To avoid conflicts, all devices that access memory must follow a *cache coherence protocol* that coordinates the values. For example, when processor 2 reads from an address, A, the coherence protocol requires cache 2 to inform cache 1. If it currently holds address A, cache 1 updates the value in memory. That is, a *read* operation on any processor triggers a write-back in any cache that currently holds a cached copy of the address. Thus, in addition to requiring additional hardware and a mechanism that allows the caches to communicate, cache coherency introduces additional delay.

12.19 L1, L2, and L3 Caches

We said that arranging multiple caches into a hierarchy can improve overall performance. Indeed, most computer memory systems have at least two levels of cache hierarchy. To understand why computer architects added a second level of cache to the memory hierarchy, we must consider four facts:

- A traditional memory cache was separate from both the memory and the processor.

- To access a traditional memory cache, a processor used pins that connect the processor chip to the rest of the computer.

- Using pins to access external hardware takes much longer than accessing functional units that are internal to the processor chip.

- Advances in technology have made it possible to increase the number of transistors per chip, which means a processor chip can contain more hardware.

The conclusion should be clear. We know that adding a second cache on the processor chip can improve the performance of the memory system, and we know that technology has allowed chip vendors to add more functionality to their chips. So, it makes sense to embed a second memory cache in the processor chip itself. If the hit ratio is high, most data references never leave the processor chip — the effective cost of accessing memory is approximately the same as the cost of accessing a register.

Manufacturers adopted the term *Level 1 cache* (*L1 cache*) to refer to the cache onboard the processor chip, *Level 2 cache* (*L2 cache*) to refer to an external cache, and *Level 3 cache* (*L3 cache*) to refer to a cache built into the physical memory. We say that an L1 cache is *on-chip* and an L2 or L3 cache is *off-chip*. We can summarize:

> *Computer systems use a multi-level cache hierarchy in which an L1 cache is embedded on the processor chip, an L2 cache is external to the processor, and an L3 cache is built into the physical memory. In the best case, a multi-level cache makes the cost of accessing memory approximately the same as the cost of accessing a register.*

Chip sizes have become so large that the latest processors can incorporate a cache hierarchy on the chip itself. Thus, the distinction between L1 and L2 caches is fading.

12.20 Sizes Of L1, L2, And L3 Caches

Most personal computers employ a cache hierarchy. Of course, the cache at the top of the hierarchy is the fastest, but also the smallest. Figure 12.5 lists example cache memory sizes.

Processor	L1 Cache	L2 Cache	L3 Cache
Itanium 2	32KB	256KB	3MB, 4MB, or 6MB
Itanium	32KB	96KB	2MB or 4MB
Xeon MP	8KB	256KB or 512KB	512KB, 1MB or 2MB
P4	8KB	512KB	-

Figure 12.5 Example cache sizes. The amount of cache needed also depends on the applications that are run.

12.21 Instruction And Data Caches

Should all memory references pass through a single cache? To understand the question, imagine instructions being executed and data being accessed.

Instruction fetch tends to behave with high locality — in many cases, the next instruction to be executed is found at an adjacent memory address. Furthermore, the most time-consuming loops in a program are usually small, which means the entire loop can fit into a cache.

Although the data access in some programs exhibits high locality, the data access in others does not. For example, when a program accesses a hash table, the locations referenced appear to be random (i.e., the location referenced in one instant is not necessarily close to the location referenced in the next).

Apparent differences in instruction and data behavior raises the question of how intermixing the two types of references affects a cache. In essence, the more random the sequence of requests becomes, the worse the cache performs (because the cache will save each value, even though the value will not be needed again). We can state a general principle:

Inserting random references in the series of requests tends to worsen cache performance; reducing the number of random references that occurs tends to improve cache performance.

So the question above can be stated in terms of performance: is overall performance improved if we use two separate caches, one for instructions and one for data? Some architects assert that separate caches are better, and they design processors with two caches. Other architects suggest that the size of the cache matters more than the reference string. That is, once the cache becomes large enough, intermixing instruction and data references makes no difference. Thus, computer systems that mix instruction and data references usually require a larger cache.

12.22 Virtual Memory Caching And A Cache Flush

If caching is used with virtual memory, should the cache be placed between the processor and the MMU or between the MMU and physical memory? That is, should a cache use virtual or physical addresses to identify an item? The answer is complex. On one hand, using virtual addresses increases memory access speed because the cache can respond before the MMU translates the virtual address into a physical address. More important, if the MMU is off-chip, an L1 cache must use virtual addresses.

On the other hand, a cache that uses virtual addresses needs extra hardware that allows the cache to interact with the virtual memory system. To understand why, observe that a virtual memory system usually supplies the same address range to each application program (i.e., each application has addresses that start at zero). When the operating system changes from one application program to another, it must also change items in the cache because the new application uses the same addresses to refer to a new set of values.

How can a cache resolve the ambiguity that occurs because multiple applications use the same range of addresses? Architects use two solutions:

- A cache *flush* operation
- A disambiguating identifier

Cache Flushing. One way to ensure that a cache does not report incorrect values consists of removing all values from the cache. We say that the cache is *flushed*. In architectures that use flushing, the cache must be flushed whenever the operating system changes to a new virtual address space.

Disambiguation. An alternative to cache flushing involves the use of extra bits that identify the address space. The processor contains an extra hardware register that contains an address space ID. The processor assigns each running program a unique number, and whenever it starts running an application, the operating system loads the applications number into the address space ID register. As Figure 12.6 shows, the cache prepends the contents of the ID register onto the virtual address when it stores an item in the cache.

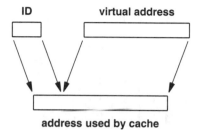

address used by cache

Figure 12.6 Illustration of an ID register used to disambiguate among virtual address spaces. Each address space is assigned a unique ID, which the operating system loads into the register.

As the figure shows, the processor creates artificially longer addresses before passing an address to the cache. From the cache's point of view, there is no ambiguity: even if two applications reference the same virtual address, the ID bits distinguish between the two addresses.

12.23 Implementation Of Memory Caching

Conceptually, each entry in a memory cache contains two values: a memory address and the value of the byte found at that address. In practice, however, storing a complete address with each entry is inefficient. Therefore, memory caches use clever techniques to reduce the amount of space needed. The two most important implementations are known as:

- Direct mapping memory cache
- Set associative memory cache

We will see that, like virtual memory schemes, both cache implementations use powers of two to avoid arithmetic computation.

12.24 Direct Mapping Memory Cache

Although memory caches are used with byte-addressable memories, a cache does not record individual bytes. Instead, a cache divides both the memory and the cache into a set of equal-size blocks, where the block size, B, is chosen to be a power of two. For example, if B is four, we can view the memory as Figure 12.7 illustrates.

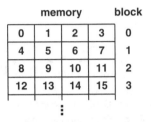

Figure 12.7 An example of memory as viewed by a cache. In the example, memory is divided into fixed-sized blocks of four bytes per block.

The blocks in memory are numbered modulo C, where C is the number of slots in the cache. That is, blocks are numbered from zero through $C-1$. To distinguish blocks with the same number, a unique *tag value* is assigned to each group of C blocks, and the tag is used in the cache to identify entries. For example, Figure 12.8 illustrates a cache of four entries and a memory that has block numbers and tag numbers assigned†.

The key to understanding a *direct mapping memory cache* arises from a restriction: only a memory block numbered i can be placed in cache slot numbered i. Thus, any of the memory blocks numbered 0 can be placed in the cache slot numbered 0, any of the blocks numbered 1 can be placed in the cache slot numbered 1, and so on. To identify the block currently in a slot of the cache, each cache entry contains a tag. Thus, if slot zero in the cache contains tag K, the value in slot zero corresponds to block zero from the area of memory that has tag K.

Why use tags? Because it identifies a large group of bytes rather than a single byte, a tag uses fewer bits to identify a section of memory than a full memory address. Furthermore, as the next section explains, choosing the block size and the size of memory identified by a tag to be powers of two makes cache lookup extremely efficient.

---

†A memory cache usually holds more than four items; a small cache size has been chosen merely as a simplified example.

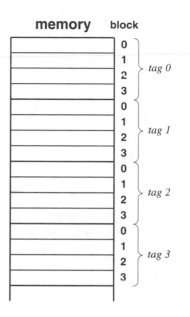

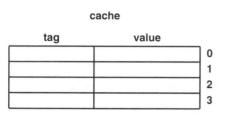

Figure 12.8 An example memory cache with space for four blocks and a memory divided into conceptual blocks. Each group of four blocks in memory is assigned a unique tag.

12.25 Using Powers Of Two For Efficiency

Although the direct mapping described above may seem complex, using powers of two simplifies the hardware implementation. Instead of modulo arithmetic, tag and block numbers can be computed by extracting groups of bits from a memory address. The high-order bits of the address are used as the tag number, the next set of bits forms a block number, and the final set of bits gives a byte offset within the block. Figure 12.9 illustrates the division.

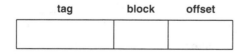

Figure 12.9 Illustration of the how using powers of two allows a cache to divide a memory address into three separate fields that correspond to a tag, a block number, and a byte offset within the block.

The algorithm for using cache lookup is straightforward:

Algorithm 12.1

Given:

    A memory address

Find:

    The data byte at that address

Method:

    Extract the tag number, t, block number, b, and offset, o, from the address.

    Examine the tag in slot b of the cache. If the tag matches t, extract the value from slot b of the cache.

    If the tag in slot b of the cache does not match t, use the memory address to extract the block from memory, place a copy in slot b of the cache, replace the tag with t, and use o to select the appropriate byte from the value.

Algorithm 12.1 Cache Lookup In A Direct Mapping Cache

12.26 Set Associative Memory Cache

The chief alternative to a direct mapping memory cache is known as a *set associative memory cache*. In essence, a set associative cache uses hardware parallelism to provide more flexibility. Instead of maintaining a single cache, the set associative approach maintains multiple underlying caches, and provides hardware that can search all of them simultaneously. More important, because it provides multiple underlying caches, a set associative cache can store more than one block that has the same number.

As a trivial example, consider a set associative cache in which there are two copies of the underlying hardware. Figure 12.10 illustrates the architecture.

To understand the advantages of the set associative approach, consider a reference string in which a program alternately references two addresses, A_1 and A_2, that have different tags, but both have block number zero. In a direct mapped cache, the two addresses contend for a single slot in the cache. A reference to A_1 loads the value of A_1 in the cache, and a reference to A_2 loads the value of A_2. Thus, in an alternating sequence of references, every reference results in a cache miss. In a set associative cache, however, A_1 can be placed in one of the two underlying caches, and A_2 can be placed in the other. Thus, every reference results in a cache hit.

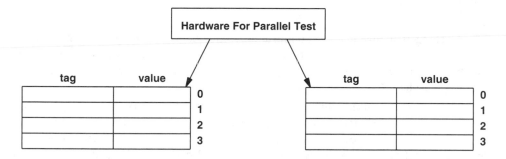

Figure 12.10 Illustration of a set associative cache with two copies of the underlying hardware. The cache includes hardware to search both copies in parallel.

As the amount of parallelism increases, performance of a set associative cache increases. In the extreme case, a cache is classified as *fully associative*, if each of the underlying caches contains only one slot, but the slot can hold an arbitrary value. Note that the amount of parallelism determines a point on a continuum: with no parallelism, we have a direct mapped cache, and with full parallelism, we have the equivalent of a Content Addressable Memory (CAM).

12.27 Consequences For Programmers

Experience has shown that caching works well for most computer programs. The code that programmers produce tends to contain loops, which means the processor will repeatedly execute a small set of instructions before moving on to another set. Similarly, programs tend to reference data items multiple times before moving on to a new data item. Furthermore, some compilers are aware of caching, and help optimize the generated code to better use the cache.

Despite the overwhelming success of caching, programmers who understand how a cache works can write code that exploits a cache. For example, consider a program that must perform many operations on each element of a large array. It is possible to perform one operation at a time (in which case the program iterates through the array many times) or to perform all the operations on a single element of the array before moving to the next element (in which case the program iterates through the array once). From the point of view of caching, the latter is preferable because the element will remain in the cache. Fortunately, a single iteration also works best for demand paging†.

---

†If a system has both extensive caching and demand paging, it can be difficult to measure the effect of either technique alone.

12.28 Summary

Caching is a fundamental optimization technique used throughout computer systems. A cache intercepts requests, automatically stores values, and answers requests quickly, whenever possible. Variations include a multi-level cache hierarchy and preloaded caches.

Caching can be used with both physical and virtual memory systems. A Translation Lookaside Buffer and demand paging are both forms of caching. Most computer systems employ a two-level memory cache. Originally, an L1 cache resided on an integrated circuit along with the processor, and an L2 cache was located external to the processor; as integrated circuits became larger, manufacturers moved L2 caches onto the processor chip. An L3 cache is built into the physical memory.

A technology known as a direct mapped memory cache allows hardware to perform cache lookup rapidly. A set associative cache extends the concept of direct mapping to permit parallel access.

EXERCISES

12.1   Consider a computer where each memory address is thirty-two bits long and the memory system has a cache that holds up to 4K entries. If a naive cache is used in which each entry of the cache stores an address and a byte of data, how much total storage is needed for the cache? If a direct mapped cache is used in which each entry stores a tag and a block of data that consists of four bytes, how much total storage is needed?

12.2   Extend the previous exercise. Assume the size of the cache is fixed, and find an alternative to the naive solution that allows the storage of more data items. Hint: what values are placed in the cache if the processor accesses a four-byte integer in memory?

12.3   Consult vendors' specifications and find the cost of memory access and the cost of a cache hit for a modern memory system (C_h and C_m in Section 12.8).

12.4   Use the values obtained in the previous exercise to plot the effective memory access cost as the hit ratio varies from zero to one.

12.5   Using the values of C_h and C_m obtained in Exercise 12.3, what value of the hit ratio, r, is needed to achieve an improvement of 30% in the mean access time of a memory system (as compared to the same memory system without a cache)?

12.6   State two ways to improve the hit ratio of a cache.

Input And Output

External Connections And Data Movement

13

Input/Output Concepts And Terminology

13.1 Introduction

Previous chapters of the text describe two of the major components found in a computer system: processors and memories. In addition to describing technologies used for each component, the chapters illustrate how processors and memory interact.

This chapter introduces the third major aspect of architecture, connections between a computer and the external world. We will learn that on most computers, the connection between a processor and memory uses the same basic paradigm as the connection between a processor and an I/O device, and we will see that although they operate under control of a processor, I/O devices can interact directly with memory.

13.2 Input And Output Devices

The earliest electronic computers, which consisted of a numerical processor plus a memory, resembled a calculator more than a modern computer. The human interface was crude — values were entered through a set of manual switches, and results of calculations were viewed through a series of lights. By the 1950s, it had become obvious that better interfaces were needed before digital computers could be useful for more than basic calculations. Engineers began devising ways to connect computers to external devices, which became known as *input* and *output* (*I/O*) devices. Modern I/O devices include keyboards, mice, monitors, hard disks, DVD drives, printers, cameras, and audio speakers.

13.3 Control Of An External Device

The earliest external devices attached to computers consisted of independent units that operated under control of the CPU. That is, an external device usually occupied a separate physical cabinet, had an independent source of electrical power, and contained internal circuitry that was separate from the computer. The small set of wires that connected the computer to the external device, only carried control signals (i.e., signals from the digital logic in the computer to the digital logic in the device). Circuitry in the device monitored the control signals, and changed the device accordingly.

For example, we said that many early computers provided a set of lights that displayed values. Typically, the display contained one light for each bit in the computer's accumulator — the light was on when the bit was set to one, and off when the bit was zero. However, it is not possible to connect a light bulb directly to an accumulator because even a small light bulb requires more power than a digital circuit can deliver. Therefore, a display unit needed a set of parallel circuits that each received a digital logic signal and controlled a light bulb accordingly. Figure 13.1 illustrates the connection.

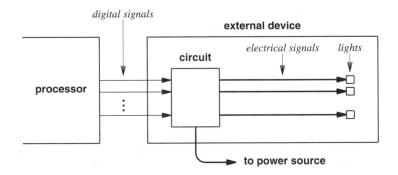

Figure 13.1 Example of an early external device: a set of lights controlled by a processor. The device contains circuitry that converts incoming signals into the signals needed to operate the device.

As the figure illustrates, we think of an external device as independent from the processor except for digital signals that pass between them. In practice, of course, some devices reside in the same enclosure with the processor, and both receive power from a common source. However, we will ignore such details and concentrate on the control signals.

Modern computers also arrange for the processor to control external devices. For example, a processor can start a disk spinning, control the volume on an external speaker, or turn off a printer. In the next chapter, we will learn how a modern computer communicates control information to external devices.

13.4 Data Transfer

Although control of external devices is essential, for most devices, control functions are secondary. The primary function of external devices is *data transfer*. Indeed, most of the architectural choices surrounding external devices focus on mechanisms that permit the device and processor to exchange data.

We will consider several questions regarding data transfer. First, exactly how is data communicated? Second, how is the transfer controlled (i.e., does the processor or the device initiate the operation)? Third, what techniques and mechanisms are needed for the highest-speed transfers?

What voltages are used to communicate with an external device, and how is data encoded? The answers depend on the type of device, the speed with which data must be transferred, the type of cabling used, and the distance between the processor and the device. In most cases, the digital signals used internally by a processor are not sufficient for communication with an external device.

Because the voltages and encodings used for external connections differ from those used internally, special hardware is needed to translate between the two representations. We use the term *interface controller* to refer to the hardware that provides the interface to an external device. Figure 13.2 illustrates that controllers are needed at both ends of a physical connection.

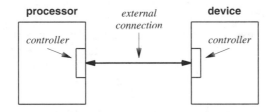

Figure 13.2 Illustration of controller hardware on each end of an external connection. The voltages and signals used on the external connection can differ from the voltages used internally.

13.5 Serial And Parallel Data Transfers

All the I/O interfaces on a computer can be classified in two broad categories:

- Parallel interface
- Serial interface

Parallel Interface. An interface between a computer and an external device is classified as *parallel* if the interface allows the transfer of multiple bits of data simultaneously. In essence, a parallel interface contains many wires — at any instant, each wire carries one bit of data.

Architects use the term *interface width* to refer to the number of parallel wires an interface uses. Thus, one might hear an architect talk about an eight-bit interface or a sixteen-bit interface. We will learn more about how interfaces use parallel wires in the next chapter.

Serial Interface. The alternative to a parallel interface is one in which only one bit of data can be transferred at any time; an interface that transfers one bit at a time is classified as *serial*.

The chief advantage of a serial interface is fewer wires. Only two wires are needed for serial data transmission — one to carry the signal and a second to serve as an electrical ground against which voltage can be measured. The chief disadvantage of a serial interface arises from increased delay: when sending multiple bits, serial hardware must wait until one bit has been sent before sending another.

13.6 Self-Clocking Data

Recall that digital circuits operate according to a *clock*, a signal that pulses continuously. Clocks are especially significant for I/O because each I/O device and processor can have a separate clock rate (i.e. each controller can have its own clock). Thus, one of the most significant aspects of an external interface concerns how the interface accommodates differences in clock rates.

The term *self-clocking* describes a mechanism in which signals sent across an interface contain information that allows the receiver to determine exactly how the sender encoded the data. For example, some external devices use an extra set of wires to contain clocking information: when transmitting data, the sender uses the extra wires to inform the receiver about the location of bit boundaries in the data.

13.7 Full-Duplex And Half-Duplex Interaction

Many external I/O devices provide *bidirectional transfer* which means the processor can send data to the device or the device can send data to the processor. For example, a disk drive supports both *read* and *write* operations. Interface hardware uses two methods to accommodate bidirectional transfer:

- Full-duplex interaction
- Half-duplex interaction

Full-Duplex Interaction. An interface that allows transfer to proceed in both directions simultaneously is known as a *full-duplex* interface. In essence, full-duplex hardware consists of two parallel devices with two independent sets of wires connecting them. One set is used to transfer data in each direction.

Half-Duplex Interaction. The alternative to a full-duplex interface, known as a *half-duplex* interface, only allows transfer to proceed in one direction at a time. That is, a single set of wires that connects the processor and the external device must be shared. In the next chapter, we will see that sharing requires negotiation — before it can perform a transfer, a processor or device must wait for the current transfer to finish, and must obtain exclusive use of the underlying wires.

13.8 Interface Latency And Throughput

Because it can only send one bit at a time, a serial interface operates slower than a parallel interface. As we have seen with memories, however, we must be careful to distinguish between *latency* and *throughput*. Latency refers to the delay between the time a bit is sent and the time the bit is received (i.e., how long it takes to transfer a single bit). Thus, latency is usually measured in nanoseconds (ns). Throughput refers to the number of bits that can be transferred per unit time, and is usually measured in *Megabits per second* (*Mbps*) or *Megabytes per second* (*MBps*).

We can summarize:

> *The latency of an interface is a measure of the time required to perform a transfer, the throughput of an interface is a measure of the data that can be transferred per unit time.*

13.9 The Fundamental Idea Of Multiplexing

It may seem that choosing an interface is trivial: a full-duplex, parallel interface offers more performance than any other combination. The difference in performance between a serial and a parallel interface can be dramatic: a parallel interface with width N has a throughput that is N times higher than a serial interface. Similarly, increasing the width of a parallel interface increases performance (e.g., doubling the width of an interface doubles the throughput).

Despite higher performance, many other factors make the choice of interfaces complex. Recall, for example, each integrated circuit has a fixed number of *pins* that provide external connections. A wider interface uses more pins, which means fewer pins for other functions. Similarly, an interface that provides full-duplex capability uses approximately twice as many pins as an interface that provides half-duplex capability.

Most architects choose a compromise for external connections. The connection has *limited parallelism*, and the hardware uses a technique known as *multiplexing* to send data. Although details are complex, the concept of multiplexing is easy to understand. The idea is that the hardware breaks a large data transfer into pieces and sends one piece at a time. We use the terms *multiplexor* and *demultiplexor* to describe the hardware that handles data multiplexing. For example, Figure 13.2 illustrates the multiplexing hardware needed to transfer sixty-four bits of data over an interface that has a width of sixteen bits.

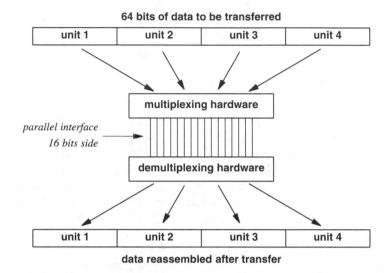

Figure 13.3 Illustration of the transfer of sixty-four bits of data over a sixteen bit interface. Multiplexing hardware divides the data into sixteen bit units and sends one unit at a time.

In practice, most physical connections between a processor and external devices use multiplexing. Doing so allows the processor to transfer arbitrary amounts of data without devoting many physical pins to the connection. In the next section, we will learn how multiplexing also improves CPU performance.

To summarize:

> *Multiplexing is used to construct an I/O interface that can transfer arbitrary amounts of data over a fixed number of parallel wires. Multiplexing hardware divides the data into blocks, and transfers each block independently.*

13.10 Multiple Devices Per External Interface

The examples in this chapter imply that each external connection from a processor attaches to one device. To help conserve pins and external connections, most processors do not have a single device per external connection. Instead, a set of devices attaches to the connection, and the controller must be able to handle communication with all of them. In the next chapter, we will see an example in detail.

13.11 A Processor's View Of I/O

We said that interface controller hardware is associated with each external connection. Thus, when a processor interacts with an external device, the processor must do so through the controller. The processor makes requests to the controller, and receives replies; the controller translates each request into the appropriate external signals that perform the requested function on the external device. The point is that the processor can only interact with the interface controller and not with the external device.

To capture the architectural concept, we say that the controller presents a *programming interface* to the processor. Interestingly, the programming interface does not need to exactly model the operations of the underlying device. In the next chapter, we will see an example of a widely-used programming interface that casts all external interactions into a simplified paradigm.

The point to remember is:

> *A processor does not access external devices directly. Instead, the processor uses a programming interface to pass requests to an interface controller, which translates the requests into the appropriate external signals.*

13.12 Summary

Computer systems interact with external devices either to control the device (e.g., to change the status) or to transfer data. An external interface can use a serial or parallel approach; the number of bits that can be sent simultaneously is known as the width of a parallel interface. A bidirectional interface can use full-duplex or half-duplex interaction.

There are two measures of interface performance. Latency refers to the time required to send a bit from a given source to a given destination (e.g., from memory to a printer), and throughput refers to the number of bits that can be sent per unit time.

Because the number of pins is limited, a processor does not have arbitrarily wide external connections. Instead, interface hardware is designed to multiplex large data transfers over fewer pins. In addition, multiple external devices can attach to a single external connection; the interface controller hardware communicates with each device separately.

14

Buses And Bus Architectures

14.1 Introduction

The chapters on memory discuss the external connection between a processor and the memory system. The previous chapter discusses connections with external I/O devices, and shows how a processor uses them to control the device or transfer data. It reviews concepts such as serial and parallel transfer, defines terminology, and introduces the idea of multiplexing communication over a set of wires.

This chapter extends the ideas by explaining a fundamental architectural feature present in all computer systems, a bus. It describes the motivation for using a bus, explains the basic operation, and shows how both memory and I/O devices can share a common bus. We will learn that a bus defines an address space, and understand the relationship between a bus address space and a memory address space.

14.2 Definition Of A Bus

A *bus* is a digital communication mechanism that allows two or more functional units to transfer control signals or data. Most buses are designed for use inside a single computer system; some are used within a single integrated circuit. Many bus designs exist because a bus can be optimized for a specific purpose. For example, a *memory bus* is intended to interconnect a processor with a memory system, and an *I/O bus* is intended to interconnect a processor with a set of I/O devices. We will see that general-purpose designs are possible.

14.3 Processors, I/O Devices, And Buses

The notion of bus is broad enough to encompass most external connections (i.e., a connection between a processor and another functional unit). Thus, instead of viewing the connection between a processor and a device as a set of wires (as in Chapter 13), we can be more precise: the two units are interconnected by a bus. Figure 14.1 illustrates the concept.

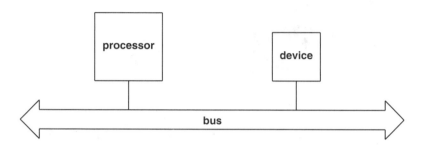

Figure 14.1 Illustration of a bus used to connect a processor and an external device. Buses are used for most external connections.

We can summarize:

> A bus *is the digital communication mechanism used within a computer system to interconnect functional units. A computer contains one or more buses that interconnect the processors, memories, and external I/O devices.*

14.4 Proprietary And Standardized Buses

A bus design is said to be *proprietary* if the design is owned by a private company and not available for use by other companies (i.e., covered by a patent). The alternative to a proprietary bus is known as a *standardized bus*, which means the specifications are available. Because they permit equipment from two or more vendors to communicate and interoperate, standardized buses allow a computer system to contain devices from multiple vendors. Of course, a bus standard must specify all the details needed to construct hardware, including the exact electrical specifications (e.g., voltages), timing of signals, and the encoding used for data. Furthermore, to ensure correctness, each device that attaches to the bus must implement the standard precisely.

14.5 Shared Buses And An Access Protocol

We said that a bus can be used to connect a processor to an I/O device. In fact, most buses are *shared*, which means that a single bus is used to connect the processor to a set of I/O devices. Similarly, if a computer contains multiple processors, all the processors can connect to a shared bus.

To permit sharing, an architect must define an *access protocol* to be used on the bus. The access protocol specifies how an attached device can determine whether the bus is available or is in use, and how a set of attached devices take turns using the bus.

14.6 Multiple Buses

A typical computer system contains multiple buses. For example, in addition to a central bus that connects the processor, I/O devices, and memory, some computers have a special-purpose bus used to access coprocessors. Other computers have multiple buses for convenience and flexibility — a computer with several standard buses can accommodate a wider variety of devices.

Interestingly, most computers also contain buses that are *internal* (i.e., not visible to the computer's owner). For example, many processors have one or more internal buses on the processor chip. A circuit on the chip uses an onboard bus to communicate with another circuit (e.g., with an onboard cache).

14.7 A Parallel, Passive Mechanism

As Chapter 13 describes, an interface is either classified as using *serial* data transfer or *parallel* data transfer. Although it is possible to devise a serial bus, almost all buses used in computer systems are parallel. That is, a bus is capable of transferring multiple bits of data at the same time†.

The most straightforward buses are classified as *passive* because the bus itself does not contain electronic components. Instead, each device that attaches to a bus contains the electronic circuits needed to communicate over the bus. Thus, we can imagine a bus to consist of parallel wires to which devices attach‡.

14.8 Physical Connections

Physically, a bus can consist of tiny wires etched in silicon on a single chip, a cable that contains multiple wires, or a set of parallel metal wires on a circuit board. Most computers use the third form: a bus is implemented as a set of parallel wires on

---

†Using a parallel bus within a single system is straightforward because all components in the computer have access to the same clock and short distances mean the system is less prone to clock skew.

‡In practice, some buses do contain a digital circuit known as a *bus arbiter* that coordinates devices attached to the bus. However, such details are beyond the scope of this text.

the computer's main circuit board, which is known as a *mother board*. In addition to a bus, the mother board contains the processor, memory, and other functional units.

A set of sockets on the mother board connects to the bus to allow devices to be plugged in or removed easily. Typically, the bus and the sockets are positioned near the edge of the mother board to make them easily accessible from outside. Figure 14.2 illustrates a bus and sockets on a mother board.

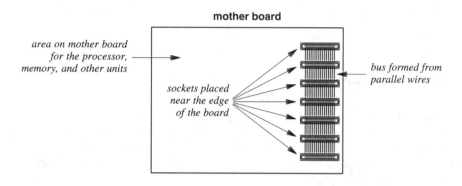

Figure 14.2 Illustration of a bus that consists of sixteen parallel wires on a mother board. The mother board contains other components that are not shown.

14.9 Bus Interface

Attaching a device to a bus is nontrivial. Recall that a bus uses an *access protocol* to determine when a given device can use the bus. Therefore, each device must have an additional digital circuit that attaches to the bus and follows the bus protocol. Known as a *bus interface* or a *bus controller*, the circuit implements the bus protocol and allows the device to access the bus. If the bus protocol is complicated, the interface circuit can be large; many bus interfaces require multiple chips.

How does an interface plug into the socket of a bus? Interestingly, the sockets of many buses are chosen to make it possible to plug a printed circuit board directly into the socket. The circuit board must have a region cut to the exact size of a socket, and must have metal *fingers* that touch metal contacts in the socket. Figure 14.3 illustrates the concept.

The figure helps us envision how a physical computer system can be constructed. If the mother board lies in the bottom of a cabinet, individual circuit boards that plug into the mother board are vertical. The arrangement is used in a typical PC — the back of the cabinet contains a series of slots that can each be occupied by a circuit board.

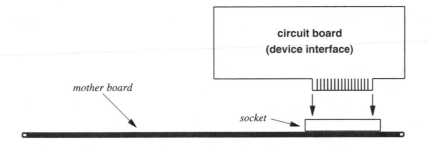

Figure 14.3 Side view of a mother board illustrating how a printed circuit board can plug directly into the socket of a bus. Metal strips on the circuit board press against metal contacts in the socket.

14.10 Address, Control, And Data Lines

Although the physical structure of a bus provides interesting engineering challenges, we are more concerned with the logical structure. We will examine how the wires are used, the operations the bus supports, and the consequences for programmers.

The wires that comprise a bus are called *lines*, and are used for three conceptual functions:

- Control of the bus
- Specification of address information
- Transfer of data

To help us understand how a bus operates, we will assume that the bus contains three separate sets of lines that correspond to the three functions†. Figure 14.4 illustrates the concept.

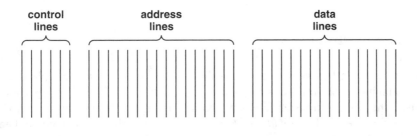

Figure 14.4 Conceptual division of wires that comprise a bus into lines for control, addresses, and data.

---

†A later section explains how the functionality can be achieved without physically separate groups of wires.

As the figure implies, lines need not be divided equally among the three uses. We will see that the control function usually requires fewer lines than other functions.

14.11 The Fetch-Store Paradigm

Recall from Chapter 9 that memory systems use the *fetch-store* paradigm in which a processor can either *fetch* (i.e., *read*) a value from memory, or *store* (i.e., *write*) a value to memory. A bus uses the same basic paradigm. That is, a bus only supports *fetch* and *store* operations. As unlikely as it seems, we will learn that when a processor communicates with a device or transfers data across a bus, the communication always uses *fetch* or *store* operations.

The point is:

> *Like a memory system, a bus employs the fetch-store paradigm; all control or data transfer operations are performed as either a* fetch *or a* store.

14.12 Fetch-Store Over A Bus

Knowing that a bus uses the fetch-store paradigm helps us understand the purpose of the three conceptual categories of lines that Figure 14.4 illustrates. All three categories are used for either a *fetch* or *store* operation. Control lines are used to ensure that only one pair of devices attempts to communicate over the bus at any time, and to allow two communicating devices to interact. The address lines are used to pass an address, and the data lines are used to transfer a value.

Figure 14.5 explains how the three categories of lines are used during a *fetch* or *store* operation. The figure lists the steps that are taken for each operation, and specifies which group of lines is used for each step.

14.13 The Width Of A Bus

We said that a bus uses parallel transfer — the bus contains multiple data lines, and can simultaneously transfer one bit over each data line. Thus, if a bus contains K data lines, the bus can transfer K bits at a time. Using the terminology from Chapter 13, we say that the bus has a *width* of K bits. Thus, a bus that has thirty-two data lines (i.e., can transfer thirty-two bits at the same time) is called a thirty-two bit bus.

Fetch

1. Use the control lines to obtain access to the bus

2. Place an address on the address lines

3. Use the control lines to request a fetch operation

4. Test the control lines to wait for the operation to complete

5. Read the value from the data lines

6. Set the control lines to allow another device to use the bus

Store

1. Use control lines to obtain access to the bus

2. Place an address on the address lines

3. Place a value on the data lines

4. Use the control lines to specify a store operation

4. Test the control lines to wait for the operation to complete

5. Set the control lines to allow another device to use the bus

Figure 14.5 The steps taken to perform a *fetch* or *store* operation over a bus, and the group of lines used in each step.

14.14 Multiplexing

How wide should a bus be? Recall from Chapter 13 that parallel interfaces represent a compromise: although increasing the width increases the throughput, greater width also takes more space and requires more electronic components in the attached devices. Thus, an architect chooses a bus width as a compromise between space, cost of electronics, and performance.

One technique stands out as especially helpful in reducing the number of lines in a bus: *multiplexing*. Multiplexing can be used in two ways: *data multiplexing* and *address and data multiplexing*.

Data Multiplexing. We have already seen how data multiplexing works. In essence, when a device attached to a bus has a large amount of data to transfer, the device divides the data into blocks that are exactly as large as the bus is wide. The device then uses the bus repeatedly, by sending one block at a time.

Address And Data Multiplexing. The motivation for multiplexing addresses and data is the same as the motivation for data multiplexing: a reduced number of lines. To understand how it works, consider the steps in Figure 14.5 carefully. In the case of a *fetch* operation, the address lines and data lines are never used at the same time (i.e., in the same step). Thus, an architect can use the same lines to send an address and receive data. Similarly, a *store* operation can use a single set of lines to communicate both address and data information provided the hardware first sends the address, and then sends the data†.

---

†Of course, a device that uses a multiplexed bus must have additional hardware to store the address while the data is transferred.

Most buses make heavy use of multiplexing. Thus, instead of three conceptual sets of lines, a typical bus has two: a few lines used for control, and a set of lines used to send either an address or data. Figure 14.6 illustrates the bus architecture used in practice.

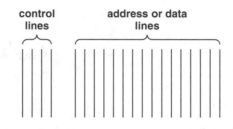

Figure 14.6 Illustration of a bus in which a single set of lines is used for both data and addresses. Using one set of lines helps reduce cost.

Multiplexing offers two advantages. On one hand, multiplexing allows an architect to design a bus that has fewer lines. On the other hand, if the number of lines in a bus is fixed, multiplexing produces higher overall performance. To see why, consider a data transfer. If K of the lines in the bus are reserved for addresses, those K lines cannot be used during a data transfer. If all the lines are shared, however, an additional K bits can be transferred on each bus cycle, which means higher overall throughput.

Despite its advantages, multiplexing does have two disadvantages. First, multiplexing takes more time because a *store* operation requires two bus cycles (i.e., one to transfer the address and another to transfer the data item). Second, multiplexing requires a more sophisticated bus protocol, and therefore, more complex bus interface hardware. Despite the disadvantages, however, most architects choose designs that use multiplexing. In the extreme case, a bus can be designed that multiplexes control information over the same set of lines used for data and addresses.

14.15 Bus Width And Size Of Data Items

The use of multiplexing helps explain another aspect of computer architecture: uniform size of all data objects, including addresses. We will see that data transfers in a computer each occur over a bus. Furthermore, because the bus multiplexes the transfers over a fixed number of lines, a data item that exactly matches the bus width can be transferred in one cycle, but any item that is larger than the bus width requires multiple cycles. Thus, it makes sense for an architect to choose a single size for the bus width, the size of a general purpose register, and the size of a data value that the ALU or functional units use (e.g., the size of an integer or a floating point value). More important, because addresses are also multiplexed over the bus lines, it makes sense for the architect to choose the same size for an address as for other data items. The point is:

Addresses and data values are multiplexed over a bus. To optimize performance of the hardware, an architect chooses a single size for both data items and addresses.

14.16 Bus Address Space

The easiest form of bus to understand consists of a *memory bus* (i.e., a bus that the processor uses to access memory). Previous chapters discuss the concepts of memory access and a memory address space; we will see how a bus is used to implement the concepts. As Figure 14.7 illustrates, a memory bus provides a physical interconnection among a processor and one or more memories.

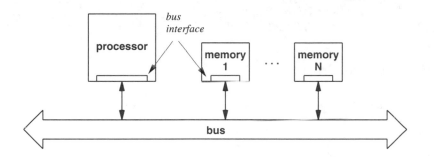

Figure 14.7 Physical interconnections of a processor and memory using a memory bus. A controller circuit in each device handles the details of bus access.

As the figure shows, each device connected to a memory bus contains an interface circuit. The interface implements the bus protocol, and handles all communication. The interface uses the control lines to gain access to the bus, and sends addresses or data values as instructed by the processor or memory. Thus, only the interface understands the bus details.

From a processor's point of view, the bus interface provides a programming interface. Because a bus uses the fetch-store paradigm, the programming interface for a bus consists of only two operations: *fetch* and *store*. When a program contains an instruction that references memory, the processor hardware passes control to the bus interface. For example, on many architectures, a *move* instruction extracts data from memory or moves data to memory. If a program moves data from a memory location to a general-purpose register, the processor issues a *fetch* instruction to the bus interface; if a program moves data to a memory location, the processor issues a *store* instruction to the bus interface.

From a programmer's point of view, the interface hardware is invisible. Instead, the programmer thinks of the bus as defining an *address space*. From an architect's point of view, the address space must be created from independent memories.

The key to creating a single address space lies in memory configuration — each memory is configured to respond to a specific set of addresses. That is, the interface for memory 1 is assigned a different set of addresses than the interface for memories 2, 3, 4, and so on. When a processor places a *fetch* or *store* request on the bus, all memory controllers receive the request. However, only one memory responds. That is, each memory interface compares the address in the request to the set of addresses for which the memory has been configured. If the address in the request lies within the controller's set, the controller responds. The point is:

> *Although an interface receives all requests that pass across the bus, the interface only responds to requests that contain an address for which the interface has been configured.*

14.17 Potential Errors

Figure 14.8. lists the conceptual steps that each memory interface implements.

```
Let R be the range of addresses assigned to the memory
Repeat forever  {
        Monitor the bus until a request appears;
        if ( the request specifies an address in R )  {
                respond to the request
        } else  {
                ignore the request
        }
}
```

Figure 14.8 The steps a memory interface follows.

Unfortunately, allowing each memory interface to follow the steps in Figure 14.8 means two types of errors can occur:

- Address conflict
- Unassigned address

An error that the bus hardware reports is referred to as a *bus error*; a typical bus protocol includes mechanisms that detect and report each type of bus error.

Address Conflict. We use the term *address conflict* to describe a bus error that results when interfaces are misconfigured so they respond to the same address. Most bus protocols include a test for address conflicts — if two or more interfaces attempt to respond to a given request, the bus hardware detects the problem, and sets a control line to indicate that an error occurred. When it uses a bus, the processor hardware checks the control lines to determine whether an error occurred, and if so, reports the error.

Unassigned Address. An *unassigned address* bus error occurs if a processor attempts to access an address that has not been configured into any interface. To detect an unassigned address, most bus protocols use a *timeout* mechanism — after sending a request over the bus, the processor starts a timer. If no interface responds, the timer expires, which causes the processor hardware to report the bus error†.

14.18 Address Configuration And Sockets

It may seem that the easiest way to prevent most bus errors consists of installing enough memory to cover all possible addresses. Then, when the computer boots, arrange for the processor to test all memory locations. In practice, however, architects usually design a memory bus to accommodate expansion. That is, a bus typically contains enough wires to accommodate more physical memory than is installed in the computer. Second, we will learn that devices other than memory can attach to a bus, and many devices do not occupy contiguous bus addresses.

Fortunately, architects have devised a scheme that helps avoid memory configuration problems: *special sockets*. The idea is straightforward. Memory is manufactured on small printed circuits that each plug into a socket on the mother board. To avoid problems caused by misconfiguration, all memory boards are identical, and no configuration is required before a board is plugged in. Instead, circuitry and wiring is added to the mother board so that the first socket only receives requests for address 0 through $K-1$, the second socket only receives requests for address K through $2K-1$, and so on. The point is:

> *To avoid memory configuration problems, architects can place memory on small circuit boards that each plug into a socket on the mother board. An owner can install memory without configuring the hardware because each socket is configured with the range of addresses to which the memory should respond.*

As an alternative, some computers contain sophisticated circuitry that allows the MMU to configure socket addresses when the computer boots. The MMU determines which sockets are populated, and assigns each an address. Although it adds cost, the extra circuitry provides additional flexibility because an owner can place memory in any socket rather than filling sockets in a particular order.

---

†The timeout mechanism also detects malfunctioning hardware (i.e., a memory that is not responding to requests).

14.19 Many Buses Or One Bus

Computers designed for high performance (e.g., mainframe computers) usually contain several buses. Each bus is optimized for a specific purpose. For example, a mainframe computer might have one bus for memory, another for high-speed I/O devices, and another for slow-speed I/O devices. As an alternative, less powerful computers (e.g., personal computers) often use a single bus for all connections. The chief advantages of a single bus are lower cost and more generality. A processor does not need multiple bus interfaces, and a single bus interface can be used for both memory and devices.

Of course, designing a single bus for all connections means choosing a compromise. That is, the bus may not be optimal for any given purpose. In particular, if the processor uses a single bus to access instructions and data as well as perform I/O, the bus can easily become a bottleneck. Thus, a system that uses a single bus often needs a large memory cache that can answer most of the memory requests without using the bus.

14.20 Using Fetch-Store With Devices

We said that a bus is used as the primary connection between a processor and an I/O device, and that all operations on a bus must use the fetch-store paradigm. The two statements may seem contradictory — although it works well for data transfer, fetch-store does not appear to handle device control. For example, consider an operation like starting or stopping a disk, or testing whether a wireless network is currently in range of an access point. How can such operations be performed unless a bus provides additional commands beyond *fetch* and *store*?

To understand how a bus works, we must remember that a bus only provides a way to communicate a small set of bits from one unit to another and does not specify what each bit means. Instead, the interface hardware on each device provides a unique interpretation of the bits. Thus, a device can interpret certain bits as a control operation rather than as a request to transfer data.

14.21 An Example Of Device Control Using Fetch-Store

An example will clarify the relationship between fetch-store and device control. Imagine a simplistic hardware device that contains sixteen status lights, and suppose we want to attach the device to a bus. Because the bus only offers *fetch* and *store* operations, we need to build interface hardware that uses the fetch-store paradigm for control. An engineer who designs a device interface begins by listing the operations to be performed. For example, assume that Figure 14.9 lists the functions that our imaginary status light device offers.

- **Turn the display on**
- **Turn the display off**
- **Set the display brightness**
- **Turn the ith status light on or off**

Figure 14.9 An example of functionality provided by an imaginary hardware device. Before the unit can be attached to a bus, control functions must be implemented using the fetch-store paradigm.

To cast control operations in the fetch-store paradigm, a designer chooses a set of addresses that are not used by other devices, and assigns meanings to each address. For example, if our imaginary status light device is attached to a bus that has a width of thirty-two bits, a designer might choose bus addresses 100 through 111, and might assign meanings according to Figure 14.10†.

Address	Operation	Meaning
100–103	store	nonzero data value turns the display on, and a zero data value turns the display off
100–103	fetch	returns zero if display is currently off, and nonzero if display is currently on
104–107	store	Change brightness. Low-order four bits of the data value specify brightness value from zero (dim) through sixteen (bright)
108–111	store	The low order sixteen bits each control a status light, where zero sets the corresponding light off and one sets it on.

Figure 14.10 Example assignment of addresses, operations, and meanings for the device control functions listed in Figure 14.9.

14.22 Operation Of An Interface

Although the bus operations are named *fetch* and *store*, a device interface is not a memory — data is not stored for later recall. That is, from the perspective of a device, the address in a request merely consists of a set of bits. The interface contains logic circuits that compare the address bits in each request to the addresses assigned to the device. If a match occurs, the interface enables a circuit that handles the operation (*fetch* or *store*). For example, the first item in Figure 14.10 can be implemented by hardware that tests the address, operation, and data items in each request. We think of the test as a conditional operation:

---

†Many other assignments are possible; the meanings assigned here merely provide one possibility.

if (address == 100 && op == store && data != 0) turn_on_display;

Similarly, the hardware must also check the case where the data item is zero:

if (address == 100 && op == store && data == 0) turn_off_display;

Although we have used programming language syntax to express the operations, interface hardware does not perform the test sequentially. Instead, an interface is constructed from Boolean circuits that can test the address, operation, and data values in parallel and take the appropriate action.

14.23 Asymmetric Assignments

Note that Figure 14.10 does not define the effect of *fetch* or *store* operations on some of the addresses. For example, the specification does not define a *fetch* operation for address 104. To capture the idea that either *fetch*, *store*, or both can be defined for a given address, we say that the assignment is *asymmetric* if it defines *fetch*, but not *store*, or vice versa. The specification in Figure 14.10 is asymmetric because the processor can store a value to the four bytes starting at address 104, but an error results if the processor attempts to read from address 104.

14.24 Unified Memory And Device Addressing

We said that in some computers, a single bus provides access to both memory and I/O devices. In such an architecture, the assignment of addresses on the bus defines the processor's view of the address space. For example, imagine a computer system with a processor, two memories, and two I/O devices attached to a bus as Figure 14.11 illustrates.

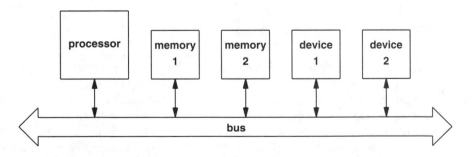

Figure 14.11 Illustration of a computer architecture that uses a single bus. Both memories and devices attach to the bus.

The bus in the figure defines a single address space. Therefore, to avoid address conflicts, each of the memories and devices attached to the bus must be assigned a unique address range. For example, if we assume the memories are each 1 MByte and the devices each require twelve memory locations, four address ranges can be assigned for use on the bus as Figure 14.12 lists.

Device	Address Range		
Memory 1	0x000000	through	0x0fffff
Memory 2	0x100000	through	0x1fffff
Device 1	0x200000	through	0x20000b
Device 2	0x20000c	through	0x200017

Figure 14.12 One possible assignment of bus addresses for the set of devices shown in Figure 14.11.

We can also imagine the address space drawn graphically like the illustrations of a memory address space in Chapter 9. However, because the space occupied by a device is extremely small compared to the space occupied by a memory, the result is not very instructive. For example Figure 14.13 shows the address space that results from the assignments in Figure 14.12.

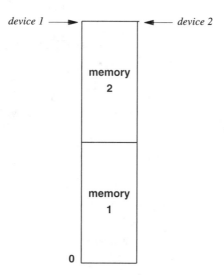

Figure 14.13 Illustration of the address space that results from the assignments in Figure 14.12. The amount of space taken by each device (sixteen bytes) is insignificant compared to the amount of space taken by each memory (1 Mbyte).

14.25 Holes In The Address Space

The address assignment in Figure 14.12 is said to be *contiguous*, which means that the address ranges do not contain gaps — the first byte assigned to one range is the immediate successor of the last byte assigned to the previous range. Because a bus protocol handles unassigned addresses, contiguous assignment is not required — if the software accidentally accesses a nonexistent address, the bus hardware detects the problem, and reports a bus error.

Using the terminology from Chapter 11, we say that if an assignment of addresses is not contiguous, the assignment leaves one or more *holes* in the address space. In many architectures, for example, the lowest part of the bus address space is reserved for memory, and devices are assigned to high addresses.

14.26 Address Map

As part of the specification for a bus, an architect chooses exactly which type of hardware can be used at each address. We call the specification an *address map*. Note that an address map is not the same as an address assignment because a map only shows what assignments are possible. For example, Figure 14.14 gives an example of an address map for a sixteen-bit bus.

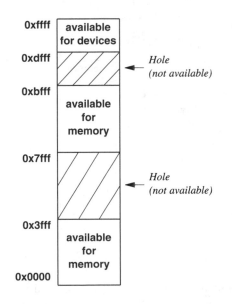

Figure 14.14 One possible address map for a sixteen-bit bus. Two areas are available for memory, and one area is available for devices.

In the figure, the two areas of the address space available for memory are not contiguous. Instead, a hole is located between them. Furthermore, a hole is located between the second memory area and the device area.

When a computer system is constructed, the owner must follow the address map. For example, the sixteen-bit bus in Figure 14.14 only allows two blocks of memory that total 32,768 bytes. The owner can choose to install less than a full complement of memory, but not more.

The device space in a bus address map is especially interesting because the space reserved for devices is often much larger than necessary. In particular, most address maps reserve a large piece of the address space for devices, making it possible for the bus to accommodate extreme cases with thousands of devices. However, a typical computer has fewer than a dozen devices, and a typical device uses a few addresses. The consequence is:

> *In a typical computer, the part of the address space available to devices is sparsely populated — only a small percentage of the addresses are used.*

14.27 Program Interface To A Bus

From a programmer's point of view there are two bus architectures. A processor that has multiple buses provides special instructions used to access each bus. A processor that provides a single, general-purpose bus interprets all memory operations as references to the bus.

As an example of using a general-purpose bus, consider how a programmer can reference the status light device described in Figure 14.10†. To turn the device on, the program must store a nonzero value in bytes 100 through 103. If we assume an integer consists of four bytes (i.e., thirty-two bits) and the processor uses little-endian byte order, the program only needs to store a nonzero value into the integer at location 100. An example of C code that performs the operation follows:

```
int      *ptr;      /* declare ptr to be a pointer to an integer */

ptr = (*int)100;   /* set pointer to address 100 */
*ptr = 1;          /* store nonzero value in addresses 100 - 103 */
```

We can summarize:

> *A processor that has multiple buses provides special instructions to access each; a processor that has one bus interprets normal memory operations as referencing locations in the bus address space.*

---

†Figure 14.10 appears on page 227.

14.28 Bridging Between Two Buses

Although a single bus offers the advantage of simplicity and lower cost, a computer that has multiple buses can accommodate a wider variety of commercial devices. Thus, architects seek inexpensive ways to attach multiple buses to a computer. One approach uses a hardware device, known as a *bridge*, that interconnects two buses as Figure 14.15 illustrates.

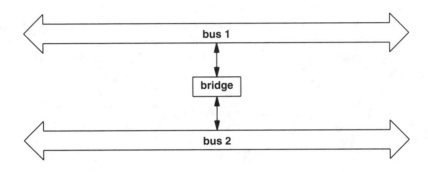

Figure 14.15 Illustration of a bridge connecting two buses. The bridge must follow the standard for each bus.

Like a device or memory, a bridge is assigned an equivalent range of addresses on each bus. Unlike a conventional device, a bridge does not answer requests directly. Instead, when it receives a request on one bus, the bridge translates the address and forwards the request to the other bus. Similarly, when it receives a reply on one bus, the bridge translates the address and forwards the reply to the other bus.

14.29 Main And Auxiliary Buses

Logically, a bridge performs a one-to-one mapping from the address space of one bus to the address space of another. That is, the bridge makes a set of addresses on one bus appear in the address space of the other. To understand why bridging is popular, consider a common case where an architect needs to add a new device to a computer that already has a bus. If the interface on the new device does not match the computer's main bus, the architect can design adapter hardware or use a bridge to add an *auxiliary bus* to the system. Using a bridge has two advantages: a computer owner can add other devices to the auxiliary bus without changing the hardware, and an architect has less work because bridges are available for most buses. Figure 14.16 illustrates the concept of address mapping.

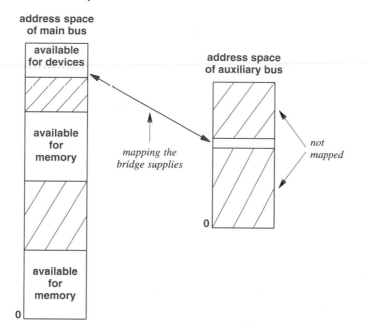

Figure 14.16 Illustration of a mapping that a bridge can provide between the address space of an auxiliary bus and the address space of a main bus. Only some bus addresses need to be mapped.

In the figure, both bus address spaces start at zero, and the address space of the auxiliary bus is smaller than the address space of the main bus. More important, the architect has chosen to map only a small part of the auxiliary bus address space, and has specified that it maps onto a region of the main bus that is reserved for devices. As a result, any device on the auxiliary bus that responds to addresses in the mapped region appears to be connected to the computer's main bus.

To summarize:

> *A bridge is a hardware device that interconnects two buses and maps addresses between them. Bridging allows a computer to have one or more auxiliary buses that are accessed through the computer's main bus.*

14.30 Consequences For Programmers

As Figure 14.16 shows, the set of mapped addresses do not need to be identical in both address spaces. The goal is to make a bridge *transparent* so the processor does not know about the auxiliary bus. From a programmer's point of view, however, the software may need to accommodate the mapping. For example, when a device is installed in an auxiliary bus, the device is configured with an address, A. If the computer's owner enters A as the device address, software must understand the mapping and use the corresponding address on the main bus. Similarly, if the interaction between the device and the processor involves addresses, the processor must use addresses that the auxiliary device understands†.

14.31 Switching Fabrics

Although a bus is fundamental to most computer systems, a bus has a disadvantage: bus hardware can only perform one transfer at a time. That is, although multiple hardware units can attach to a given bus, at most one pair of attached units can communicate at any time. The basic paradigm always consists of three steps: wait for exclusive use of the bus, perform a transfer, and release the bus so another transfer can occur.

Some buses extend the paradigm by permitting multiple attached units to transfer N bytes of data each time they obtain the bus. For situations where bus architectures are insufficient, architects have invented alternative technologies that permit multiple transfers to occur simultaneously. Known as *switching fabrics*, the technologies use a variety of forms. Some fabrics are designed to handle a few attached units, and other fabrics are designed to handle hundreds or thousands. Similarly, some fabrics restrict transfers so only a few attached units can initiate transfers at the same time, and other fabrics permit many simultaneous transfers. One of the reasons for the variety arises from economics: higher performance (i.e., more simultaneous exchanges) can cost much more, and the higher cost may not be justified.

Perhaps the easiest switching fabric to understand consists of a *crossbar switch*. We can imagine a crossbar to be a matrix with N inputs and M outputs. The crossbar contains $N \times M$ electronic switches that each connect an input to an output. At any time, the crossbar can turn on switches to connect pairs of inputs and outputs as Figure 14.17 illustrates.

---

†Chapter 15 explains why a processor and a device exchange address information.

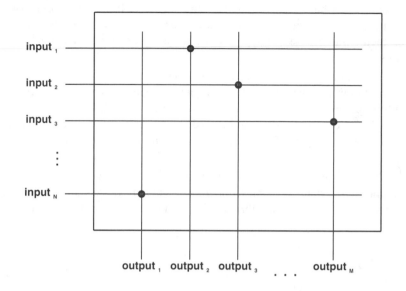

Figure 14.17 A conceptual view of a crossbar switch with N inputs and M
outputs with a dot showing an active connection. The crossbar
mechanism ensures that only one connection is active for a
given row or a given column at any time.

The figure helps us understand why switching fabrics are expensive. First, each
line in the diagram represents a parallel data path composed of multiple wires. Second,
each potential intersection between an input and output requires an electronic switch
that can connect the input to the output at that point. Thus, a crossbar requires $N \times M$
switching components, each of which must be able to switch a parallel connection. By
comparison, a bus only requires $N + M$ electronic components (one to connect each input and each output to the bus).

14.32 Summary

A bus is the fundamental mechanism used to interconnect memory, I/O devices,
and processors within a computer system. Most buses operate in parallel, meaning that
the bus consists of parallel wires that permit multiple bits to be transferred simultaneously.

Each bus defines a protocol that attached devices use to access the bus. Most bus
protocols follow the fetch-store paradigm; an I/O device connected to a bus is designed
to receive *fetch* or *store* operations and interpret them as control operations on the device.

Conceptually, a bus protocol specifies three separate forms of information: control information, address information, and data. In practice, a bus does not need separate wires for each type because a bus protocol can multiplex communication over a small set of wires.

A bus defines an address space that may contain holes (i.e., unassigned addresses). A computer system can have a single bus to which memory and I/O devices attach, or can have multiple buses that each attach to specific types of devices. As an alternative, a hardware device called a bridge can be used to add multiple auxiliary buses to a computer by mapping all or part of the auxiliary bus address space onto the address space of the computer's main bus.

The chief alternative to a bus is known as a switching fabric. Although they achieve higher throughput by using parallelism, switching fabrics are restricted to high-end systems because a switching fabric is significantly more expensive than a bus.

EXERCISES

14.1   A hardware architect asks you to choose between a single, thirty-two bit bus design that multiplexes both data and address information across the bus, or two sixteen-bit buses, one used to send address information and one used to send data. Which design do you choose? Why?

14.2   If a bus has can transfer 64 bits in each cycle and runs at a rate of 66 MHz, what is the bus throughput measured in megabytes per second?

14.3   How many simultaneous transfers can occur over a crossbar switching fabric of N inputs and M outputs?

15

Programmed And Interrupt-Driven I/O

15.1 Introduction

Earlier chapters introduce I/O. The previous chapter explains how a bus provides the connection between a processor and a set of I/O devices. The chapter discusses the bus address space, and shows how an address space can hold a combination of both memory and I/O devices. Finally, the chapter explains that a bus uses the fetch-store paradigm, and shows how *fetch* and *store* operations can be used to interrogate or control an external device.

This chapter continues the discussion. The chapter describes and compares the two basic styles of interaction between a processor and an I/O device. It focuses on interrupt-driven I/O, and explains how device driver software in the operating system interacts with an external device.

The next chapter takes a different approach to the subject by examining I/O from a programmer's perspective. The chapter looks at individual devices, and describes how they interact with the processor.

15.2 I/O Paradigms

We know from Chapter 14 that I/O devices connect to a bus, and that a processor can interact with the device by issuing *fetch* and *store* operations to bus addresses that have been assigned to the device. Although the basic mechanics of I/O are easy to specify, several questions remain unanswered. What control operations should each device support? How does application software running on the processor access a given device without understanding the hardware details? Can the interaction between a processor and I/O devices affect overall system performance?

15.3 Programmed I/O

The earliest computers took a straightforward approach to I/O: an external device consisted of basic digital circuits that controlled the hardware in response to *fetch* and *store* operations; the CPU handled all the details. For example, to print a new line of text on a printer, the CPU needed to perform several steps. The CPU activated a set of circuits, one at a time. The circuits advanced the paper, moved the print head to the beginning of the line, selected a character to print, and caused the hammer to strike the character.

To capture the idea that an early peripheral device consisted only of basic circuits that respond to commands from the CPU, we say that the device contained no intelligence†. We also characterize the form of interaction by saying that the I/O is *programmed*.

15.4 Synchronization

It may seem that writing software to perform programmed I/O is trivial: at each step, the program merely assigns a value to an address on the bus. To understand I/O programming, however, we need to remember two things. First, a nonintelligent device cannot remember a list of commands. Instead, circuits in the device perform each command precisely when the processor sends the command. Second, a processor operates much faster than an I/O device — even a slow processor can execute hundreds of instructions in the time it takes for a motor or mechanical actuator to move a physical mechanism (e.g., to retract the read head in a CD-ROM drive).

If a processor issues instructions too rapidly, the results can be unpredictable. In our example above, if the processor issues instructions to move the print mechanism, select a character, and print, the instructions will arrive much faster than the device can respond. The printer may attempt to print the character while the print head is moving or the hardware may malfunction.

To prevent problems, programmed I/O relies on *synchronization*. That is, once it issues a command, the processor must interact with the device to determine when the device is ready for another command. We can summarize:

> *Because a processor operates orders of magnitude faster than an I/O device, programmed I/O requires the processor to synchronize with the device that is being controlled.*

---

†Colloquially, engineers and architects use the term *dumb* to refer to nonintelligent hardware.

15.5 Polling

The basic form of synchronization that a processor uses with an I/O device is known as *polling*. In essence, polling requires the processor to repeatedly ask the device whether an operation has completed before the processor starts the next operation. Thus, to perform the *print* operation described below, a processor must use polling at each step. Figure 15.1 lists the steps required.

- Cause the printer to advance the paper
- Poll to determine when paper has advanced
- Move the print head to the beginning of the line
- Poll to determine when the print head reaches the
  beginning of the line
- Specify a character to print
- Poll to determine when the character is locked in position
- Cause the hammer to strike the character
- Poll to determine when the hammer is finished striking

Figure 15.1 Illustration of synchronization between a processor and an I/O
device. The processor must wait for each step to complete.

15.6 Code For Polling

How does software perform polling? Because I/O devices connect to a bus, and a bus follows the fetch-store paradigm, polling uses a *fetch* operation. That is, one or more of the addresses assigned to the device correspond to status information — when the processor fetches a value from the address, the device responds by giving its current status.

Before we can see an example of code that uses polling, we need to specify the exact details of a hardware device. To keep the example simple, we will assume our imaginary printing device uses sixteen bytes which it interprets as Figure 15.2 lists.

Addresses	Operation	Meaning
0 through 3	store	Nonzero starts paper advance
4 through 7	store	Nonzero starts head moving to beginning of line
8 through 11	store	Character to print (low-order byte)
9 through 12	store	Nonzero starts hammer striking
13 through 16	fetch	Busy: nonzero when device is busy

Figure 15.2 An example specification that shows how the fetch-store paradigm can allow a processor to control a device or determine the
current status. The specification is for an imaginary printing
device.

In the figure, addresses cover sixteen bytes starting at zero. Of course, when an I/O device is attached to a bus, it is unlikely that the device will be assigned location zero on the bus. Thus, the values shown are relative, not absolute, numbers. We will soon see how the values are used in a program.

Once we are given a hardware specification, writing code that controls a device is straightforward. For example, assume a printing device that uses sixteen bytes, as specified in Figure 15.2, has been assigned a starting address on a bus of 0x110000. Figure 15.3 shows C code that performs the steps in Figure 15.1 for a computer that uses little-endian arithmetic and has an integer size of four bytes.

```
int        *p;          /* declare an integer pointer */

p = 0x110000;           /* point to lowest address of device */
*p = 1;                 /* start paper advance */
while (*(p+4) != 0)     /* poll for paper advance */
    ;

*(p+1) = 1;             /* start print head moving */
while (*(p+4) != 0)     /* poll for print head movement */
    ;

*(p+2) = 'C';           /* select character "C" */
while (*(p+4) != 0)     /* poll for character selection */
    ;

*(p+3) = 1;             /* start hammer striking */
while (*(p+4) != 0)     /* poll for hammer striking */
    ;
```

Figure 15.3 An example of C code that carries out the steps from Figure 15.1 on an imaginary printing device as specified in Figure 15.2.

To understand the code, remember how the C programming language defines pointer arithmetic: adding K to an integer pointer advances the pointer by KN, where N is the number of bytes in an integer. Thus, if variable p has the value 0x110000, $p+1$ equals 0x110004.

Programmers who have not written a program to control a device may find the code shocking because it contains four occurrences of a while statement that each appear to be an infinite loop. If such a statement appeared in a conventional application program, the statement would be in error and the program would fail. In the example, however, pointer p references a device instead of a memory location. Thus, when the processor fetches a value from location $p+4$, the request passes to a device, which interprets it as a request for status information. So, unlike a value in memory, the value returned by the device will change over time — if the processor polls enough times, the device will complete its current operation, and will return zero as the status value.

15.7 Control And Status Registers

We use the term *Control and Status Registers (CSRs)* to refer to the set of addresses that a device uses. More specifically, a *control register* corresponds to a contiguous set of addresses (usually the size of an integer) that respond to a *store* operation, and a *status register* corresponds to a contiguous set of addresses that respond to a *fetch* operation.

In practice, CSRs are usually more complicated than the simplified version listed in Figure 15.2. For example, a typical status register assigns meanings to individual bits (e.g., the low-order bit of the status word specifies whether the device is in motion, the next bit specifies whether an error has occurred, and so on). More important, to conserve addresses, many devices combine control and status functions into a single set of addresses. That is, a single address can serve both functions — a *store* operation to the address controls the device, and a *fetch* operation to the same address reports the device status.

As a final detail, some devices interpret a *fetch* operation as both a request for status information and a *control* operation. For example, as it moves, a mouse delivers bytes to indicate the relative motion. The processor uses a *fetch* operation to obtain a byte that the mouse has sent. Furthermore, each *fetch* automatically resets the hardware to accept the next byte from the mouse.

15.8 Processor Use And Polling

The chief advantage of a programmed I/O architecture arises from the economic benefit: because they do not contain sophisticated digital circuits, devices that rely on programmed I/O are inexpensive. The chief disadvantage of programmed I/O arises from the computational overhead: each step requires the processor to interact with the I/O device.

To understand why polling is especially undesirable, we must recall the fundamental mismatch between I/O devices and computation: because they are electromechanical, I/O devices operate several orders of magnitude slower than a processor. Furthermore, if a processor uses polling to control an I/O device, the amount of time the processor waits is fixed, and is independent of the processor speed. The important point is:

> *Because a typical processor is much faster than an I/O device, the speed of a system that uses polling depends only on the speed of the I/O device; using a fast processor will not increase the rate at which I/O is performed.*

Turning the statement around, we can immediately see a corollary: if a processor uses polling to wait for an I/O device, using a faster processor merely means that the processor will execute more instructions waiting for the device (i.e., loops, such as those in Figure 15.3, will run faster). Thus, a faster processor merely "wastes" more cycles waiting for an I/O device — if the processor did not need to poll, the processor could be performing computation instead†.

15.9 First, Second, And Third Generation Computers

In the 1950s and 1960s, computer architects became aware of the mismatch between the speed of processors and I/O devices. The difference was particularly important when the first generation of computers, which used vacuum tubes, was replaced by a second generation that used solid-state devices. Although the use of solid state devices (i.e., transistors) increased the speed of processors, the speed of I/O devices remained approximately the same. Thus, architects explored ways to overcome the mismatch between I/O and processor speeds.

One approach emerged as superior, and led to a third revolution in computer architecture. Known as an *interrupt* mechanism, the facility is now standard in computers. Figure 15.4 summarizes the three main generations of computer architecture.

Generation	Description
1	Vacuum tubes used to build digital circuits
2	Transistors used to build digital circuits
3	Interrupt mechanism used to control I/O

Figure 15.4 The three main generations of computer systems and the characteristics of each.

15.10 Interrupt-Driven I/O

The central premise of interrupt-driven I/O is straightforward: instead of wasting time polling, allow a processor to continue to perform computation while an I/O device operates. In practice, however, interrupt-driven I/O requires substantial changes to all aspects of the system, including:

- I/O device hardware
- Bus architecture and functionality
- Processor architecture
- Programming paradigm

I/O Device Hardware. Instead of merely operating under control of a processor, an interrupt-driven I/O device must operate independently once it has been started. Later, when it finishes, a device must be able to inform the processor.

---

†Programmers who work on computers that use polling optimize programs by placing computation between I/O operations, which means the processor can execute useful instructions instead of spending as much time polling.

Bus Architecture And Functionality. A bus must support two-way communication that allows a processor to start an operation on a device and allows the device to inform the processor when the operation completes.

Processor Architecture. A processor needs a mechanism that can cause the processor to temporarily stop normal processing and handle a device.

Programming Paradigm. Perhaps the most significant change involves a shift in programming paradigm. Polling uses a sequential, *synchronous* style of programming in which the programmer specifies each step of the operation an I/O device performs. As we will see in the next chapter, interrupt-driven programming uses an *asynchronous* style of programming in which the programmer writes code to handle events.

15.11 A Hardware Interrupt Mechanism

We use the term *interrupt* to capture the idea that device events are temporary. The processor starts a device, and then continues to execute conventional instructions. When it needs service (e.g., when an operation completes), the device hardware sends an interrupt signal over the bus to the processor. The processor temporarily stops executing instructions, and saves all the state information needed to resume execution later. The hardware tells the processor which device interrupted, and allows the processor to handle the device. Finally, when it finishes handling the interrupt, the processor uses the saved state information to resume executing instructions as if no interrupt had occurred. That is:

> *As the name implies, an interrupt mechanism temporarily borrows the processor to handle an I/O device. When an interrupt occurs, the hardware saves the state of the computation, and restarts the computation when interrupt processing finishes.*

15.12 Interrupts And The Fetch-Execute Cycle

From an application programmer's point of view, an interrupt is *transparent*. That is, a programmer writes a series of instructions as if interrupts do not exist. The hardware is designed so the result of computation is the same if no interrupts occur during the execution of the instructions, one interrupt occurs, or many interrupts occur. Of course, a programmer who writes code executed during an interrupt must adhere to rules that guarantee transparency (e.g., if the interrupt code stored zero in random memory locations, the interrupt would not be transparent).

How does I/O hardware interrupt a processor? In fact, it does not. Instead, interrupts are implemented by a modified fetch-execute cycle as Algorithm 15.1 explains. In essence, an interrupt occurs *between* the execution of two instructions.

Algorithm 15.1

Repeat forever {

    Test: if any device has requested interrupt, handle the interrupt and then continue with the next iteration of the loop.

    Fetch: access the next step of the program from the location in which the program has been stored.

    Execute: Perform the step of the program.

}

Algorithm 15.1

15.13 Handling An Interrupt

To handle an interrupt, a processor takes five steps as Figure 15.5 illustrates.

- Save the current execution state
- Determine which device interrupted
- Call the procedure that handles the device
- Clear the interrupt signal on the bus
- Restore the current execution state

Figure 15.5 Five steps that processor hardware performs to handle an interrupt. The steps are hidden from a programmer.

Saving and restoring state is easiest to understand: the hardware saves information when an interrupt occurs (usually in memory), and a special *return from interrupt* instruction reloads the saved state. In some architectures, the hardware saves complete state information, including all the registers. In other architectures, the hardware saves basic information, such as the instruction counter, and requires software to explicitly save and restore values, such as the general-purpose registers. In any case, saving and restoring state are symmetric operations — hardware is designed so the instruction that returns from an interrupt reloads exactly the state information that the hardware saves when an interrupt occurs. We say that the processor temporarily *switches the execution context* when it handles an interrupt.

15.14 Interrupt Vectors

How does the processor know which device is interrupting? The processor uses the bus to find out. When it detects an interrupt signal, the processor sends a special command to determine which device needs service. The bus is arranged so that exactly one device can respond at a time. Each device is assigned a unique number, and the device responds by giving its number.

Numbers assigned to devices are not random. Instead, the processor hardware interprets the number as an index into an array of pointers at a reserved location in memory. An item in the array, which is known as an *interrupt vector*, is a pointer to software that handles the device; we say that the interrupts are *vectored*. The software is known as an *interrupt handler*. Figure 15.6 illustrates the data structure.

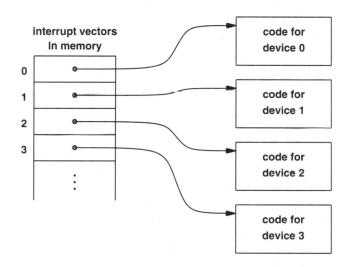

Figure 15.6 Illustration of interrupt vectors. Each vector points to code that serves as an interrupt handler for the device.

The figure shows the simplest interrupt vector arrangement in which each physical device is assigned a unique interrupt vector. In practice, computer systems designed to accommodate many devices often use a variation in which multiple devices share a common interrupt vector. After the interrupt occurs, code in the interrupt handler uses the bus a second time to determine which physical device interrupted. Once it determines the physical device, the handler chooses an interaction that is appropriate for the device. The chief advantage of sharing an interrupt vector among multiple devices arises from scale — a processor with a fixed set of interrupt vectors can accommodate an arbitrary number of devices.

15.15 Initialization And Enabling And Disabling Interrupts

How are values installed in an interrupt vector table? Software must initialize interrupt vectors because neither the processor nor the device hardware enters or modifies the table. Instead, the hardware blindly assumes that the interrupt vector table has been initialized — when an interrupt occurs, the processor saves state, uses the bus to request a vector number, uses the value as an index into the table of vectors, and then branches to the code at that address. No matter what address is found in a vector, the processor will jump to the address and attempt to execute the instruction.

To ensure that no interrupts occur before the table has been initialized, most processors start in a mode that has interrupts *disabled*. That is, the processor continues to run the fetch-execute cycle without checking for interrupts. Later, once the software (usually the operating system) has initialized the interrupt vectors, the software must execute a special instruction that explicitly *enables* interrupts. In many processors, the interrupt status is controlled by the *mode* of the processor; interrupts are automatically enabled when the processor changes from the initial startup mode to a mode suitable for executing programs.

15.16 Preventing Interrupt Code From Being Interrupted

We pointed out earlier that a computer can have many devices, including multiple copies of the same type of device (e.g., a computer might have two identical disk drives). Imagine what might happen if a second device interrupts while the processor is handling an interrupt. To avoid problems and make interrupt handlers easier to write, some hardware follows a straightforward policy: further interrupts are automatically disabled once an interrupt occurs. Interrupts are not enabled again until the processor returns from the interrupt. Thus, if two identical disk devices attempt to interrupt simultaneously, the processor handles one of them at a time — the processor only starts servicing a second interrupt after it completes servicing the first.

15.17 Multiple Levels Of Interrupts

Another potential problem arises in situations where a computer system includes multiple types of devices. Some devices require that interrupts be serviced within a short time, and other devices do not require service immediately, but take a long time to service. Therefore, a general-purpose processor that allows an owner to connect arbitrary devices creates a potential problem: a slow device may take longer to service than a fast device can wait. If a processor follows the policy of only allowing one device to interrupt at a time, the processor cannot have both a slow device and a fast device.

To overcome the differences in devices, architects have introduced a modification of the interrupt scheme that provides *multiple level interrupts*, which are also known as *multiple interrupt priorities*. Typically, a processor offers seven or fifteen levels, and allows a computer owner to assign each device to one of the levels. The processor hardware is designed to give higher priority to higher-numbered levels and allows an interrupt handler at one level to be interrupted by a device at a higher level†.

When multiple levels of interrupts are used, the processor hardware is more sophisticated. At any given time, the processor is said to be operating at one of the priority levels. Priority zero means the processor is not currently handling an interrupt; priority N means the processor is currently handling an interrupt from a device that has been assigned to level N. The rule is:

> *When operating at priority level K, a processor can only be interrupted by a device that has been assigned to level K + 1 or higher.*

To see how multiple interrupt priorities work, consider the two device types described above. Assume we assign the slow device interrupt priority one and the fast device interrupt priority two. If the processor is running an application when the slow device interrupts, the processor changes from priority zero to priority one. If the fast device interrupts before the slow device has been serviced, the processor changes to priority two and jumps to the interrupt handler for the fast device. When the handler for the fast device finishes, the processor returns to level one and finishes handling the slow device. Finally, when the handler for the slow device finishes, the processor returns to level zero.

The consequence of multiple interrupts is:

> *A processor that has interrupt priority levels zero through N and uses zero for application programs can have up to N interrupts in progress at a time. However, only one interrupt can be in progress at any priority level.*

15.18 Assignment Of Interrupt Vectors And Priorities

We said that each device must be assigned an interrupt vector and an interrupt priority. Furthermore, both the hardware in the device and the software running on the processor must agree on the assignments — when a device returns an interrupt vector number, the corresponding interrupt vector must point to the handler for the device.

---

†The notion of priorities can be extended to assign each application program a priority; priorities are especially important in real-time systems.

How are interrupt assignments made? There are two answers:

- Fixed, manual assignment used on small, embedded systems
- Flexible, automated assignment used on general-purpose systems

Manual Assignment. As the name implies, manual assignment means that a person configures both the hardware and software. For example, some devices are manufactured with physical switches on the circuit board, and the interrupt vector address is entered by setting switches.

Automated Assignment. An automated interrupt vector assignment is used on a general-purpose computer, such as a PC, where a user can install an arbitrary set of devices. When the computer boots, the processor uses the bus to determine which devices are attached. The processor assigns an interrupt vector and priority to each device, places a copy of the appropriate device hander software in memory, and builds the interrupt vector in memory.

Because it saves space, reduces software complexity, and eliminates startup delays, manual assignment works well for small, embedded systems, such as a video game system where the set of external devices does not change. Because it eliminates human error, automated assignment works well for general-purpose computers. Of course, automated assignment means higher delay when booting the computer.

15.19 Dynamic Bus Connections And Pluggable Devices

The interrupt mechanism described above assumes that interrupt vectors and priorities are assigned at startup and remain in place as the computer operates. What about devices that can be dynamically attached or detached? For example, consider a *Universal Serial Bus* (*USB*) that permits a user to plug in a device at any time.

How does a USB operate? In essence, a USB appears as a single device on the computer's main bus. When the computer boots, the USB is assigned an interrupt vector as usual, and a handler is placed in memory. Later, when a user attaches a device, the USB hardware generates an interrupt, and the processor executes the handler. The handler, in turn, interrogates the USB to determine which device has been attached, and loads a secondary handler for the new device. When the device needs service, the USB generates an interrupt, control passes to the USB handler, the handler interrogates the USB to determine which device needs service, and invokes the appropriate secondary handler.

15.20 The Advantage Of Interrupts

Why did the interrupt mechanism cause a revolution in computer architecture? The answer is easy. First, as we will learn in the next chapter, I/O had become an important aspect of computing. Second, interrupt-driven I/O automatically overlaps computation and I/O without requiring a programmer to take any special action. More important, interrupts adapt to any speed processor and I/O devices automatically. Because a programmer does not need to estimate how many instructions can be performed during an I/O operation, interrupts never underestimate or overestimate. We can summarize:

A computer that uses interrupts is both easier to program and offers better I/O performance than a computer that uses polling.

15.21 Smart Devices And Improved I/O Performance

Although a basic interrupt mechanism provides better performance than polling, architects realized that further improvements are possible. In general, the more digital logic an I/O device contains, the less the device relies on the processor. Informally, architects use the term *smart device* to characterize a device that can perform a series of operations on its own.

As an example of how a smart device works, consider a disk drive. The underlying hardware requires several steps to read data from the disk and place it in memory. The simplest disk hardware requires a processor to start each step, and generates an interrupt when the step finishes. Figure 15.7 illustrates the sequence of events that occur†.

- Processor starts the disk spinning
- Disk interrupts when it reaches full speed
- Processor starts disk arm moving to the desired location
- Disk interrupts when arm is in position
- Processor starts a *read* operation to transfer data to memory
- Disk interrupts when the transfer completes

Figure 15.7 Example of the interaction between a dumb disk device and a processor. The processor controls each step of the operation.

A smart version of a disk device contains sufficient logic (perhaps even an embedded processor) to handle a series of steps. Thus, a smart device does not interrupt as

---

†Only events involving the disk are shown; the processor can execute another program between the time a step is started and an interrupt occurs.

often, and does not require the processor to handle each step. Figure 15.8 illustrates the interaction between a processor and a smart disk device.

- Processor requests a *read* operation by specifying the location on the disk and the location in memory
- Disk performs all steps of the operation and interrupts when the operation completes

Figure 15.8 Example of the interaction between a smart disk device and a processor. The disk device performs individual steps of the operation without interrupting the processor.

Our discussion of dumb and smart devices has omitted many details. For example, most I/O devices detect and report errors (e.g., a disk does not spin or a flaw on a surface prevents the hardware from reading a disk block). Thus, interrupt processing is more complex than described: when an interrupt occurs, the processor must interrogate the CSRs associated with the disk to determine whether the operation was successful or an error occurred. Furthermore, for devices that report *soft errors* (i.e., temporary errors), the processor must retry the operation to determine whether an error was temporary or permanent.

15.22 Direct Memory Access (DMA)

Our discussion above assumes that a smart I/O device can transfer data into memory without using the CPU. The technology for such transfers is known as *direct memory access (DMA)*, and is a key aspect of high-speed I/O.

To understand DMA, recall that in most architectures, both memory and I/O devices attach to a central bus. Thus, there is a direct path between an I/O device and memory. If we imagine that a smart I/O device contains an embedded processor, the idea behind DMA should be clear: the embedded processor in the I/O device issues *fetch* or *store* requests to which the memory responds. Of course, the bus must provide a mechanism that allows multiple units to access the bus without interfering (i.e., a mechanism that guarantees only one processor can send a request at any time). If the bus supports such a mechanism, an I/O device can transfer data to memory without using the processor.

To summarize:

A technology known as Direct Memory Access (DMA) *allows a smart I/O device to access memory directly. A device that uses DMA can transfer data between the device and memory without using the processor.*

15.23 Buffer Chaining

It may seem that a smart device using DMA is sufficient to guarantee high performance: data can be transferred between the device and memory without using the processor, and the device does not interrupt for each step of the operation. However, further optimization is possible.

To understand situations in which a single DMA transfer is insufficient, consider a high-speed network. Packets arrive from the network in *bursts*, which means a set of packets arrives back-to-back with minimum time between packets. If the device that connects to the network can only perform one operation at a time, the device must interrupt the processor after a packet arrives. During the interrupt, the processor must allocate a buffer to hold the next packet, and must start the device reading the packet. The sequence of events must occur quickly (i.e., before the next packet arrives). Unfortunately, if multiple devices attempt to interrupt simultaneously, the processor may not be able to service the network device interrupt in time to capture the next packet.

To solve the problem of back-to-back arrivals, some smart I/O devices use a technique known as *buffer chaining*. The processor allocates multiple buffers, and creates a linked list in memory. The processor then passes the list to the I/O device, and allows the device to fill each buffer. Figure 15.9 illustrates the concept.

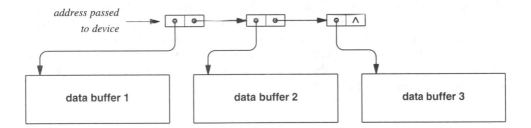

Figure 15.9 Illustration of buffer chaining. A processor passes a list of
buffers to a smart I/O device, and the device fills each buffer on
the list without waiting for the processor.

The example above describes the use of buffer chaining for high-speed input. A buffer chain can also be used with output: a processor places data in a set of buffers, places the buffers on a linked list, and starts an I/O device. The device moves through the list, writing the data from each buffer.

15.24 Scatter Read And Gather Write Operations

Buffer chaining is especially helpful for computer systems in which the buffer size used by software is smaller than the size of a data block used by an I/O device. On input, chained buffers allow a device to divide a large data transfer into a set of smaller buffers. On output, chained buffers allow a device to extract data from a set of small buffers and combine the data into a single block.

We use the term *scatter read* to capture the idea of dividing a large block of incoming data into multiple small buffers, and the term *gather write* to capture the idea of combining data from multiple small buffers into a single output block.

15.25 Operation Chaining

Although buffer chaining handles situations in which a given operation is repeated over many buffers, further optimization is possible in cases where a device can perform multiple operations. To understand, consider a disk device that offers *read* or *write* operations. To optimize performance, we need to start another operation as soon as the current operation completes.

The technology used to start a new operation without delay is known as *operation chaining*. Like buffer chaining, a processor that uses operation chaining must create a linked list in memory, and must pass the list to a smart device. Unlike buffer chaining, however, nodes on the linked list specify a complete operation: in addition to a buffer pointer, the node contains an operation and necessary parameters. For example, a node on the list used with a disk might specify a *read* operation and a disk block. Figure 15.10 illustrates operation chaining.

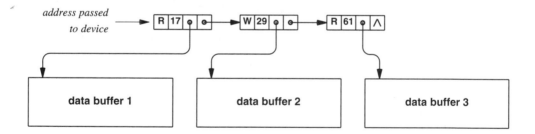

Figure 15.10 Illustration of operation chaining. Each node specifies an operation (*R* or *W*), a disk block number, and a buffer in memory.

15.26 Summary

Two paradigms are used to handle I/O devices: programmed I/O and interrupt-driven I/O. Programmed I/O requires a processor to handle each step of an operation. More important, because a processor is much faster than an I/O device, the processor must wait for the device.

Third generation computers introduced interrupt-driven I/O that allows a device to perform a complete operation before informing the processor. A processor that uses interrupts tests for an interrupt during the fetch-execute cycle.

Interrupts are vectored, which means the interrupting device supplies a unique integer that the processor uses as an index into an array of pointers to handlers. To guarantee that interrupts do not affect a running program, the hardware saves and restores state information during an interrupt. Multi-level interrupts are used to give some devices priority over others.

Smart I/O devices contain additional logic that allows them to perform a series of steps without assistance from the processor. Smart devices use the techniques of buffer chaining and operation chaining to further optimize performance.

EXERCISES

15.1   Assume a RISC processor take two microseconds to execute each instruction and an I/O device can wait at most 1 millisecond before its interrupt is serviced. What is the maximum number of instructions that can be executed with interrupts disabled?

15.2   Read about devices on a bus and the interrupt priorities assigned to each. Does a disk or mouse have higher priority? Why?

15.3   In most systems, part or all of the device driver code must be written in assembly language. Why?

16

A Programmer's View Of Devices, I/O, And Buffering

16.1 Introduction

Previous chapters cover the hardware aspects of I/O. They explain the bus architecture that is used to interconnect devices, processors, and memory, as well as the interrupt mechanism that an external device uses to inform a processor when an operation completes.

This chapter changes the focus to software, and considers I/O from a programmer's perspective. The chapter examines both the software needed to control a device and the application software that uses I/O facilities. We will understand the important concept of a device driver, and see how a driver implements operations like *read* and *write*. We will learn that devices can be divided into two broad types: byte-oriented and block-oriented, and we will understand the interaction used with each.

Although few programmers write device drivers, understanding how a device driver operates and how low-level I/O occurs can help programmers write more efficient applications. Once we have looked at the mechanics of device drivers, we will focus on the concept of buffering, and see why it is essential for programmers to use buffering.

16.2 Definition Of A Device Driver

The previous chapter explains the basic hardware interrupt mechanism. We are now ready to consider how low-level software uses the interrupt mechanism to perform I/O operations. We use the term *device driver* to refer to software that provides an interface between an application program and an external hardware device. In most cases, a computer system has a device driver for each external device, and all applications that access a given device use the same driver. Typically, device drivers are part of the computer's operating system, which makes each driver accessible to any application.

Because a device driver understands the details of a particular hardware device, we say that a driver contains *low-level code*. The driver interacts with the device over a bus, understands the device's *Control And Status Registers* (*CSRs*), and handles interrupts from the device.

16.3 Device Independence, Encapsulation, And Hiding

The primary purpose of a device driver is *device independence*. That is, the device driver approach removes all hardware details from application programs and relegates them to a driver.

To understand why device independence is important, we need to know how early software was built. Each application program was designed for a specific brand of computer, a specific memory size, and a specific set of I/O devices. An application contained all the code needed to use the bus to communicate with particular devices. Unfortunately, a program written to use a specific set of devices could not be used with any other devices. For example, upgrading a printer to a newer model required all programs to be rewritten.

A device driver solves the problem by providing a device-independent interface to applications. For example, because all applications that use a printer rely on the printer's device driver, an application does not have detailed knowledge of the hardware built in. Consequently, changing a printer only requires changing the device driver; all applications remain unchanged. We say that the device driver *hides* hardware details from applications or that the driver *encapsulates* the hardware details.

To summarize:

> *A device driver consists of software that understands and handles all the low-level details of communication with a particular device. Because the driver provides a high-level interface to applications, an application program does not need to change if a device changes.*

16.4 Conceptual Parts Of A Device Driver

A device driver contains multiple functions that must all work together, including code to communicate over a bus, code to handle device details, and code to interact with an application. Furthermore, the driver must interact with the computer's operating system. To help manage complexity, programmers think of a driver as partitioned into three parts:

- A *lower half* comprised of a handler that is invoked when an interrupt occurs
- An *upper half* comprised of functions that are invoked by applications to request I/O operations
- A set of *shared variables* that hold state information needed to coordinate the two halves

The names *upper half* and *lower half* reflect a programmer's view that hardware is "low level" and application programs are "high level". Thus, a programmer thinks of applications at the top of a hierarchy and hardware at the bottom. Figure 16.1 illustrates a programmer's view.

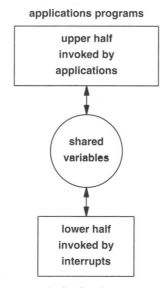

Figure 16.1 The conceptual organization of device driver software into three parts. A driver provides the interface between applications that operate at a high level and the underlying device hardware.

16.5 Two Types Of Devices

Before we can understand more about device drivers, we need to know more about the interface the hardware presents to the driver. Devices can be divided into two broad categories, depending on the style of interface the device uses:

- Character-oriented devices
- Block-oriented devices

A *character-oriented* device transfers a single byte of data at a time. For example, the serial interface used to connect a keyboard to a computer transfers one character (i.e., byte) for each keystroke. Similarly, the serial interface used to connect a dialup modem to a computer is character-oriented. From a device driver's point of view, a character-oriented device generates an interrupt each time a character is sent or received — sending or receiving a block of N characters generates N interrupts.

A *block-oriented* device transfers an entire block of data at a time. In some cases, the device specifies a block size, B, and all blocks must contain exactly B bytes. For example, a disk device defines a block size equal to the disk's sector size. In other cases, however, blocks are of variable size. For example, a network interface defines a block to be as large as a packet†. From a device driver's point of view, a block-oriented device only generates one interrupt each time a block is sent or received.

16.6 Example Flow Through A Device Driver

The details of programming device drivers are beyond the scope of this text. However, to help us understand the concept, we will consider how a simplified device driver might handle basic output. For our example, we will assume that an application performs a *write* operation to a block-oriented device, and specifies data to be written. Figure 16.2 illustrates a device driver, and lists the steps that are taken for output.

As the figure shows, even a trivial operation requires a complex sequence of steps. When an application writes to a device, execution transfers to an operating system function which, in turn, passes control to the upper half of the appropriate device driver. In our simplified example, the driver waits for the device to become ready, starts the output operation, and returns to the application.

How does a driver wait for a device to become ready? If the device has a CSR that reports status, the driver can use polling to repeatedly test the device CSR. As an alternative, the driver can be written so the upper half sets a bit in the shared variable area when an operation is started, and the lower half clears the bit when the operation completes. The driver can be written to use polling to repeatedly test the bit in the shared variable area.

---

†Most networking technologies do not enforce a fixed packet size. Instead, the network sets an upper bound, and allows the size of a given packet to be smaller than the upper bound, depending on the amount of data being sent.

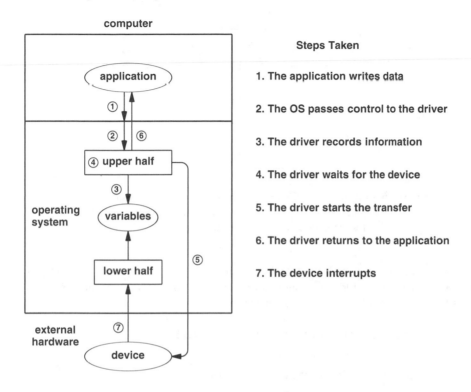

Figure 16.2 A simplified example of the steps that occur when an application requests an output operation. A device driver located in the operating system handles all communication with the device.

16.7 Queued Output Operations

Although the design used in our example driver will work, the approach is too inefficient to use in a production system. In particular, our driver can waste significant amounts of time polling for a device to become ready.

To avoid waiting, drivers used in production systems implement a *queue of requests*. On output, the upper half never waits for the device. Instead, the upper half deposits the data to be written in a queue, ensures that the device will generate an interrupt, and returns to the application. Later, when the device finishes its current operation and generates an interrupt, the lower half extracts the next request from the queue, starts the device, and returns from the interrupt. Figure 16.3 illustrates the organization.

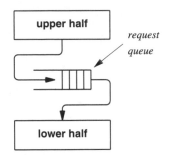

Figure 16.3 Illustration of a device driver that uses a request queue. On output, the upper half deposits items in the queue without waiting for the device, and the lower half controls the device.

A driver that uses an output queue is elegant — the queue of requests provides coordination between the upper and lower halves of the driver. Figure 16.4 lists the steps that each half of a driver takes for output.

Initialization (computer system starts)

    1. Initialize input queue to empty

Upper half (application performs write)

    1. Deposit data item in queue

    2. Use the CSR to request an interrupt

    3. Return to application

Lower half (interrupt occurs)

    1. If the queue is empty, stop the device from interrupting

    2. If the queue is nonempty, extract an item and start output

    3. Return from interrupt

Figure 16.4 The steps that the upper and lower halves of a driver take for an output operation when queueing is used. The upper half forces an interrupt, but does not start output on the device.

As the figure shows, the steps for each half of the driver are straightforward. Notice that the lower half performs most of the work: in addition to handling interrupts from the device, the lower half checks the queue and, if the queue is not empty, extracts the next item and starts the device. Because the device interrupts each time it completes an operation, the lower half will be invoked once per output operation, which allows it to start the next operation. Thus, the lower half will continue to be invoked until the queue is empty.

What happens after the last item has been removed from the queue? The lower half will be invoked after the last output operation completes, but will find the queue empty. At that point, the device is not restarted. Instead, the lower half stops the device from interrupting. Later, when an application calls the upper half to place a new item in the queue, the upper half starts the device interrupting again, and output proceeds.

16.8 Forcing An Interrupt

Because a request queue is used in so many drivers, architects have designed hardware that works well with the programming paradigm outlined in Figure 16.4. In particular, a device often includes a CSR bit that a processor can set to force the device to interrupt†. The mechanism is designed to work in the following way:

- A device has a CSR bit, B, that is used to force the device to interrupt

- If the device is idle, setting bit B causes the device to generate an interrupt

- If the device is currently performing an operation, setting bit B has no effect

In other words, if an interrupt is already destined to occur when the current operation completes, the device waits for the operation to complete, and generates an interrupt as usual. Otherwise, setting the CSR bit will force an interrupt to occur. Arranging for a CSR to have no effect on a busy device greatly simplifies programming. To see why, look at the steps Figure 16.4 lists. The upper half does not need to test whether the device is busy (i.e., whether an operation is in progress). Instead, the upper half always sets the CSR bit. If an operation is already in progress, the device hardware ignores the bit being set, and waits until the operation completes. If the device is idle, setting the bit causes the device to interrupt immediately, which forces the lower half to process the next request in the queue.

16.9 Queued Input Operations

A device driver can also use queueing for input. However, additional coordination is required for two reasons. First, to accept input before an application is ready, the device must be started. Second, if input does not arrive before an application reads, the driver must temporarily stop the application until input does arrive‡. Figure 16.5 lists the steps a driver uses to handle input when a queue is present.

---

†Recall from Chapter 15 that the code required to set a CSR bit is trivial — it consists of a single assignment statement.

‡On some systems, an application can determine whether data is available (i.e., the application can use polling to avoid waiting for input).

Initialization (computer system starts)

1. Initialize input queue to empty

2. Force the device to interrupt

Upper half (application performs read)

1. If input queue is empty, temporarily stop the application

2. Extract the next item from the input queue

3. Return the item to the application

Lower half (interrupt occurs)

1. If the queue is not full, start another input operation

2. If an application is stopped, allow the application to run

3. Return from interrupt

Figure 16.5 The steps that the upper and lower half of a driver take for an input operation when queueing is used. The upper half temporarily stops an application until data becomes available.

Although our description of device drivers omits many details, it gives an accurate picture of the general approach that device drivers use. We can summarize:

> *A production device driver uses an input or output queue to store items. The upper half places a request in the queue, and the lower half handles the details of communication with a device.*

16.10 Devices That Support Bi-Directional Transfer

Some devices allow both input and output — the device allows data transfer from the processor to the device, or vice versa. We use the term *bi-directional device* to characterize a device that supports data transfer in two directions, and the term *uni-directional* device to characterize a device that supports data transfer in one direction.

The distinction between bi-directional and uni-directional devices is subtle because many uni-directional devices provide feedback to the processor. For example, consider a printer. Although a printer is uni-directional (i.e., only used for output), typical printer hardware provides status information to the processor. For example, most printers allow the processor to determine the *paper status* (i.e., whether paper remains available) or the *ink level* (i.e., the amount of ink remaining). Although it can transfer status information to the computer, such a device is still classified as *uni-directional*.

How does a driver handle a bi-directional device? There are two approaches:

- Treat the device as two separate devices, one used for input and one used for output

- Treat the device as a single device that handles two types of commands, one for input and one for output

Two Devices. Treating a device as two devices works well for devices in which the hardware distinguishes between input interrupts and output interrupts. For example, many serial line interfaces contain parallel hardware that handles input and output independently. The two directions use separate CSRs and separate interrupt vectors.

In cases where parallel hardware handles input and output separately, a device driver simply maintains two queues: one for incoming data and one for outgoing data. In essence, the driver contains code for two separate drivers that each handle one direction of transfer.

One Device. The alternative approach treats a bi-directional device as a single, unified entity. The driver maintains a single queue of requests, and each request specifies a direction. A unified approach is needed if the hardware can only perform one operation at a time (i.e., does not contain parallel hardware to handle the two directions). For example, although a disk device provides bi-directional transfer, the underlying hardware handles one operation at a time. Thus, the queue of requests that a driver maintains for a disk device must specify the operation to be performed (i.e., *read* or *write*).

A disk drive provides a special case of bi-directional transfer because an application can issue requests to read and write the same block of data. Thus, a driver that queues output must handle a situation in which an application writes data and then reads the data back before the driver has actually written the data to disk (i.e., the data is still in the output queue). To optimize performance, whenever it receives a *read* request, a disk driver searches the queue of requests to determine if the requested data is waiting to be written.

16.11 Asynchronous Vs. Synchronous Programming Paradigm

In Chapter 15, we said that an interrupt mechanism requires the use of an *asynchronous programming model*. We can now understand why. Like a conventional program, polling is *synchronous* because control passes through the code from beginning to end. A device driver that handles interrupts is *asynchronous* because the programmer writes separate pieces of code that respond to events. One of the upper half routines is invoked when an application requests I/O, a lower half routine is invoked when an input or output operation occurs and when an interrupt occurs, and an initialization routine is invoked when a device is started.

Asynchronous programming is more challenging than synchronous programming. Because events can occur in any order, a programmer must use shared variables to encode the current state of the computation (i.e., the events that have occurred in the past and their effect). It can be difficult to test asynchronous programs because a programmer cannot easily control the sequence of events. More important, applications running on the processor and device hardware can generate events simultaneously.

16.12 Asynchrony, Smart Devices, And Mutual Exclusion

Simultaneous events make programming asynchronous device drivers especially difficult. For example, consider a smart device that uses command chaining. The processor creates a linked list of operations in memory, and the device follows the list and performs the operations automatically.

A programmer must coordinate the interaction between a processor and a smart device. To understand why, imagine a smart device extracting items from a list at the same time the upper half of a driver is adding items. A problem can occur if the smart device reaches the end of the list and stops processing just before the driver adds a new item. Similarly, if two independent pieces of hardware attempt to manipulate pointers in the list simultaneously, links can become invalid.

To avoid errors caused by simultaneous access, a driver that interacts with a smart device must implement *mutual exclusion*. That is, a driver must ensure that the smart device will not access the list until changes have been completed, and the smart device must ensure that the driver will not access the list until changes have been completed. A variety of schemes are used to ensure exclusive access. For example, some devices have special CSR values that the processor can set to temporarily stop the device from accessing the command list. Other systems have a facility that allows the processor to temporarily restrict use of the bus (if it cannot use the bus, a smart device cannot make changes to a list in memory). Finally, some processors offer *test-and-set* instructions that can be used to provide mutual exclusion.

16.13 I/O As Viewed By An Application

The sections above describe how a device driver is programmed. We said earlier that few programmers write device drivers. Thus, the details of CSR addresses, interrupt vectors, and request queues remain hidden from a typical programmer. The motivation for considering drivers and low-level I/O is background: it helps us understand how to create applications that use low-level services efficiently.

Because they tend to use high-level languages, few programmers invoke low-level I/O facilities directly — to express I/O operations, the programmer uses *abstractions* that the programming language offers. For example, application programs seldom use a disk device. Instead, the programming language or the underlying system presents a programmer with a high-level abstraction known as a *file*. Similarly, instead of exposing a programmer to display hardware, most systems present the programmer with an abstraction known as a *window*.

The point is:

> *In many programming systems, I/O is hidden from the programmer. Instead of manipulating hardware devices, such as disks and display screens, a programmer only uses abstractions such as files and windows.*

16.14 Run-Time I/O Libraries

In systems that do allow application programmers to control I/O devices, the software is designed to hide as many details as possible from the programmer. In particular, an application can only specify generic, high-level I/O operations. When a compiler translates the program into a binary form for use on a specific computer, the compiler maps each high-level I/O operation into a sequence of low-level steps.

Interestingly, a typical compiler does not translate each I/O operation directly into a sequence of basic machine instructions. Instead, the compiler generates code that invokes library functions to perform I/O operations. Therefore, before it can be executed, the program must be combined with the appropriate library functions.

We use the term *run-time library* to refer to the set of library functions that accompany a compiled program. Of course, the compiler and run-time library must be designed to work together — the compiler must know which functions are available, the exact arguments used by each function, and the meaning of the function.

As an example, consider the following statement which is used in the high-level language APL. The statement displays the decimal value 13 on an output device (e.g., the user's screen)†:

$$\square \leftarrow 13$$

The statement does not specify the exact device to be used, nor does it specify the exact character encoding that the device expects. Instead, the compiler or interpreter is required to translate the statement into binary code and choose the device details. Rather than generate instructions to use a specific device, a compiler usually translates such statements into library calls. That is:

> *Instead of encoding I/O details into a program, a compiler relies on a run-time library to act as an intermediary. When the application performs an I/O operation, the generated code invokes a library function, which then performs the actual I/O operation.*

---

†APL uses a nonstandard character set that includes a "box" character.

The chief advantage of using a run-time library as an intermediary arises from the flexibility and ease of change. Only the library function understands how to use the underlying I/O mechanisms (i.e., the device driver). If the I/O hardware and/or the device drivers change, only the run-time library needs to be updated — the compiler can remain unchanged. In fact, a run-time library allows a single compiler to be used with two different run-time libraries (e.g., two versions of an operating system).

16.15 The Library/Operating System Dichotomy

We know that a device driver resides in the operating system and the run-time library functions that an application uses to perform I/O reside outside the operating system (because they are linked with the application). Conceptually, we imagine three layers of software on top of the device hardware as Figure 16.6 illustrates.

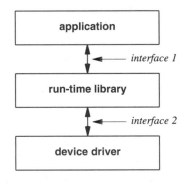

Figure 16.6 The conceptual arrangement of application code, run-time library code, and a device driver. The run-time library acts as an intermediary.

Several questions arise. What services does each layer of software provide? What is the interface between an application and the run-time library, or the interface between the run-time library and the operating system? What are the relative costs of using the two interfaces?

16.16 I/O Operations The OS Supports

We begin by examining the interface between the run-time library and the operating system. In a low-level programming language such as C, the operating system interface is directly available to applications. Thus, a programmer can choose to use an I/O library or make operating system calls directly†.

Although the exact details of I/O operations depend on the operating system, a general approach has become popular. Known as the *open/read/write/close* paradigm, the approach offers six basic functions. Figure 16.7 lists the functions with the names used by the Unix operating system.

Operation	Meaning
open	Prepare a device for use (e.g., power up)
read	Transfer data from the device to the application
write	Transfer data from the application to the device
close	Terminate use of the device
seek	Move to a new location of data on the device
ioctl	Miscellaneous control functions (e.g., change volume)

Figure 16.7 Six basic I/O functions that comprise the open/read/write/close paradigm. The names are taken from the Unix operating system.

As an example, consider a device that can read or write a *Compact Disc (CD)*. The *open* function can be used to start the drive motor and ensure that a disc has been inserted. Once the drive has been started, the *read* function can be used to read data from the disc, and the *write* function can be used to write data onto the disc. The *seek* function can be used to move to a new position (e.g., a specific song on a music CD), and the *close* function can be used to power down the disc. Finally, the *ioctl* function (an abbreviation of I/O control) can be used for all other functions (e.g., the eject function).

Of course, each of the operations take arguments that specify details. For example, a *write* operation needs arguments that specify the device to use, the location of data, and the amount of data to write. More important, the device driver must understand how to map each operation and arguments to operations on the underlying device. For example, when the driver receives a *control* operation, such as an eject, the driver must know how to implement the operation with the device hardware (e.g,, how to assign values to the device's CSR registers).

---

†A later section discusses the standard I/O library used with C.

16.17 The Cost Of I/O Operations

When an application program invokes a function in the run-time library, the cost is exactly the same as calling a procedure because a copy of the code for the library function is incorporated into the application when the program is built. Thus, the cost of invoking library functions is relatively low.

When an application program or a run-time library function invokes an I/O operation such as *read* or *write*, however, control must pass through a *system call*† to the appropriate device driver in the operating system. Unfortunately, invoking an operating system function through a system call incurs extremely high overhead. There are three reasons. First, the processor must change privilege mode because the operating system runs with greater privilege than an application. Second, the processor must change the address space from the application's virtual address space to the operating system's address space. Third, the processor must copy data between the application's address space and the operating system's address space.

We can summarize:

> *The overhead involved in using a system call to communicate with a device driver is extremely high; a system call is much more expensive than a conventional procedure call, such as the call used to invoke a library function.*

More important, much of the system call overhead is associated with making the call rather than the work performed by the driver. Therefore, to optimize performance, programmers seek ways to minimize the number of system calls.

16.18 Reducing The System Call Overhead

To understand how we can reduce the overhead of system calls, consider a worst-case example. Suppose an application needs to print a document, and suppose printing requires the application to send a total of N bytes of data to the printer. The highest cost occurs if the application makes a separate system call to transfer each byte of data because the application will make a total of N system calls. As an alternative, if the application generates a complete line of text and then makes a system call to transfer the entire line, the overhead is reduced from N system calls to L system calls, where L is the number of lines in the document (i.e., $L < N$).

Can we further reduce the overhead of printing a document? Yes. The application can be redesigned to allocate enough memory to hold an entire page of the document, generate the page, and then make one system call to transfer the entire page to the device driver. The result is an application that only makes P system calls, where P is the number of pages in the document (presumably $P << N$).

---

†Some computer architectures use the term *trap* in place of system call.

A general principle can be stated:

> *To reduce overhead and optimize I/O performance, a programmer must reduce the number of system calls that an application invokes. The key to reducing system calls involves transferring more data per system call.*

Of course, it is not always possible to reduce the number of system calls used for I/O. For example, an application like a text editor or email composer displays characters as the user enters them. The application cannot wait until the user enters an entire line or an entire screenful because each character must appear on the screen immediately. Similarly, input from a keyboard often requires a program to accept one character at a time without waiting for a user to enter an entire line or page. Fortunately, such applications often involve user interaction in which I/O is relatively slow, so optimization is unimportant.

16.19 The Important Concept Of Buffering

The above discussion shows that an application programmer can optimize I/O performance by rewriting code in such a way that the number of systems calls is lower. The optimization is so important for high-speed I/O that it has been incorporated into most computer software. Instead of requiring a programmer to rewrite code, I/O runtime libraries have been designed to handle the optimization automatically.

We use the term *buffering* to describe the concept of accumulating data before an I/O transfer, and the term *buffer* to refer to the area of memory in which the data is placed. The terminology is used for the general principle as well.

> *The buffering principle: to reduce the number of system calls on output, accumulate data in a buffer, and transfer more data each time a system call is made.*

To automate buffering, we need a scheme that works for any application. Thus, we use a fixed-size buffer and a set of library functions. Instead of making system calls to perform I/O operations, an application program uses the library functions. In the case of a programming language that contains built-in I/O facilities, the run-time library implements buffering, and the compiler generates code that invokes the appropriate library routines; in the case of a programming language that does not have built-in I/O facilities, the programmer must call buffering library routines instead of system calls.

Library routines that implement buffering usually provide five conceptual operations that Figure 16.8 lists.

Operation	Meaning
setup	Initialize the buffer
input	Perform an input operation
output	Perform an output operation
terminate	Discontinue use of the buffer
flush	Force contents of buffer to be written

Figure 16.8 The conceptual operations provided by a typical library that offers buffered I/O.

The operations listed in the figure are analogous to those that an operating system offers as an interface to a device. In fact, we will see that at least one implementation of a buffered I/O library uses function names that are variants of *open*, *read*, *write*, and *close*. Figure 16.8 uses alternate terminology to help clarify the distinction.

16.20 Implementation of Buffering

To understand how buffering works, consider how an application uses the above functions for buffered output. When it begins, the application calls function *setup* to initialize buffering. Some implementations provide an argument that allows the application to specify a buffer size; in other implementations, the buffer size is a constant†. In any case, we will assume *setup* allocates a buffer, and initializes the buffer to empty. Once the buffer has been initialized, the application can call function *output* to transfer data. On each call, the application supplies an argument, D, that is a single byte of data. Finally, when it finishes transferring data, the application calls function *terminate‡*.

The amount of code required to implement buffered I/O is trivial. Figure 16.9 describes the steps used to implement each output function. In a language such as C, each can be implemented with one or two lines of code.

The motivation for a *terminate* function should now be clear: because output is buffered, the buffer may be partially full when the application finishes. Therefore, the application must force the remaining contents of the buffer to be written.

---

†Typical buffer sizes range from 8 Kbytes to 128 Kbytes, depending on the computer system.
‡A later section describes the use of function *flush*.

Setup(N)

1. Allocate a buffer of N bytes.

2. Create a global pointer, p, and initialize p to the address of the first byte of the buffer.

Output(D)

1. Place data byte D in the buffer at the position given by pointer p, and move p to the next byte.

2. If the buffer is full, make a system call to write the contents of the entire buffer, and reset pointer p to the start of the buffer.

Terminate

1. If the buffer is not empty, make a system call to write the contents of the buffer prior to pointer p.

2. If the buffer was dynamically allocated, deallocate it.

Figure 16.9 The steps taken to achieve buffered output.

16.21 Flushing A Buffer

It may seem that output buffering cannot be used with some applications. For example, consider an application that allows a user to communicate over a computer network. When it emits a message, an application assumes the message will be transmitted and delivered to the other end. Unfortunately, if buffering is used, the message may wait in the buffer unsent.

Of course, a programmer can rewrite an application to buffer data internally and make system calls directly. However, designers of general-purpose buffering libraries have devised another alternative — use conventional functions for buffered I/O, but allow a programmer to specify when a system call is needed. That is, the library includes an extra function that an application can call to force output, even if the buffer is not full.

Programmers use the term *buffer flushing* to describe the process of forcing output of a partially full buffer. Most buffered I/O libraries include a *flush* function that the application can call to invoke buffer flushing. If the buffer is empty, the *flush* function has no effect. If the buffer contains data, however, the *flush* function makes a system call to write the data, and then resets the global pointer to indicate that the buffer is empty. Figure 16.10 lists the steps of a *flush* operation.

Flush

1. If the buffer is currently empty, return to the caller without taking any action.

2. If the buffer is not currently empty, make a system call to write the contents of the buffer and set the global pointer p to the address of the first byte of the buffer.

Figure 16.10 The steps required to implement a *flush* function in a buffered I/O library. *Flush* allows an application to force data to be written before the buffer is full.

Look back at the implementation of the *terminate* function given in Figure 16.9. If the library offers a *flush* function, the first step of *terminate* can be replaced by a call to the *flush* function.

To summarize:

> *A programmer uses a* flush *function to specify that outgoing data in a buffer should be sent to the device driver in the operating system. A* flush *operation has no effect if a buffer is currently empty.*

16.22 Buffering On Input

The descriptions above explain how buffering can be used with output. In many cases, buffering can also be used to reduce the overhead on input. To understand how, consider reading data sequentially. If an application reads N bytes of data, one byte at a time, the application will make N system calls.

Assuming the underlying device allows transfer of more than one byte of data, the application can use buffering to reduce the number of system calls. The application allocates a large buffer, makes one system call to fill the buffer, and then satisfies requests from the buffer. Figure 16.11 lists the steps required. As with output buffering, the implementation is straightforward. In a language such as C, each step can be implemented with a trivial amount of code.

16.23 Effectiveness Of Buffering

Why is buffering so important? Because even a small buffer can have a large effect on I/O performance. To see why, observe that when buffered I/O is used, a system call is only needed once per buffer†. As a result, a buffer of N bytes reduces the number of system calls by a factor of N. Thus, if an application makes S system calls, a buffer of only 100 bytes reduces the number of system calls to $S/100$.

---

†Assuming calls to the *flush* function are ignored.

Setup(N)

    1. Allocate a buffer of N bytes.

    2. Create a global pointer, p, and initialize p to indicate that the buffer is empty.

Input(N)

    1. If the buffer is empty, make a system call to fill the entire buffer, and set pointer p to the start of the buffer.

    2. Extract a byte, D, from the position in the buffer given by pointer p, move p to the next byte, and return D to the caller.

Terminate

    1. If the buffer was dynamically allocated, deallocate it.

Figure 16.11 The steps required to achieve buffered input.

We said that in practice, a buffer size of 8 Kbytes is considered minimal and that some run-time libraries use larger buffers. Using a buffer of 8 Kbytes reduces the number of system calls to $S/8192$, where S is the original number of system calls. Thus, the number of system calls required to transfer 2 Mbytes of data drops from 2,097,162 to 256.

The point is:

Using a buffer of N bytes reduces the number of system calls by a factor of N. A large buffer can mean the difference between an I/O mechanism that is fast and one that is intolerably slow.

16.24 Buffering In An Operating System

Buffering is so important that device drivers in an operating system often implement buffering. For example, in some disk drivers, the driver maintains a copy of the disk block in memory, and allows an application to read or write data from the block.

Of course, buffering in an operating system does not eliminate system calls. However, such buffering does improve performance because external data transfers are slower than system calls. The important point is that buffering can be used to reduce I/O overhead whenever a less expensive operation can be substituted for an expensive operation.

16.25 Relation To Caching

Buffering is closely related to the concept of caching that is described in Chapter 12. The chief difference arises from the way items are accessed: a cache system is optimized to accommodate random access, and a buffering system is optimized for sequential access.

In essence, a cache stores an item that has been referenced, and a buffer stores an item that is referenced plus the next $N-1$ sequential items. Thus, in a virtual memory system, a cache stores entire pages of memory — when any byte on the page is referenced, the entire page is placed in the cache. In contrast, a buffer stores sequential bytes. Thus, when a byte is referenced, a buffering system preloads the next bytes — if the referenced byte lies at the end of a page, the buffering system preloads bytes from the next page.

16.26 An Example: The Unix Standard I/O Library

One of the best-known examples of a buffering I/O library was created for the Unix operating system. Known as the *standard I/O library* (*stdio*), the library supports both input and output buffering. Figure 16.12 lists a few of the functions found in the standard I/O library along with their purpose.

Function	Meaning
fopen	Set up a buffer
fgetc	Buffered input of one byte
fread	Buffered input of multiple bytes
fwrite	Buffered output of multiple bytes
fprintf	Buffered output of formatted data
fflush	Flush operation for buffered output
fclose	Terminate use of a buffer

Figure 16.12 Examples of functions included in the standard I/O library used with the Unix operating system. The library includes additional functions not listed here.

16.27 Summary

Two aspects of I/O are pertinent to programmers. A systems programmer who writes device driver code must understand the low-level details of the device, and an application programmer who uses I/O facilities must understand the relative costs.

A device driver is divided into three parts: an upper half that interacts with application programs, a lower half that interacts with the device itself, and a set of shared variables. A function in the upper half receives control when an application reads or writes data; the lower half receives control when the device generates an input or output interrupt.

The fundamental technique programmers use to optimize sequential I/O performance is known as buffering. Buffering can be used for both input and output, and is often implemented in a run-time library. Because it gives an application control over when data is transferred, a *flush* operation allows buffering to be used with arbitrary applications.

Buffering reduces system call overhead by transferring more data per system call. Buffering provides significant performance improvement because a buffer of N bytes reduces the number of system calls that an application makes by a factor of N.

EXERCISES

16.1   Measure the execution time needed to copy a large file using *write* and *fwrite*.

16.2   The standard I/O function *fseek* allows random access. Measure the difference in the time required to use *fseek* within a small region of a file and within a large region.

16.3   Build an output buffering routine, *fputc*, that accepts a single character to be printed. Store characters in a buffer, and call *write* once for the entire buffer. Compare the performance of your buffered routine to a program that uses *write* for each character.

Advanced Topics

The Fundamental Concepts Of Parallelism And Pipelining

17

Parallelism

17.1 Introduction

Previous chapters cover the three key components of computer architecture: processors, memory systems, and I/O. This chapter begins a discussion of fundamental concepts that cross the boundaries among architectural components.

The chapter focuses on the use of parallel hardware, and shows that parallelism can be used throughout computer systems to increase speed. The chapter introduces terminology and concepts, presents a taxonomy of parallel architectures, and examines computer systems in which parallelism is the fundamental paradigm around which the entire system is designed. Finally, the chapter discusses limitations and problems with parallel architectures.

The next chapter extends the discussion by examining a second fundamental technique, pipelining. We will see that both parallelism and pipelining are important in high-speed designs.

17.2 Parallel And Pipelined Architectures

Some computer architects assert that there are only two fundamental techniques used to achieve high speed: *parallelism* and *pipelining*. We have already encountered examples of each technique, and seen how they can be used.

Other architects take a broader view of parallelism and pipelining, using the techniques as the fundamental basis around which a system is designed. In many cases, the architecture is so completely dominated by one of the two techniques that the resulting system can be called a *parallel computer* or *pipelined computer*.

17.3 Characterizations Of Parallelism

Rather than classify an architecture as *parallel* or *nonparallel*, computer architects use a variety of terms to characterize the type and amount of parallelism that is present in a given design. In many cases, the terminology describes the possible extremes for a type of parallelism. We can classify an architecture by saying where the architecture lies between the two extremes. Figure 17.1 lists the key characterizations using nomenclature defined by Flynn [Flynn 1996]; later sections explain each of the terms and give examples.

- Microscopic vs. macroscopic
- Symmetric vs. asymmetric
- Fine-grain vs. coarse-grain
- Explicit vs. implicit

Figure 17.1 Terminology used to characterize the amount and type of parallelism present in a computer architecture.

17.4 Microscopic Vs. Macroscopic

Parallelism is so fundamental that an architect cannot design a computer without thinking about parallel hardware. Interestingly, the importance of parallelism means that unless a computer uses an unusual amount of parallel hardware, we do not bother to discuss the parallel aspects. To capture the idea that much of the parallelism in a computer remains hidden inside subcomponents, we use the term *microscopic parallelism*. Like microbes in the world around us, microscopic parallelism is present, but does not stand out without closer inspection.

The point is:

> *Parallelism is so fundamental that virtually all computer systems contain some form of parallel hardware. We use the term* microscopic parallelism *to characterize parallel facilities that are present, but not especially visible.*

To be more precise, we say that *microscopic parallelism* refers to the use of parallel hardware within a specific component (e.g., inside a processor or inside an ALU), whereas *macroscopic parallelism* refers to the use of parallelism as a basic premise around which a system is designed.

17.5 Examples Of Microscopic Parallelism

ALU. We have already seen examples of using *microscopic parallelism* within a processor, a memory system, and an I/O system. For example, consider the design of an Arithmetic Logic Unit that handles logical and arithmetic operations. Most ALUs perform integer arithmetic by processing multiple bits at the same time. Thus, an ALU that is designed to operate on integers might contain parallel hardware that allows the ALU to compute the *exclusive-or* of a pair of thirty-two bit values in a single operation. The alternative consists of an ALU that processes one bit at a time, analogous to the way a human performs arithmetic by considering one digit at a time. The approach is sometimes called *bit serial processing*. It should be easy to see that computing one bit at a time takes longer than computing bits in parallel. Therefore, bit serial arithmetic is usually reserved for special cases.

Registers. The general-purpose registers in a CPU make heavy use of microscopic parallelism. Each bit in a register is implemented by a separate digital circuit. Furthermore, to guarantee the highest-speed computation, parallel hardware is used to move data between general-purpose registers and the ALU.

Physical Memory. As another example of microscopic parallelism, recall that a physical memory system uses parallel hardware to implement *fetch* and *store* operations — the hardware is designed to transfer an entire word on each operation. As in an ALU, microscopic parallelism increases memory speed dramatically. For example, a memory system that implements sixty-four bit words can access or store approximately sixty-four times as much data in the same time as a memory system that accesses a single bit at a time.

Parallel Bus Architecture. As we have seen, the central bus in a computer uses parallel hardware to achieve high-speed transfers among the processor, memory, and I/O devices. A typical modern computer has a bus that is either thirty-two or sixty-four bits wide, which means that either thirty-two or sixty-four bits of data can be transferred across the bus in a single step.

17.6 Examples Of Macroscopic Parallelism

As the examples above demonstrate, microscopic parallelism is essential for high performance — without parallel hardware, various components of a computer system cannot operate at high speed. Architects are aware, however, that the global architecture often has a greater impact on overall system performance than the performance of any single subsystem. That is, adding more parallelism to a single subsystem may not improve the overall performance†.

To achieve the greatest impact, parallelism must span multiple components of a system — instead of merely using parallelism to improve the performance of a single component, the system must allow multiple components to work together. We use the term *macroscopic parallelism* to characterize the use of parallelism across multiple,

---

†Chapter 19 discusses performance in more detail.

large-scale components of a computer system. A few examples will clarify the concepts.

Multiple, Identical Processors. As we will see, systems that employ macroscopic parallelism usually employ multiple processors in one form or another. For example, some PCs are advertised as *dual processor* computers, meaning that the PC contains two identical CPU chips. The hardware is arranged to allow both processors to function at the same time. The hardware does not control exactly how the two CPUs are used. Instead, the operating system assigns each processor code to execute. For example, the operating system can assign one processor the task of handling I/O (i.e., running device drivers), and assign the other processor the task of running applications.

Multiple, Dissimilar Processors. Another example of macroscopic parallelism arises in systems that make extensive use of special-purpose coprocessors. For example, a computer optimized for high-speed graphics might have four displays attached, with a special graphics processor running each display. A graphics processor, typically found on an interface card, does not use the same architecture as a CPU because the graphics processor needs instructions optimized for graphics operations.

17.7 Symmetric Vs. Asymmetric

We use the term *symmetric parallelism* to characterize a design that uses replications of identical elements, usually processors, that can operate simultaneously. For example, the *dual-processor* PC, mentioned above, is said to be symmetric provided the two processors are identical.

The alternative to a symmetric parallel design is a parallel design that is *asymmetric*. As the name implies, an asymmetric design contains multiple elements that function at the same time, but differ from one another. For example, a PC with a graphics coprocessor and a math coprocessor is classified as using asymmetric parallelism because the three processors can operate simultaneously, but differ from one another internally†.

17.8 Fine-grain Vs. Coarse-grain Parallelism

We use the term *fine-grain parallelism* to refer to computers that provide parallelism on the level of individual instructions or individual data elements, and the term *coarse-grain parallelism* to refer to computers that provide parallelism on the level of programs or large blocks of data. For example, a graphics processor that uses sixteen parallel hardware units to update sixteen bytes of an image at the same time is said to use fine-grain parallelism. A dual processor PC that uses one processor to print a document while another processor is used to compose an email message is described as using coarse-grain parallelism.

---

†Some architects also apply the term *asymmetric* to a design that uses identical hardware but does not grant each copy the same privileges (e.g., provides high-speed paths from memory to some copies, or only allows some copies to access I/O devices).

17.9 Explicit Vs. Implicit Parallelism

An architecture in which the hardware handles parallelism automatically without requiring a programmer to initiate or control parallel execution is said to offer *implicit parallelism*, and an architecture in which a programmer must control each parallel unit is said to offer *explicit parallelism*. We will consider the advantages and disadvantages of explicit and implicit parallelism later.

17.10 Parallel Architectures

In some architectures, parallelism is the central feature around which the entire system is designed. Architects use the term *parallel architecture* to characterize such systems. Parallel architecture involves a replication of complete processors or substantial parts of processors.

Although many systems contain multiple processors of one type or another, the term *parallel architecture* is usually reserved for designs that permit arbitrary *scaling*. That is, when they refer to a parallel architecture, architects usually mean a design in which the number of processors can be arbitrarily large (or at least reasonably large). As a particular example, consider a design that allows a second processor to be added to a conventional PC. Although the resulting system uses parallelism, such an architecture is usually classified as a *dual-processor computer* rather than a parallel architecture. Similarly, a PC with four processors is classified as a *quad-processor PC*. However, a computer that has thirty-two processors or a computer that can scale to sixty-four thousand processors is classified as a parallel architecture.

17.11 Types Of Parallel Architectures (Flynn Classification)

The easiest way to understand parallel architectures is to divide architectures into broad groups, where each group represents a type of parallelism. Of course, no division is absolute — we will learn that a practical parallel computer system is usually a hybrid that contains facilities from more than one group. Nevertheless, we use the classification to define basic concepts and nomenclature that allow us to discuss and characterize systems.

A popular way to describe parallelism that is attributed to Flynn focuses on whether data or processing is replicated. That is, does the computer have multiple, independent processors each running a separate program, or is a single program being applied to multiple data items? Figure 17.2 lists terms often used to define types of parallelism; the next sections explain the terminology and give examples.

Name	Meaning
SISD	Single Instruction Single Data stream
SIMD	Single Instruction Multiple Data streams
MIMD	Multiple Instructions Multiple Data streams

Figure 17.2 Terminology used to characterize computers according to the amount and type of parallelism. In practice, hybrids exist that span multiple types†.

17.12 Single Instruction Single Data (SISD)

The phrase *Single Instruction Single Data stream (SISD)* is used to describe an architecture that does not support macroscopic parallelism. The term *sequential architecture* or *uniprocessor architecture* is often used in place of SISD to emphasize that the architecture is not parallel. In essence, SISD refers to a conventional (i.e., Von Neumann) architecture — the processor runs a standard fetch-execute cycle and performs one operation at a time. The term refers to the idea that a single, conventional processor is executing instructions that each operate on a single data item. That is, unlike a parallel architecture, a conventional processor can only execute one instruction at any time, and each instruction refers to a single computation.

Of course, we have seen that an SISD computer can use parallelism internally. For example, the ALU may be able to perform operations on multiple bits in parallel, the CPU may invoke a coprocessor, or the CPU may have mechanisms that allow it to fetch operands from two banks of memory at the same time. However, the overall effect of an SISD architecture is sequential execution of instructions that each operate on one data item.

17.13 Single Instruction Multiple Data (SIMD)

The phrase *Single Instruction Multiple Data streams (SIMD)* is used to describe a parallel architecture in which each instruction specifies a single operation (e.g., integer addition), but the instruction is applied to many data items at the same time. Typically, an SIMD computer has sufficient hardware to handle sixty-four simultaneous operations (e.g., sixty-four simultaneous additions).

Vector Processors. An SIMD architecture is not useful for applications such as a word processor. Instead, SIMD is only used with applications that apply the same operation to a set of values. For example, some scientific applications work well on an SIMD architecture that can apply a floating point operation to a set of values. The architecture is sometimes called a *vector processor* or an *array processor* after the mathematical concept of vectors and the computing concept of arrays.

---

†Some architects list a fourth class, MISD, to describe the possibility of computers that execute multiple instructions on the same data. We have chosen to omit MISD because it is impractical except in special cases (e.g., redundant processors used to increase reliability).

As an example of how an SIMD machine works, consider normalizing the values in a vector, *V* that contains *N* elements. Normalization requires that each item in the vector be multiplied by a floating point number, *Q*. On a sequential architecture (i.e., an SISD architecture), the algorithm required to normalize the vector consists of a loop as Figure 17.3 shows.

```
for i from 1 to N {
    V[i] ← V[i] × Q;
}
```

Figure 17.3 The algorithm for vector normalization used on a sequential computer.

On an SIMD architecture, the underlying hardware can simultaneously apply an arithmetic operation to all the values in an array, provided the size of the array does not exceed the parallelism in the hardware. For example, in a single step, hardware that has sixteen parallel units can multiply each value in a sixteen-element array by a constant. Thus, the algorithm to perform normalization of an array on an SIMD computer is trivial:

$$V \leftarrow V \times Q;$$

Of course, if vector V is larger than the hardware capacity, multiple steps will be required. The important point is that a vector instruction on an SIMD architecture is not merely a shorthand for a loop. Instead, the underlying system contains multiple hardware units that operate in parallel to provide substantial speedup; the performance improvement can be significant, especially for computations that use large matrices.

Of course, not all instructions in an SIMD architecture can be applied to an array of values. Instead, an architect identifies a subset of operations to be used with vectors, and defines a special *vector instruction* for each. For example, normalization of an entire array is only possible if the architect chooses to include a vector multiplication instruction that multiplies each value in the vector by a constant.

In addition to operations that use a constant and a vector, SIMD computers often provide instructions that use two vectors. That is, a vector instruction takes one or more operands that each specify a vector. For example, SIMD architectures are used for problems involving matrix multiplication. On most SIMD machines, an operand that specifies a vector gives two pieces of information: the location of the vector in memory and an integer that specifies the size of the vector (i.e., number of items in the vector). On some machines, vector instructions are controlled by special-purpose registers — the address and size of each vector are loaded into registers before a vector instruction is invoked. In any case, software determines the number of items in a vector up to the maximum size supported by the hardware†.

---

†An exercise considers speedup in cases where vectors exceed the capacity of the hardware; a definition of *speedup* can be found in Section 17.16.

Graphics Processors. SIMD architectures are also popular for use with graphics. To understand why, it is important to know that typical graphics hardware uses sequential bytes in memory to store values for pixels on a screen. To move a rectangular window (e.g., a window being dragged by a mouse), software must copy the bytes that correspond to the window from one location in memory to another. A sequential architecture requires a programmer to specify a loop that copies one location at a time. On an SIMD architecture, however, a programmer can specify a vector size, and then issue a single *copy* command. The underlying SIMD hardware then copies multiple bytes.

17.14 Multiple Instructions Multiple Data (MIMD)

The phrase *Multiple Instructions Multiple Data streams (MIMD)* is used to describe a parallel architecture in which each of the processors performs independent computations at the same time. Although many computers contain multiple internal processing units, the MIMD designation is reserved for computers in which the processors are visible to a programmer. That is, an MIMD computer can run multiple, independent programs at the same time.

Symmetric Multiprocessor (SMP). The most well-known example of an MIMD architecture consists of a computer known as a *Symmetric Multiprocessor (SMP)*. An SMP contains a set of *N* processors that can each be used to run programs. In a typical SMP design, the processors are identical: they each have the same instruction set, operate at the same clock rate, have access to the same (modules of) memory, and have access to the same external devices. Thus, any processor can perform exactly the same computation as any other processor. Figure 17.4 illustrates the concept.

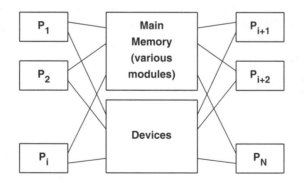

Figure 17.4 Illustration of a symmetric multiprocessor with N identical processors. Each processor has access to memory and I/O devices.

In the 1980s, while some researchers explored ways to increase the speed and power of a silicon chip, other researchers investigated symmetric multiprocessors as an alternate way to provide more powerful computers. One of the most well-known projects, which was conducted at Carnegie Mellon University, produced a prototype known as the *Carnegie multiminiprocessor* (*C.mmp*). During the 1980s, vendors first created commercial products, informally called multiprocessors, that used the SMP approach. Sequent Corporation (currently owned by IBM) created a symmetric multiprocessor that runs the Unix operating system, and Encore Corporation created a symmetric multiprocessor named *Multimax*.

Asymmetric Multiprocessor (AMP). Although SMPs are popular, other forms of MIMD architectures are possible. The chief alternative to an SMP design is an *Asymmetric Multiprocessor* (*AMP*). An AMP contains a set of *N* programmable processors that can operate at the same time, but does not require all processors to have identical capabilities. For example, an AMP design can choose a processor that is appropriate to a given task (i.e., one processor can be optimized for management of high-speed disk storage devices, and another processor can be optimized for graphics display).

In most cases, AMP architectures follow a *master-slave* approach in which one processor (or in some cases a set of processors) controls the overall execution and invokes other processors as needed. The processor that controls execution is known as the *master*, and other processors are known as *slaves*.

In theory, an AMP architecture that has *N* processors can have *N* distinct types of processors. In practice, however, most AMP designs have between two and four types of processors. Typically, a general-purpose AMP architecture includes at least one processor optimized for overall control (the master), and others optimized for subsidiary functions such as arithmetic computation or I/O.

Math And Graphics Coprocessors. Commercial computer systems have been created that use an asymmetric architecture. One of the most widely-known AMP designs became popular in the late 1980s and early 1990s when PC manufacturers began selling *math coprocessors*. The idea of a math coprocessor is straightforward: the coprocessor is a special-purpose chip that the CPU can invoke to perform floating point computation. Because it is optimized for one task, a coprocessor can perform the task faster than the CPU.

I/O Processors. Most mainframe computers use an AMP architecture to handle I/O at high speed without slowing down the CPU. Each external I/O connection is equipped with a dedicated, programmable processor. Instead of manipulating a bus or handling interrupts, the CPU merely downloads a program into the programmable processor. The processor then handles all the details of I/O. For example, the mainframe computers sold by IBM corporation use programmable I/O processors called *channels*.

CDC Peripheral Processors. Control Data Corporation helped pioneer the idea of using an AMP architecture in mainframes when they created the 6000 series of mainframe computers. The CDC architecture uses ten *peripheral processors* to handle I/O. Figure 17.5 illustrates the architecture†.

---

†The CDC computer is no longer manufactured, but the basic idea of programmable I/O processors continues to be used.

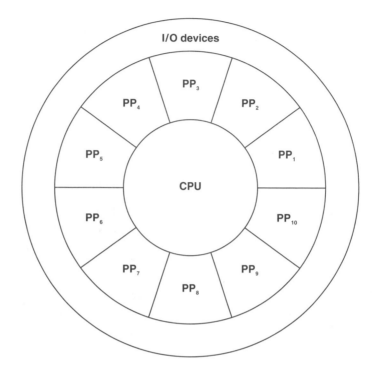

Figure 17.5 Illustration of the asymmetric architecture used in the CDC 6000
mainframe computers. The CPU was more powerful than the
peripheral processors.

Interestingly, CDC's peripheral processors were not limited to I/O — a peripheral
processor resembled a minicomputer with a general-purpose instruction set that could be
used however a programmer chose. The peripheral processors had access to memory,
which meant a peripheral processor could read or store values in any location.
Although they were much slower than the CPU, all ten peripheral processors could execute simultaneously. Thus, it was possible to optimize program performance by dividing tasks among the peripheral processors as well as the CPU.

17.15 Communication, Coordination, And Contention

It may seem obvious that multiprocessor architectures always have better performance than a uniprocessor architecture. Consider, for example, a symmetric multiprocessor, M. Intuitively, computer M can outperform a uniprocessor because M can perform N times as many operations at any time. Moreover, if a chip vendor finds a way
to make a single processor run faster than M, the vendor who sells M merely needs to

replace each of the processors in M with the new, faster processor. Indeed, many companies that sell multiprocessors make these statements to attract customers.

Unfortunately, our intuition about computer performance can be misleading. Architects have found three main challenges in designing a high-performance parallel architecture:

- Communication
- Coordination
- Contention

Communication. Although it may seem trivial to envision a computer that has dozens of independent processors, the computer must also provide a mechanism that allows the processors to communicate with each other, with memory, and with I/O devices. More important, the communication mechanism must be able to scale to handle a large number of processors. Typically, an architect must spend a significant amount of effort to create a parallel computer system that does not have severe communication bottlenecks.

Coordination. In a parallel architecture, processors must work together to perform computation. Therefore, a coordination mechanism is needed that allows processing to be controlled. We said that asymmetric designs usually designate one of the processors to act as a master that controls and coordinates all processing; some symmetric designs also use the master-slave approach. Other architectures use a distributed coordination mechanism in which the processors must be programmed to coordinate among themselves without a master.

Contention. When two or more processors attempt to access a resource at the same time, we say that the processors *contend* for the resource. Resource *contention* creates one of the greatest challenges in designing a parallel architecture because contention increases as the number of processors increases.

To understand why contention is a problem, consider memory. If a set of N processors all have access to a given memory, a mechanism is needed that only permits one processor to access the memory at any time. When multiple processors attempt to use the memory simultaneously, the hardware contention mechanism blocks all except one of them. That is, $N-1$ of the processors are idle during the memory access. In the next round, $N-2$ processors remain idle. It should be obvious that:

> *In a parallel architecture, contention for shared resources lowers performance dramatically because only one processor can proceed to use a given resource at any time; the hardware contention mechanism forces other processors to remain idle while they wait for access.*

17.16 Performance Of Multiprocessors

Multiprocessor architectures have not fulfilled the promise of scalable, high-performance computing. There are several reasons: operating system bottlenecks, contention for memory, and I/O. Operating system bottlenecks are the easiest to understand. The operating system controls all processing, including allocating tasks to processors and performing I/O. Only one copy of an operating system can run because a device cannot take orders from multiple processors simultaneously. Thus, in a multiprocessor, at most one processor can run operating system software at any time. As a consequence, processors must access the operating system serially — if K processors need access, $K-1$ of them must wait.

Contention for memory has proven to be an especially difficult problem. First, hardware for a multiported memory is extremely expensive. Second, one of the more important optimizations used in memory systems, caching, causes problems when used with a multiprocessor. To understand why problems occur, consider what happens when two processors access memory. If processor 1 caches a value from location X and processor 2 changes the value in location X, the value in the cache of processor 1 becomes invalid. Thus, whenever a processor stores a value into memory, the processor must notify all other processors to disregard cached values. Unfortunately, the notification itself introduces overhead, and discarding values from a cache reduces the effectiveness.

Many multiprocessor architectures suffer from another weakness: the architecture only works better than a uniprocessor when performing intensive computation. Surprisingly, most applications are not limited by the amount of computation they perform. Instead, most applications are *I/O bound*, which means the application spends more time waiting for I/O than performing computation. For example, most of the delay in common applications, such as word processors, spreadsheets, and web browsing, arises when the application waits for I/O from a file or the network. Thus, adding additional computational power to the underlying computer does not lower the time required to perform the computation — the extra processors sit idle waiting for I/O.

To assess the performance of an N-processor system, we define the notion of *speedup* to be the ratio of the performance of a single processor to the performance of a multiprocessor. Specifically, we define speedup as:

$$Speedup \; = \; \frac{\tau_1}{\tau_N}$$

where τ_1 denotes the execution time required on a single processor, and τ_N denotes the execution time required on a multiprocessor†. In each case, we assume performance is measured using the best algorithm available (i.e., we allow the program to be rewritten to take advantage of parallel hardware).

When multiprocessors are measured performing general-purpose computing tasks, an interesting result emerges. In an ideal situation, we would expect performance to in-

---

†Because we expect the processing time on a single processor to be greater than the processing time on a multiprocessor, we expect the speedup to be greater than one.

crease linearly as more processors are added to a multiprocessor system. Experience has shown, however, that problems like memory contention, inter-processor communication, and operating system bottlenecks mean that multiprocessors do not achieve linear speedup†. Instead, performance often reaches a limit as Figure 17.6 illustrates.

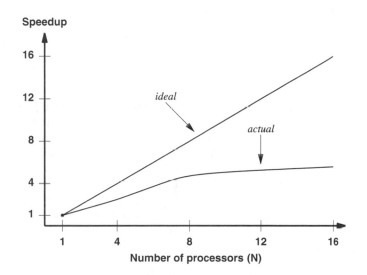

Figure 17.6 Illustration of the ideal and typical performance of a multiprocessor as the number of processors is increased. Values on the y-axis list the relative speedup compared to a single processor.

Surprisingly, the performance illustrated in the figure may not be achievable in practice. In some multiprocessor designs, communication overhead and memory contention dominate the running time: as more and more processors are added, the performance starts to decrease. For example, a particular symmetric multiprocessor design exhibited a small speedup with a few processors. However, when sixty-four processors were used, communication overhead made the performance worse than a single processor system.

We can summarize:

> *When used for general-purpose computing, a multiprocessor may not perform well. In some cases, added overhead means performance decreases as more processors are added.*

---

†Performance anomalies do exist where a multiprocessor can always perform better than a uniprocessor; the exercises explore one possible anomaly.

17.17 Consequences For Programmers

17.17.1 Locks And Mutual Exclusion

Writing code that uses multiple processors is inherently more complex than writing code for a single processor. To understand the complexity, consider using a shared variable. For example, suppose two processors use a variable x to store a count. A programmer writes a statement such as:

$$x = x + 1;$$

A compiler translates the statement into a sequence of machine instructions, such as the sequence that Figure 17.7 lists.

```
load    x, R5
incr    R5
store   R5, x
```

Figure 17.7 An example sequence of machine instructions used to increment a variable in memory. In most architectures, increment entails a *load* and a *store* operation.

Unfortunately, if two processors attempt to increment x at nearly the same time, the value of x might be incremented by one instead of two. To see why, observe that because the two processors operate independently, they compete for access to memory. Thus, the operations can be performed in the order that Figure 17.8 lists.

- Processor 1 loads x in to its register 5
- Processor 1 increments its register 5
- Processor 2 loads x in to its register 5
- Processor 1 stores its register 5 into x
- Processor 2 increments its register 5
- Processor 2 stores its register 5 into x

Figure 17.8 A sequence of steps that can occur when two independent processors access variable x in shared memory.

As the figure shows, each processor loads the original value of x, each increments the value, and each stores the new value. Thus, although two processors execute instructions to increment variable x, the value following the sequence is only one greater than the value at the beginning of the sequence.

To prevent problems like the one illustrated in Figure 17.8, multiprocessor hardware offers *hardware locks*. A programmer must associate a lock with each shared item, and use the lock to ensure that no other processors can change the item while an update is in progress. For example, if lock 17 is associated with variable x, a programmer must obtain lock 17 before updating x. The idea is called *mutual exclusion*, and we say that a processor must gain *exclusive use* of a variable before updating the value. Figure 17.9 illustrates the concept.

```
lock     17
load     x, R5
incr     R5
store    R5, x
release  17
```

Figure 17.9 Illustration of the instructions used to guarantee exclusive access to a variable. A separate lock is assigned to each shared item.

The key to understanding locks is to realize that the underlying hardware only keeps one copy of each lock and guarantees that only one processor will be granted a lock at any time. Thus, if two or more processors both attempt to obtain a given lock at the same time, only one will be granted access. The hardware forces the other processors to wait (i.e., places the other processors in a queue). When a processor releases a lock, the hardware checks the queue. If other processors are waiting for the lock, the hardware selects the next processor from the queue, and grants the lock to that processor. Thus, at most one processor can hold a given lock at any time.

Locking adds a nontrivial amount of complexity to programs for several reasons. First, because locking is unusual, a programmer not accustomed to programming multiprocessors can easily forget to lock a shared variable (and because they depend on timing, such errors can be difficult to detect). Second, locking can severely reduce performance — if K processors attempt to access a shared variable at the same time, the hardware will keep $K-1$ of them idle while they wait for access. Third, because separate instructions are used to obtain and release a lock, locking adds overhead. Thus, a programmer must decide whether to obtain a lock for each individual operation or whether to obtain a lock, hold the lock while performing a series of operations on the variable, and then release the lock.

17.17.2 Programming Explicit And Implicit Parallel Computers

The most important aspect of parallelism for a program concerns whether software or hardware is responsible for managing parallelism: a system that uses implicit parallelism is significantly easier to program than a system that uses explicit parallelism. For example, consider a processor designed to handle packets arriving from a computer network. In an implicit design, a programmer writes code to handle a single packet, and the hardware automatically applies the same program to N packets in parallel. In an explicit design, the programmer must plan to read N packets, send each to a different hardware unit, start each hardware unit processing a packet, wait for the hardware units to complete, and extract the resulting packets. In many cases, the code required to start and control parallel hardware units and determine when they finish is more complex than the code to perform the desired computation. More important, code to control parallel units must allow hardware to operate in arbitrary order. For example, because the time required to process a packet depends on the packet's contents, a controller must be ready for the hardware units to complete processing in arbitrary order. The point is:

> *From a programmer's point of view, a system that uses explicit parallelism is significantly more complex to program than a system that uses implicit parallelism.*

17.17.3 Programming Symmetric And Asymmetric Multiprocessors

One of the most important advantages of symmetry arises from the positive consequences it has for programmers: a symmetric multiprocessor can be substantially easier to program than an asymmetric multiprocessor. First, if all processors are identical, a programmer only needs to learn one instruction set. Second, symmetry means a programmer does not need to consider which tasks are best suited for which type of processor. Third, when identical processors operate at the same speed, a programmer does not need to worry about the time required to perform a task on a given processor. Fourth, because all processors use the same encoding for instructions and data, a binary program or a data value can be moved from one processor to another.

From a programmer's point of view, however, any form of multiprocessor introduces a complication: in addition to everything else, a programmer must consider how coding decisions will influence performance. For example, consider a computation that processes packets arriving over a network. A conventional program keeps a global counter in memory, and updates the counter when a packet arrives. On a shared memory architecture, however, updating a value in memory is expensive: a processor must obtain a lock, update the value, and release the lock. Thus, an architecture in which multiple processors update global values can be considerably slower than a conventional architecture.

17.18 Redundant Parallel Architectures

Our discussion has focused on the use of parallel hardware to improve performance or increase functionality. However, it is also possible to use parallel hardware to improve reliability and prevent failure. That is, multiple copies of hardware can be used to verify each computation.

The term *redundant hardware* usually refers to multiple copies of a hardware unit that operate in parallel to perform an operation. The basic difference between redundant hardware and the parallel architectures described above arises from the data items being used: a parallel architecture arranges for each copy of the hardware to operate on a separate data item; a redundant architecture arranges for all copies to perform exactly the same operation.

The point of using redundant hardware is verification that a computation is correct. What happens when redundant copies of the hardware disagree? The answer depends on the details and purpose of the underlying system. One possibility uses votes: K copies of a hardware unit each perform the computation and produce a value. A special hardware unit then compares the output, and selects the value that appears most often. Another possibility uses redundant hardware merely to detect hardware failures: if two copies of the hardware disagree, the system displays an error message, and then halts until the defective unit can be repaired or replaced.

17.19 Distributed And Cluster Computers

The parallel architectures discussed in this chapter are called *tightly coupled* because the parallel hardware units are located inside the same computer system. The alternative, which is known as a *loosely coupled* architecture uses multiple computer systems that are interconnected by a communication mechanism. For example, we use the term *distributed architecture* to refer to a set of computers that are connected by a computer network or an internet. In a distributed architecture, each computer operates independently, but the computers can communicate by sending messages across a network.

A special form of distributed computing system is known as a *network cluster* or a *cluster computer*. In essence, a cluster computer consists of a set of independent computers connected by a high-speed computer network that are all dedicated to solving one problem at a time. For example, scientists sometimes use cluster computers to run computations on extremely large sets of data. If the cluster contains N computers, the data is divided into N parts, and each part is given to one computer in the cluster. Computers in the cluster run independently; when all the computers finish, the results are collected to produce the final output. Of course, the problem being solved must be amenable to division (i.e., cluster computing does not offer a performance improvement in cases where data values are sent among computers frequently).

A special case of cluster computing is used to construct a high-capacity web site. When a single computer running a web server cannot accommodate the traffic for the site, the manager installs a cluster of computers that each run a copy of the web server. A special-purpose system that is known as a *web load balancer* disperses incoming requests among computers in the cluster of servers. That is, each time it receives a request from a browser, the load balancer chooses the least-loaded computer in the cluster, and forwards the request. Thus, a web site with N computers in a cluster can respond to approximately N times as many requests per second as a single computer.

Another form of loosely-coupled distributed computing is known as *grid comput-ing*. Grid computing uses the global Internet as a communication mechanism among a large set of computers. The computers (typically personal computers) agree to provide spare CPU cycles for the grid. Each computer runs software that repeatedly accepts a request, performs the requested computation, and returns the result. To use the grid, a problem must be divided into many small pieces. Each piece of the problem is sent to a computer, which means all computers can execute simultaneously.

Grid computing is especially popular for large, scientific calculations. There are two reasons. First, because scientific calculations require intensive amounts of process-ing, using a grid reduces the running time dramatically. Second, many scientific prob-lems use representations, such as matrices, that make dividing the problem into small pieces easy. For most problems, however, the long delays required to transmit requests and data across the Internet mean that grid computing does not result in significantly faster computation.

17.20 Summary

Parallelism is one of the fundamental optimization techniques used to increase hardware performance. Most components of a computer system contain parallel hardware; an architecture is only classified as parallel if the architecture includes paral-lel processors. Explicit parallelism gives a programmer control over the use of parallel facilities; implicit parallelism handles parallelism automatically.

A conventional computer is classified as a Single Instruction Single Data (SISD) architecture because a single instruction operates on a single data item at any given time. A Single Instruction Multiple Data (SIMD) architecture allows an instruction to operate on an array of values. Typical SIMD machines include vector processors and graphics processors. A Multiple Instructions Multiple Data (MIMD) architecture em-ploys multiple, independent processors that operate simultaneously and can each exe-cute a separate program. Typical MIMD machines include symmetric and asymmetric multiprocessors. Alternatives to SIMD and MIMD architectures include redundant, dis-tributed, cluster, and grid architectures.

In theory, a general-purpose multiprocessor with N processors should perform N times faster than a single processor. In practice, however, memory contention and com-munication overhead mean that the performance of a multiprocessor does not increase linearly as the number of processors increases. In some cases, performance decreases as additional processors are added.

Programming a computer with multiple processors can be a challenge. In addition to other considerations, a programmer must use locks to guarantee exclusive access to shared items.

EXERCISES

17.1   Consider multiplying two 10 X 20 matrices on a computer that has vector capability but limits each vector to sixteen items. How is matrix multiplication handled on such a computer, and how many vector multiplications are required?

17.2   In the previous exercise, how many scalar multiplications are needed on a uniprocessor (i.e., an SISD architecture)? If we ignore addition and only measure multiplication, what is the speedup? Does the speedup change when multiplying 100 X 100 matrices?

17.3   If you have access to single processor and dual processor computers that use the same clock rate, write a program that consumes large amounts of CPU time, run multiple copies on both computers, and record the running times. What is the effective speedup?

17.4   In the previous question, change the program to reference large amounts of memory (e.g., repeatedly set a large array to a value x, then set the array to value y, and so on). How do memory references affect the speedup?

17.5   Can a multiprocessor ever achieve speedup that is *better* than linear? To find out, consider an encryption breaking algorithm that must try twenty-four (four factorial) possible encryption keys, and must perform up to 1024 operations to test each key (stopping early only if an answer is found). If we assume a multiprocessor requires K milliseconds to perform 1024 operations, on average how much time will the processor spend solving the entire problem? How much time will a 32-processor MIMD machine spend solving the problem? What is the resulting speedup?

18

Pipelining

18.1 Introduction

Earlier chapters present processors, memory systems, and I/O as the fundamental aspects of computer architecture. The previous chapter shows how parallelism can be used to increase performance, and explains a wide variety of parallel architectures.

This chapter focuses on the second major technique used to increase performance: pipelining. The chapter discusses the motivation for pipelining, explains the variety of ways pipelining is used, and shows why pipelining can increase hardware performance.

18.2 The Concept Of Pipelining

The term *pipelining* refers broadly to any architecture in which digital information flows through a series of stations (e.g., processing components) that each inspect, interpret, or modify the information as Figure 18.1 illustrates.

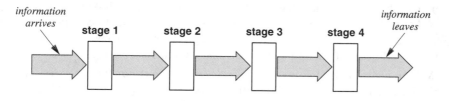

Figure 18.1 Illustration of the pipeline concept. The example has four stages, and information flows through each stage.

Although we are primarily interested in hardware architectures and the use of pipelining within a single computer system, the concept itself is not limited to hardware. Pipelining is not restricted to a single computer, a particular type or size of digital information, or a specific length of pipeline (i.e., a particular number of stages). Instead, pipelining is a fundamental concept in computing that is used in a variety of situations.

To help us understand the concept, we will consider a set of possibilities. Figure 18.2 lists ways to characterize pipelines, and succeeding paragraphs explain each of the characteristics.

- Hardware or software implementation
- Large or small scale
- Synchronous or asynchronous flow
- Buffered or unbuffered flow
- Finite chunks or continuous bit streams
- Automatic data feed or manual data feed
- Serial or parallel path
- Homogeneous or heterogeneous stages

Figure 18.2 The variety of ways a pipeline can be used. The concept arises in many ways in digital systems.

Hardware Or Software Implementation. Pipelining can be implemented in either software or hardware. For example, the Unix operating system provides a *pipe* mechanism that can be used to form a software pipeline — a set of processes creates pipes that connect the output of one process to the input of the next process. We will examine hardware pipelines in later sections. However, it should be noted that software and hardware pipelines are independent: a software pipeline can be created on a computer that does not use a pipeline hardware architecture, and pipeline hardware is not necessarily visible to programmers.

Large Or Small Scale. Stations in a pipeline can range from simplistic to powerful, and a pipeline can range in length from short to long. At one extreme, a hardware pipeline can be contained entirely within a small functional unit on a chip. At the other extreme, a software pipeline can be created by passing data through a series of programs that each run on a separate computer and use the Internet to communicate. Similarly, a short pipeline can be formed of two stages, one that generates information and one that absorbs it, and a long pipeline can contain hundreds of stages.

Synchronous Or Asynchronous Flow. A *synchronous pipeline* operates like an assembly line: at a given time, each station is processing some amount of information (e.g., a byte). A global clock controls movement, which means that all stations simultaneously forward their data (i.e., the results of processing) to the next station. The alternative, an *asynchronous pipeline*, allows a station to forward information at any time.

Asynchronous communication is especially attractive for situations where the amount of time a given stage spends on processing depends on the information. However, asynchronous communication can mean that if one stage delays for a long time, later stages must wait.

Buffered Or Unbuffered Flow. Our conceptual diagram in Figure 18.1 implies that one stage of a pipeline sends data directly to another stage. It is also possible to construct a pipeline in which a *buffer* is placed between each pair of stages. Buffering is useful with asynchronous pipelines in which information is processed in *bursts* (i.e., a pipeline in which a stage repeatedly emits steady output, then ceases emitting output, and then begins emitting steady output again).

Finite Chunks Or Continuous Bit Streams. The digital information that passes though a pipeline can consist of a sequence of small data items (e.g., packets from a computer network) or an arbitrarily long bit stream (e.g., a continuous video feed). Furthermore, a pipeline that operates on individual data items can be designed such that all data items are the same size (e.g., disk blocks that are each four Kbytes) or the size of data items is not fixed (e.g., a series of Ethernet packets that vary in length).

Automatic Data Feed Or Manual Data Feed. Some implementations of pipelines use a separate mechanism to move information, and other implementations require each stage to participate in moving information. For example, a synchronous hardware pipeline usually relies on an auxiliary mechanism to move information from one stage to another. However, a software pipeline usually requires each stage to *write* outgoing data and *read* incoming data explicitly.

Serial Or Parallel Path. The large arrows in Figure 18.1 imply that a parallel path is used to move information from one stage to another. Although some pipelines do use a parallel path, others use serial communication. Furthermore, communication between stages need not consist of conventional communication (e.g., stages can use an operating system, computer network, or shared memory to communicate).

Homogeneous Or Heterogeneous Stages. Although Figure 18.1 uses the same size and shape for each stage of a pipeline, homogeneity is not required. Some implementations of pipelines choose a type of hardware that is appropriate for each stage.

18.3 Software Pipelining

From a programmer's point of view, a software pipeline is attractive for two reasons. First, a software pipeline provides a way to handle complexity. Second, a software pipeline allows programs to be reused. In essence, both goals are achieved because a software pipeline allows a programmer to divide a large, complex task into smaller, more generic pieces.

As an example of software pipelining, consider a Unix *command interpreter* (also known as a *shell*). A shell allows a user to create a software pipeline easily. The user enters a list of program names separated by the vertical bar character to specify that the programs should be run as a pipeline (i.e., the output from one program should be connected to the input of the next). Each program can have zero or more arguments; the vertical bar separates one program from the next. For example, the following input to the shell specifies that three programs, *cat*, *sed*, and *more* are to be connected in a pipeline:

cat x | sed 's/friend/partner/g' | more

In the example, the *cat* program writes a copy of file *x* (presumably a text file) to its output, which becomes the input of the *sed* program. The *sed* program, in the middle of the pipeline, receives input from *cat* and sends output to *more*. *Sed* has an argument that specifies translating every occurrence of the word *friend* to *partner*. The final program in the pipeline, *more*, displays anything it receives as input on the user's screen.

Although the example above is trivial, it illustrates how a software pipeline helps programmers. Decomposing a program into a series of smaller, less complex programs makes it easier to create and debug software. Furthermore, if the division is chosen carefully, some of the pieces can be reused among programs. In particular, programmers often find that using a pipeline to separate input and output processing from computation allows a piece that performs computation to be reused with various forms of input and output.

18.4 Software Pipeline Performance And Overhead

It may seem that software pipelining results in lower performance than a single program. After all, the operating system must run multiple programs at the same time, and must pass data between pairs of programs. Inefficiency can be especially high if early stages of a pipeline pass large volumes of data that are later discarded. For example, consider the following software pipeline that contains one more stage than the example above: an additional invocation of *sed* that deletes any line containing the character *W*.

cat x | sed 's/friend/partner/g' | sed '/W/d' | more

If we expect ninety-nine percent of all lines to contain the character *W*, the first two stages of the pipeline will perform unnecessary work (i.e., processing lines of text that will be discarded in a later stage of the pipeline). In the example, the pipeline can be optimized by moving the deletion to an earlier stage. However, the overhead of using a software pipeline appears to remain: copying data from one program to another is less efficient than performing all computation in a single program.

Surprisingly, a software pipeline can sometimes perform better than a large, monolithic program. To understand why, consider the underlying architecture: processing, memory, and I/O are constructed from independent hardware. A modern operating system takes advantage of the independence by automatically switching the processor among programs: when one program is waiting for I/O, another program runs. Thus, if a pipeline is composed of many small programs, the operating system may be able to improve overall performance by running one of the programs in a pipeline, while another program waits for I/O.

18.5 Hardware Pipelining

Hardware pipelining offers several advantages. First, like software pipelining, hardware pipelining can help a designer manage complexity — a complex task can be divided into smaller, more manageable pieces. Second, if the division is performed carefully and the task is sufficiently general, it may be possible to reuse pieces in other hardware designs. Third, and most important, hardware pipelining typically offers higher performance†.

Before we discuss performance, it is important to understand that hardware pipelines are usually divided into two categories:

- Instruction pipeline
- Data pipeline

Instruction Pipeline. Chapter 5 explains how the fetch-execute cycle in most modern processors uses a pipeline to decode and execute instructions. To be precise, we use the term *instruction pipeline* to describe a pipeline in which the information consists of machine instructions and the stages of the pipeline execute the instructions. However, because instruction sets and operand types vary from one processor to another, there is no overall agreement on the number of stages in an instruction pipeline or the exact operations performed at a given stage‡.

Data Pipeline. The alternative to an instruction pipeline is known as a *data pipeline*. That is, instead of passing instructions, a data pipeline is designed to pass data from stage to stage. For example, if a data pipeline is used to handle packets that arrive from a computer network, each packet passes sequentially through the stages of the pipeline. Data pipelining provides some of the most unusual and most interesting uses of pipelining. As we will see, data pipelining also has the potential for the greatest overall improvement in performance.

18.6 How Hardware Pipelining Increases Performance

To understand why pipelining is fundamental in hardware design, we need to examine a key point: pipelining can dramatically increase performance. To see how, compare a data pipeline to a monolithic design. For example, consider the design of an Internet router that is used by an Internet Service Provider (ISP) to forward packets between customers and web sites. A router connects to multiple networks, some of

---

†We have already seen that pipelining does not always enhance performance: overall performance will suffer if the pipeline stalls.

‡The definition of *superpipeline*, given later in this chapter, also relates to an instruction pipeline.

which lead to customers and at least one leads to the Internet. Network packets can arrive over any network, and the router's job is to send each packet on toward its destination. For purposes of this example, we will assume the router performs six basic operations on each packet as Figure 18.3 lists.

1. Receive a packet (i.e., transfer the packet into memory).

2. Verify packet integrity (i.e., verify that no changes occurred between transmission and reception).

3. Check for routing loops (i.e., decrement a value in the header, and reform the header with the new value).

4. Route the packet (i.e., use the destination address field to select one of the possible output networks and a destination on that network).

5. Prepare for transmission (i.e. compute information that will be used to verify packet integrity).

6. Transmit the packet (i.e., transfer the packet to the output device).

Figure 18.3 An example series of steps that hardware in an Internet router performs to forward a packet.

Now consider the design of hardware that implements the steps in the figure. Because the steps involve complex computation, it may seem that a processor should be used to perform packet forwarding. However, a single processor is not fast enough for high-speed networks. Thus, most designs employ two optimizations described in earlier chapters: smart I/O devices and parallelism. A smart I/O device can transfer a packet to or from memory without using a processor, and a parallel design uses a separate processor to handle each input.

A parallel design with a smart I/O interface means that each processor implements a loop that repeatedly executes the six basic steps. Figure 18.4 illustrates how a processor connects to an input, and shows the algorithm the processor runs.

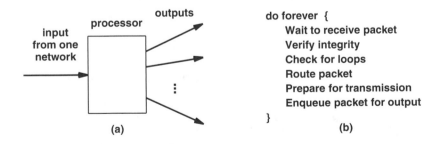

Figure 18.4 (a) Illustration of the connections on a processor used in a parallel implementation of an Internet router, and (b) the algorithm the processor executes. Each processor handles input from one network.

Suppose a parallel architecture, like the one in the figure, is still too slow. That is, suppose the processor cannot execute all the steps of the algorithm before the next packet arrives over the interface and no faster processor is available. How can we achieve higher performance? One possibility for higher speed lies in a data pipeline: use a pipeline of several processors in place of a single processor as Figure 18.5 illustrates.

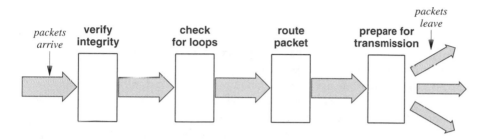

Figure 18.5 Illustration of a pipeline used in place of a single processor in an
Internet router.

It may seem that the pipeline in the figure is no faster than the single processor in Figure 18.4. After all, the pipeline architecture performs exactly the same operations on each packet as the single processor. Furthermore, if the processor in Figure 18.4 is the fastest processor available, the processors in Figure 18.5 cannot run any faster. Thus, if we assume the same type of processor is used, and ignore the delay introduced by passing packets among stages of the pipeline, the total time taken to process a packet is exactly the same. That is:

> *A data pipeline passes data through a series of stages that each examine or modify the data. If it uses the same speed processors as a nonpipeline architecture, a data pipeline will not improve the overall time needed to process a given data item.*

If the total processing time is not reduced, what is the advantage of a data pipeline? Surprisingly, even if the individual processors in Figure 18.5 are each exactly the same speed as the processor in Figure 18.4, the pipeline architecture can process more packets per second. To see why, observe that an individual processor executes fewer instructions per packet. Furthermore, after operating on one data item, a processor moves on to the next data item. Thus, a data pipeline architecture allows a given processor to move on to the next data item more quickly than a nonpipeline architecture. As a result, data can enter (and leave) a pipeline at a higher rate.

We can summarize:

> *Even if a data pipeline uses the same speed processors as a nonpipe-line architecture, a data pipeline has higher overall throughput (i.e., number of data items processed per second).*

18.7 When Pipelining Can Be Used

A pipeline will not yield higher performance in all cases. First, it must be possible to partition processing into independent stages. Second, the additional overhead required to move data from one stage to another must be insignificant. Third, the processing performed at each stage must take approximately the same time as the processing performed at other stages.

The third requirement arises because the throughput of a pipeline is limited by the slowest stage (i.e., the stage that takes the most time). For example, suppose the data pipeline in Figure 18.5 uses identical processors, and assume a processor takes exactly the same time to execute any instruction and can execute ten instructions each microsecond. Further suppose the four stages take fifty, one hundred, two hundred, and one hundred fifty instructions, respectively, to process a packet†. The slowest stage requires two hundred instructions, which means the total time the slowest stage takes to process a packet is:

$$total\ time = \frac{200\ inst}{10\ inst\ /\ \mu sec} = 20\ \mu sec$$

Looking at this another way, we can see that the maximum number of packets that can be processed per second is the inverse of the time per packet of the slowest stage. Thus, the overall throughput of the example pipeline, T_p is given by:

$$T_p = \frac{1\ packet}{20\ \mu sec} = \frac{1\ packet \times 10^6}{20\ sec} = 50,000\ packets\ per\ second$$

In contrast, the throughput of a non-pipelined architecture is:

$$T_{np} = \frac{1\ packet}{50\ \mu sec} = \frac{1\ packet \times 10^6}{50\ sec} = 20,000\ packets\ per\ second$$

---

†Although our examples and discussion assume that each stage of a pipeline uses the same processor as other stages, a pipeline can be heterogeneous as describe earlier in the chapter.

18.8 The Conceptual Division Of Processing

Conceptually, pipelining offers a special form of parallelism. By dividing a series of sequential operations into groups that are each handled by a separate stage of the pipeline, pipelining allows each of the stages to operate in parallel. Of course, a pipeline architecture differs from a conventional parallel architecture in a significant way: although the stages operate in parallel, a given data item must pass through all stages. Figure 18.6 illustrates the concept.

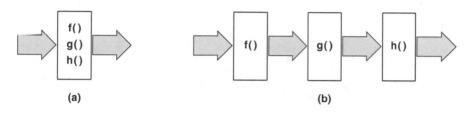

(a)   **(b)**

Figure 18.6 (a) Processing on a conventional processor, and (b) equivalent processing in a data pipeline. The functions performed in sequence are divided among stages of the pipeline.

18.9 Pipeline Architectures

Recall from the previous chapter that we distinguish between hardware architectures that merely use parallelism and architectures in which parallelism forms the central paradigm around which the entire architecture is designed. We make an analogous distinction between hardware architectures that use pipelining and architectures in which pipelining forms the central paradigm around which the entire system is designed. We reserve the name *pipeline architectures* for the latter. Thus, one might hear an architect say that a particular system uses a pipeline processor, but the architect will not characterize the system as a pipeline architecture unless the overall design centers around a pipeline.

Most hardware systems that follow a pipeline architecture are dedicated to special-purpose functions. For instance, the example above describes how pipelining can be used to improve performance of a packet processing system. Pipelining is especially important in network systems because the high data rates used when sending data over optical fibers exceeds the capacity of conventional processors.

Pipeline architectures are less relevant to general-purpose computers for two reasons. First, few applications can be decomposed into a set of independent operations that can be applied sequentially. Instead, a typical application accesses items randomly and keeps large volumes of additional state information. Second, even in situations where the functions to be performed on data can be decomposed into a pipeline, the number of stages in the pipeline and the hardware needed to implement each stage is not usually known in advance. As a result, general-purpose computers usually restrict pipeline hardware to an instruction pipeline in the processor or a special-purpose pipeline in an I/O device.

18.10 Pipeline Setup, Stall, And Flush Times

Our description of pipelines overlooks many of the practical details. For example, many pipeline implementations have overhead associated with starting and stopping the pipeline. We use the term *setup time* to describe the amount of time required to start a pipeline after an idle period. Setup may involve synchronizing processing among stages or passing a special control token through the pipeline to restart each stage. For a software pipeline, setup can be especially expensive because connections among various stages are created dynamically.

Unlike other architectures, a pipeline can require significant time to terminate processing. We use the term *flush time* to refer to the amount of time that elapses between the input being unavailable and the pipeline finishing its current processing. We say that items currently in the pipeline must be *flushed* before the pipeline can be shut down.

The need to flush items through a pipeline can arise for two reasons. First, a pipeline becomes idle when no input is available for the first stage. Second, as we have seen, later stages of a pipeline become idle when one stage *stalls* (i.e., the stage delays because it cannot complete processing). In a high-speed hardware pipeline, mundane operations such as a memory reference or an I/O operation can cause a stage to stall. Thus, high flush (or setup) times can reduce pipeline performance significantly.

18.11 Definition Of Superpipeline Architecture

A final concept completes our description of pipelines. Architects use the term *superpipeline* to describe an extension of the pipeline approach in which a given stage of the pipeline is subdivided into a set of partial stages. Superpipelining is most often used with an instruction pipeline. A traditional instruction pipeline typically has five stages that correspond to: instruction fetch, instruction decode, operand fetch, ALU operation, and memory write. A superpipeline architecture subdivides the stages into multiple pieces.

As an example, a superpipeline can subdivide the operand fetch stage into four steps: the first step decodes an operand, the second step fetches an immediate value or a value from a register, the third step fetches values from memory, and the fourth step fetches indirect operand values. As with standard pipelining, the point of the subdivision is higher throughput — because each substage has less to do, throughput of a superpipeline is higher than the throughput of a standard pipeline.

18.12 Summary

Pipelining is a broad, fundamental concept that is used with both hardware and software. A software pipeline, which arranges a set of programs in a series with data passing through them, can be used on hardware that does not provide pipelining.

A hardware pipeline is either classified as an instruction pipeline, which is used inside a processor to handle machine instructions, or a data pipeline, in which arbitrary data is transferred through the pipeline. The superpipeline technique, in which a stage of a pipeline is further subdivided into partial stages, is often used with an instruction pipeline.

Unless faster processors are used, a data pipeline does not decrease the overall time required to process a single data item. However, using a pipeline does increase the overall throughput (items processed per second). The stage of a pipeline that requires the most time to process an item limits the throughput of the pipeline.

EXERCISES

18.1   What is the maximum throughput of a homogeneous pipeline in which four processors each handle one million instructions per second and processing a data item requires 50, 60, 40, and 30 instructions, respectively? Assume a constant execution time for all types of instructions.

18.2   In the previous exercise, what is the relative gain in throughput compared to an architecture without pipelining? What is the maximum speedup?

18.3   Extend the previous problem by considering heterogeneous processors that have speeds of 1.0, 1.2, 0.9, and 1.0 million instructions per second, respectively.

19

Assessing Performance

19.1 Introduction

Earlier chapters cover the fundamental mechanisms that computer architects use to construct computer systems: processors, memories, and I/O devices. They characterize each mechanism, and explain the salient features. The previous chapters consider two techniques used to increase computational performance: parallelism and pipelining.

This chapter takes a broader view of performance. It examines how performance can be measured, and discusses how an architect evaluates an instruction set. More important, the chapter presents Amdahl's law, and explains consequences for computer architecture.

19.2 Measuring Power And Performance

How can we measure computational power? What makes one computer system perform better than another? These questions have engendered research in the scientific community, caused heated debate among representatives from the sales and marketing departments of commercial computer vendors, and resulted in a variety of answers.

The chief problem that underlies performance assessment arises from the flexibility of a general-purpose computer system: a computer is designed to perform a variety of tasks. More important, because optimization involves choosing among alternatives, optimizing the architecture for a given task means that the architecture will be less than optimal for other tasks. Consequently, the performance of a computer system depends on how the system is used.

We can summarize:

> *Because a computer is designed to perform a wide variety of tasks and no architecture is optimal for all tasks, the performance of a system depends on the task being performed.*

The dependency between performance and the task being performed has two important consequences. First, it means that many computer vendors can each claim that they have the most powerful computer. For example, a vendor whose computer performs matrix multiplication at high speed uses matrix multiplication examples when measuring performance, while a vendor whose computer performs integer operations at high speed uses integer examples when measuring performance. Both vendors can claim that their computer performs best. Second, from a scientific point of view, we can see that no single measure of computer system performance suffices for all cases. The point is fundamental to understanding performance assessment:

> *A variety of performance measures exist because no single measure suffices for all situations.*

19.3 Measures Of Computational Power

Recall that early computer systems consisted of a central processor with little or no I/O capability. As a consequence, early measures of computer performance focused on the execution speed of the CPU. Even when performance measures are restricted to a CPU, however, multiple measures apply. The most important distinction arises between computer systems optimized for:

- Integer computation
- Floating point computation

Because scientific and engineering calculations rely heavily on floating point, applications that employ floating point are often called *scientific applications*, and the resulting computation is known as *scientific computation*. When assessing how a computer performs on scientific applications, engineers focus entirely on the performance of floating point operations. That is, they ignore the speed of all other operations, and only measure the speed of floating point operations (i.e., floating point addition, subtraction, multiplication and division). Of course, addition and subtraction are generally faster than multiplication and division, and a program contains other instructions (e.g., instructions to call functions or control iteration). On many computers, however, a floating point operation takes so much longer than a typical integer instruction that floating point computation dominates the overall performance of a program.

Rather than reporting the time required to perform a floating point operation, engineers report the number of floating point operations that can be performed per unit time. In particular, the primary measure is given as the average number of floating point operations the hardware can execute per second (*FLOPS*).

Of course, floating point speed is only pertinent for scientific computation; the speed of floating point hardware is irrelevant to programs that use integers. More important, a measure of FLOPS does not make sense for a RISC processor that does not offer floating point instructions. Thus, as an alternative to measuring floating point performance, a vendor may choose the average number of (non floating point) instructions that a processor can execute per unit time. Typically, vendors measure *millions of instructions per second* (*MIPS*).

Simplistic measures of performance such as MIPS or FLOPS only provide a rough estimate of performance. To see why, consider the time required to execute an instruction. For example, consider a processor on which floating point multiplication or division takes twice as long as floating point addition or subtraction. If we assume that an addition or subtraction instruction takes Q nanoseconds and weight each of the four instruction types equally, the average time the computer takes to perform a floating point operation, T_{avg} is:

$$T_{avg} = \frac{Q + Q + 2 \times Q + 2 \times Q}{4} = 1.5\,Q \quad ns \ per \ instruction \quad (19.1)$$

However, when the computer performs addition and subtraction, the time required is only Q nanoseconds per instruction (i.e., 33% less than the average). Similarly, when performing multiplication or division, the computer requires $2 \times Q$ nanoseconds per instruction (i.e., 33% more than the average).

The point is:

> *Because some instructions take substantially longer to execute than others, the average time required to execute an instruction only provides a crude approximation of performance. The actual time required depends on which instructions are executed.*

19.4 Application Specific Instruction Counts

How can we produce a more accurate assessment of performance? One answer lies in assessing performance for a specific application. For example, suppose we need to know how a floating point hardware unit will perform when multiplying two $N \times N$ matrices. By examining the program, it is possible to derive a set of expressions that give the number of floating point additions, subtractions, multiplications, and divisions that will be performed as a function of N. For example, assume that multiplying a pair of $N \times N$ matrices requires N^3 floating point multiplications and $N^3 - N^2$ floating point additions. If each addition requires Q nanoseconds and each multiplication requires $2 \times Q$ nanoseconds, multiplying two matrices will require a total of:

$$T_{total} = 2 \times Q \times N^3 + Q \times (N^3 - N^2)$$

As an alternative to precise analysis, engineers use a weighted average. That is, instead of calculating the exact number of times each instruction is executed, an approximate percentage is used. For example, suppose a graphics program is run on many input data sets, the number of floating point operations is counted to obtain the list in Figure 19.1.

Instruction Type	Count	Percentage
Add	8513508	72
Subtract	1537162	13
Multiply	1064188	9
Divide	709458	6

Figure 19.1 Example of instruction counts for a graphics application run on many input values. The third column shows the relative percentage of each instruction type.

Once a set of instruction counts has been obtained, the performance of hardware can be assessed by using a weighted average. When the graphics application is run on the hardware described above, we expect the average time for each floating point instruction to be:

$$T_{avg'} = \frac{.72 \times Q + .13 \times Q + .09 \times 2\,Q + .06 \times 2\,Q}{4} = 0.29\, Q \ \ ns \ per \ instruction$$

As the example shows, a weighted average can differ significantly from a uniform average. In this case, the weighted average is less than 20% of the average in equation (19.1) that was obtained using uniform instruction weights†.

19.5 Instruction Mix

Although it provides a more accurate measurement of performance, the weighted average example above only applies to one specific application, and only assesses floating point performance. Can we give a more general assessment? One approach has become popular: use a large set of programs to obtain relative weights for each type of instruction, and then use the relative weights to assess the performance of a given architecture. That is, instead of focusing on floating point, keep a counter for each instruc-

---

†Equation 19.1 can be found on page 313.

tion type (e.g., integer arithmetic instructions, bit shift instructions, subroutine calls, conditional branches), and use the counts and relative weights to compute a weighted average performance.

Of course, the weights depend on the specific programs chosen. Therefore, to be as fair as possible, we must choose programs that represent a typical workload. Architects say that they choose an *instruction mix* that represents typical programs.

In addition to helping assess performance of a computer, an instruction mix helps an architect design an efficient instruction set. The architect drafts a tentative instruction set, assigns an expected cost to each instruction, and uses weights from the instruction mix to see how the proposed instruction set will perform. In essence, the architect uses the instruction mix to evaluate how the proposed architecture will perform on typical programs. If the performance is unsatisfactory, the architect can change the design.

We can summarize.

> *An instruction mix consists of a set of instructions along with relative weights that have been obtained by counting instruction execution in example programs. An architect can use an instruction mix to assess how a proposed architecture will perform.*

19.6 Standardized Benchmarks

What instruction mix should be used to compare the performance of two architectures? To answer the question, we need to know how the computers will be used: the programs the computers are intended to run, and the type of input the programs will receive. In essence, we need to find a set of applications that are "typical". Engineers and architects use the term *benchmark* to refer to such programs — a benchmark provides a standard workload against which a computer can be measured.

Of course, devising a benchmark is difficult, and the community does not benefit if each vendor creates a separate benchmark. To solve the problem, an independent not-for-profit corporation was formed in the 1980s. Named *Standard Performance Evaluation Corporation (SPEC)*, the corporation was created to "establish, maintain and endorse a standardized set of relevant benchmarks that can be applied to the newest generation of high-performance computers"†. Indeed, SPEC has devised a series of standard benchmarks that are used to compare performance. For example, the *SPECint92* benchmark is used to evaluate integer performance, and the *SPECfp92* benchmark is used to evaluate floating point performance.

The benchmarks produced by SPEC are primarily used for measurement, not design. That is, each benchmark consists of a set of programs that are run and measured. The score that results from running a SPEC benchmark, known as a *SPECmark*, is often quoted in the industry as a vendor-independent measure of computer performance.

---

†Taken from the SPEC bylaws.

Interestingly, SPEC has produced many benchmarks that each test one aspect of performance. For example, SPEC offers six separate benchmarks that focus on integer arithmetic and another fourteen benchmarks that focus on various aspects of floating point performance. In addition, SPEC provides benchmarks used to assess UNIX systems performing software development tasks and computers that use the Network File System (*NFS*) for remote file access.

19.7 I/O And Memory Bottlenecks

CPU performance only accounts for part of the overall performance of a computer system. As users of personal computers have realized, a faster CPU does not guarantee faster response for all computing tasks. A colleague of the author recently complained that although CPU speeds increase by an order of magnitude every ten years, the time required to launch an application seems to increase.

What prevents a faster CPU from increasing the overall speed? We have already seen one answer: the Von Neumann bottleneck (i.e., memory access). Recall that the speed of memory can affect the rate at which instructions can be fetched as well as the rate at which data can be accessed. Thus, rather than merely measuring CPU performance, some benchmarks are designed to measure memory performance. That is, the benchmark consists of a program that repeatedly accesses memory. Some memory benchmarks are designed to test sequential access (i.e., access to contiguous bytes), while others are designed to test random access. More important, memory benchmarks also make repeated references to a memory location to test memory caching.

As the chapters on I/O point out, peripheral devices and the buses over which peripheral devices communicate can also form a bottleneck. Thus, some benchmarks are designed to test the performance of I/O devices. For example, a benchmark to test a disk will repeatedly execute *write* and *read* operations that each transfer a block of data to the disk and then read the data back. As with memory, some disk benchmarks focus on measuring performance when accessing sequential data blocks, and other benchmarks focus on measuring performance when accessing random blocks.

19.8 Boundary Between Hardware And Software

One of the fundamental principles that underlies computer performance arises from the relative speed of hardware and software: special-purpose hardware can be designed to perform a given function much faster than the function can be performed in software. Thus, an architect can increase overall performance by adding special-purpose hardware units.

We can summarize:

> *To optimize performance, move operations that account for the most*
> *CPU time from software into hardware.*

19.9 Choosing Items To Optimize

Because adding additional hardware increases the cost of the computer system, an architect cannot use high-speed hardware to handle each operation. Similarly, using special-purpose, high-speed hardware costs more than conventional hardware. Instead, an architect must choose which functions to handle with high-speed hardware, which to handle with conventional hardware, and which to handle with software.

How should the choice be made? Computer architect Gene Amdahl observed that it is a waste of resources to optimize functions that are seldom used. For example, consider the hardware used to handle division by zero or the circuitry used to power down a computer system. There is little point in optimizing such hardware because it is seldom used.

Amdahl suggested that the greatest gains in performance are made by optimizing functions that account for the most time. His principle, which is known as *Amdahl's law*, focuses on operations that each require extensive computation or operations that are performed most frequently. Usually, the principle is stated in a form that refers to the potential for speedup:

> Amdahl's Law: *the performance improvement that can be realized*
> *from faster hardware technology is limited to the fraction of time the*
> *faster technology can be used.*

19.10 Amdahl's Law And Parallel Systems

Chapter 17 discusses parallel architectures, and explains some of the problems. As the chapter explains, MIMD architectures have serious limitations on performance. Overhead from communication among processors and contention for shared resources such as memory and I/O buses limit the effective speed of the system. As a result, parallel systems that contain N processors do not achieve N times the performance of a single processor.

Interestingly, Amdahl's Law applies directly to parallel systems and explains why adding more processors does not help. The speedup that can be achieved by optimizing the processing power (i.e., adding additional processors) is limited to the amount of time the processors are being used. Because a parallel system spends most of the time waiting for communication or bus access rather than using the processors, adding additional processors will not have much impact.

19.11 Summary

A variety of performance measures exist. Simplistic measures of processor performance include the average number of floating point operations a computer can perform per second (FLOPS) or the average number of instructions the computer can execute per second (MIPS). More sophisticated measures use a weighted average in which an instruction that is used more often is weighted more heavily. Weights can be derived by counting the instructions in a program or a set of programs; such weights are specific to the application(s) used. We say that weights, which are useful in assessing an instruction set, correspond to an instruction mix.

A benchmark refers to a standardized program or set of programs used to assess performance; each benchmark is chosen to represent a typical computation. Some of the best-known benchmarks have been produced by the SPEC corporation, and are known as SPECmarks. In addition to measuring performance of various aspects of integer and floating point performance, benchmarks are available from SPEC to measure such mechanisms as a remote file system.

Amdahl's Law helps architects select functions to be optimized (e.g., moved from software to hardware or moved from conventional hardware to high-speed hardware). The law states that functions to be optimized should account for the most time. Amdahl's Law explains why parallel computer systems do not benefit from large numbers of processors.

EXERCISES

19.1   Write a C program that measures the performance of integer addition and subtraction operators. Perform at least 10,000 operations and calculate the average time per operation.

19.2   In the previous problem, repeat the measurement with compiler optimization enabled and determine the relative speedup.

19.3   Write a program that compares the average time required to perform integer arithmetic operations and the average time required to reference memory. Calculate the ratio of the two measures.

19.4   Write a program that compares the average time required to perform floating point operations and integer operations. For example, compare the average time required to perform 10,000 floating point additions and the average time required to perform 10,000 floating point multiplications.

20

Architecture Examples And Hierarchy

20.1 Introduction

Earlier chapters explain the concepts and terminology that are essential to an understanding of computer architecture. The chapters discuss the fundamental aspects of processors, memory, and I/O, and explain the role of each. The previous chapters discuss how parallelism and pipelining are used to improve performance.

This chapter considers a few architecture examples. Instead of introducing new ideas, the chapter shows how the ideas in previous chapters can be used to describe and explain various aspects of digital systems. The examples have been chosen to show a range of possibilities.

20.2 Architectural Levels

Recall from earlier chapters that architecture can be presented at multiple levels. To help us appreciate how broadly architectural concepts apply to digital systems, we will explore a hierarchy of architectural specifications. The hierarchy ranges in size from a complete computer system to a small functional unit on a single integrated circuit. We use the terms *system-level architecture* (sometimes called *macroscopic architecture*), *board-level architecture*, and *chip-level architecture* (sometimes called *microscopic architecture*) to characterize the range. For each level, we will see that the concepts from earlier chapters allow us to understand both the basic components and their interconnection. Furthermore, we will see that at a given level, it is possible to specify a logical (i.e., conceptual) architecture or to specify a more detailed implementation. Figure 20.1 summarizes the levels.

Level	Description
System	A complete computer with processor(s), memory, and I/O devices. A typical system architecture describes the interconnection of components with buses.
Board	An individual circuit board that forms part of a computer system. A typical board architecture describes the interconnection of chips and the interface to a bus.
Chip	An individual integrated circuit that is used on a circuit board. A typical chip architecture describes the interconnection of functional units and gates.

Figure 20.1 Levels of architecture and the purpose of each. As one moves down the levels, increasing amounts of detail are specified.

20.3 System-Level Architecture: A Personal Computer

Conceptually, a personal computer consists of a processor, memory, and a set of I/O devices that all attach to a single bus. In practice, however, even a personal computer contains a complex assortment of buses and interconnection mechanisms that are each designed to fill a specific role.

Some of the variety and complexity in underlying hardware arises from special performance requirements and cost. For example, a video card needs much higher data throughput than a floppy disk, and a high-resolution screen requires more throughput than a low-resolution screen. Unfortunately, the hardware that interconnects a device to a high-speed bus costs significantly more than hardware that interconnects to a low-speed bus, which means that using multiple buses can lower the overall cost of the system.

A second motivation for multiple I/O buses arises from a vendor's desire to provide a low-cost migration path to newer, more powerful systems. That is, a vendor strives to create a processor that offers the advantages of higher performance and more capabilities, while simultaneously retaining the ability to use existing peripheral devices. We use the term *backward compatibility* to characterize the ability to use existing pieces of hardware.

20.4 Bus Interconnection And Bridging

Backward compatibility is especially important for bus architectures because a bus forms the interconnection between an I/O device and a processor. How can a computer vendor devise a new, higher speed bus while still retaining the ability to attach older peripheral devices? One possibility consists of creating a processor with multiple bus interfaces. A much less expensive answer lies in a technology known as *bridging*.

Bridging is easiest to understand through an example. At one point in history, all personal computers used an *Industry Standard Architecture* (*ISA*) bus that was developed by IBM Corporation. Peripheral devices for PCs were designed with an interface for the ISA bus. Later, a higher-speed bus architecture was developed: a *Peripheral Component Interconnect* (*PCI*) bus. The two standards for PC buses are incompatible — an interface that plugs into an ISA bus cannot be connected to a PCI bus. Thus, if a user owns ISA devices, the user is less likely to purchase a computer that only accepts PCI devices.

To entice computer owners to upgrade their computers to a computer with a PCI bus, vendors created a piece of hardware, known as a *bridge*, to interconnect the new PCI bus and the older ISA bus. Logically, the bridge provides the interconnection that Figure 20.2 illustrates.

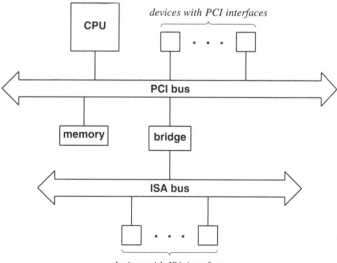

Figure 20.2 Conceptual view of the architecture of a PC that uses a bridge to interconnect an ISA bus and a PCI bus. The bridge makes it possible to use older ISA devices with a newer processor.

In the figure, the CPU connects to a PCI bus along with any I/O devices that have a PCI interface. The bridge provides a connection to an ISA bus that is used by I/O devices that have an ISA interface. In the best case, interconnection provided by a bridge is *transparent*. That is, each side uses a local bus protocol to communicate without knowing about the interconnection — the CPU addresses ISA devices as if they are connected to the PCI bus, and an ISA device responds as if the CPU is connected to the ISA bus.

20.5 Controller Chips And Physical Architecture

Although the architecture illustrated in Figure 20.2 provides a conceptual explanation of a PC architecture, an implementation is much more complex than the figure indicates. First, although a PC provides slots that external devices use to connect to each bus, the PC does not use the same technology internally. Instead, a PC usually contains two special-purpose *controller chips* that provide all the bus and memory interconnections. Second, controller chips are configured to give the illusion of multiple buses.

To understand the need for controller chips, consider some of the functionality required in a PC. An architect needs to connect the processor, memory, and I/O bus (or buses). In addition to providing electrically compatible interconnections, the architect must design a mechanism that allows one component to communicate with another. For example, both the CPU and I/O devices need to access memory.

Unfortunately, replicating hardware interfaces is expensive. In particular, an architect cannot afford to build a system in which each component has multiple interface units that each handle communication with one other component. For example, although the processor and most I/O devices need to access memory, the cost prohibits an architect from providing a memory interface for each device.

To save effort and expense, architects often adopt the approach of using a centralized *controller chip*. A controller chip contains a set of K hardware interfaces, one for each type of hardware, and forwards requests among them. When a hardware unit needs to access another hardware unit, the request always goes to the controller. The controller translates each incoming request into the appropriate form, and then forwards the request to the destination hardware unit. Similarly, the controller translates each reply.

The key idea is:

> *Architects use a controller chip to provide interconnection among components in a computer because doing so is less expensive than equipping each unit with a set of interfaces or building a set of discrete bridges to interconnect buses.*

20.6 Virtual Buses

A controller chip introduces an interesting possibility. For example, because a bus is used to communicate, we expect two or more devices to be attached to each bus (e.g., a processor and a disk). In a computer that uses a controller chip, however, it is reasonable to create a bus that contains exactly one connected device. To understand why, consider a computer in which the processor and all devices, except one, use a PCI bus. Assume the device that forms the exception uses an ISA bus. A controller chip can be created that uses the ISA protocol to communicate with the ISA device and uses the PCI protocol for all other devices. If the ISA device attaches directly to the controller, the computer will not need slots for ISA devices, and will not have an ISA bus in the usual sense. However, the controller chip can still use the ISA protocol to communicate with the ISA device. That is:

> A controller chip can provide the illusion of a bus over a direct connection; the wires and sockets normally used to construct a bus are optional.

The concept of a controller chip that can provide the illusion of a bus over a direct connection allows architects to generalize the notion of a bus. Instead of separate physical entities with parallel wires, a silicon chip can be used to create the appearance of a bus. We use the term *virtual bus* to describe the technology. For example, a controller can be created that presents the illusion of one virtual bus per attached device. As an alternative, a controller can be created that combines one or more virtual buses with connections to one or more physical buses. Later sections show examples.

Typically, PC architectures use two controller chips to enable higher speeds. The controllers are known informally as the *Northbridge* and *Southbridge* chips; the Northbridge is sometimes called a *system controller*. The Northbridge connects the higher-speed components: the CPU, memory, a streaming communications controller, and an *Advanced Graphics Port* (*AGP*) interface that is used to operate a high-speed graphics display. The Southbridge, which is attached to the Northbridge, provides connectivity for lower-speed components, such as a PCI bus, *Local Area Network* (*LAN*) interface†, six-channel audio, keyboard, mouse, printer port, floppy disk, PS/2 port, and other devices that connect to an ISA bus. Figure 20.3 illustrates the physical interconnections in a PC architecture that uses two controller chips.

---

†Although the Southbridge can connect a LAN interface that operates at 100 mbps, a LAN interface that operates at gigabit speeds must connect to the Northbridge.

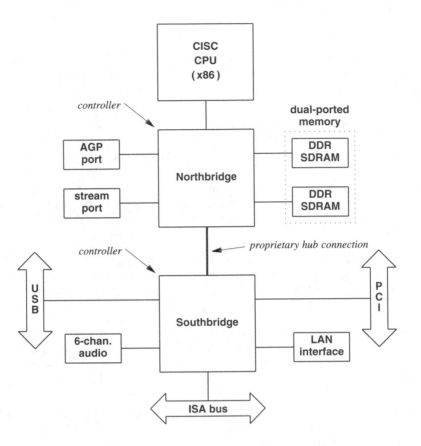

Figure 20.3 Example of a system-level architecture that shows the physical
interconnections in a PC that uses two controller chips. Components that require the highest speeds attach to the controller
labeled *Northbridge*.

As the figure shows, a controller chip must accommodate heterogeneity because a
controller can connect to multiple bus technologies. In the figure, for example, the
Southbridge provides connections for both a PCI bus and a USB bus. Of course, the
controller must follow the rules for each bus. That is, the controller must adhere to the
electrical specifications, ensure that all addresses lie within the bus address space, and
obey the protocol that defines how devices access and use the bus.

Vendors who manufacture CPUs usually offer a set of controller chips that are
designed to interconnect a CPU with standard buses. For example, Intel Corporation
offers a *82865PE* chip that provides the functionality of a Northbridge, and an *ICH5*
chip that provides the functionality of a Southbridge. More important, the Intel processor and controller chips are designed to work together: each chip contains an interface
that allows the chips to be directly interconnected, and each chip performs the translation necessary to connect heterogeneous devices.

20.7 Connection Speeds

The connections illustrated in Figure 20.3 typically use a parallel hardware inter-face that has a fixed width and is engineered to operate at a fixed clock rate to deliver a certain throughput. Figure 20.4 lists typical values for the clock rate, width, and throughput of major connections.

Connection	Clock Rate	Width	Throughput†
AGP	100-200 MHz	64-128 bits	2.0 GBps
Memory	200-800 MHz	64-128 bits	6.4 GBps
CPU	400-800 MHz	64-128 bits	3.2-6.4 GBps
Hub	100-200 MHz	64 bits	800 MBps
USB	33 MHz	32 bits	133 MBps
PCI	33 MHz	32 bits	133 MBps

Figure 20.4 Example clock rates, data widths, and throughput for connections in the architecture that Figure 20.3 illustrates.

20.8 Bridging Functionality And Virtual Buses

As the names *Northbridge* and *Southbridge* imply, the two controllers provide bridging functionality. For example, the Northbridge chip bridges memory, other high-speed devices, and the Southbridge, presenting the CPU with a single, unified address space that includes all of them. Similarly, the Southbridge combines the PCI bus, ISA bus, and USB bus into a single, unified address space.

Interestingly, a set of controllers does not need to bridge all devices into a single address space. Instead, the controller can present the CPU with the illusion of multiple virtual buses. For example, a controller might allow the CPU to access two separate PCI buses: bus number zero contains the CPU and memory, while bus number one contains I/O devices. As an alternative, a controller might present the illusion of three virtual buses: one that contains the host and memory, another that contains a high-speed graphics device, and a third that corresponds to the external PCI slots for arbitrary devices. Although it is not particularly interesting to a programmer, the separation is crucial to a hardware designer interested in performance because the controller chip can contain parallel circuitry that allows all virtual buses to operate at the same time.

20.9 Board-Level Architecture

As Figure 20.3 illustrates, a *Local Area Network* (*LAN*) interface is one of the units that can be found in a personal computer. The role of the interface is straightforward: provide a connection between the PC and a LAN (e.g., an Ethernet), and transfer data

---

†Throughput is measured in *MegaBytes per second* (*MBps*) or *GigaBytes per second* (*GBps*).

that the PC sends over the network as well as data that arrives over the network. Physically, a LAN interface can be integrated onto the computer's *motherboard*, or can consist of a separate circuit board. When a LAN interface consists of a separate circuit board, the interface can attach directly to the motherboard (in which case, the interface is known as a *daughter board*), or can plug into a bus exactly like an I/O device.

A LAN interface board contains a surprising amount of computational power. In particular, a LAN interface usually contains a processor, instructions in ROM, a buffer memory, an external host interface (typically a PCI bus), and an interface to the network. Some LAN interfaces use a conventional RISC processor; others use a *network processor*, a specialized processor optimized for handling network packets. Figure 20.5 illustrates a possible architecture for a LAN interface that uses a network processor.

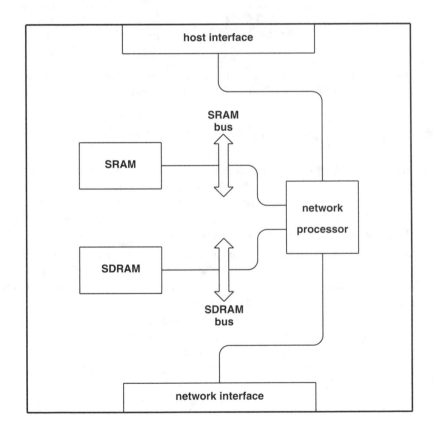

Figure 20.5 Example of a board-level architecture that shows a LAN interface. The interface passes packets between a network and a computer system.

Why might a LAN interface need two types of memory? The primary motivation is cost: although it is faster, SRAM costs more than SDRAM. Thus, a large SDRAM can be used to hold packets, and a small SRAM can be used for values that must be accessed or updated frequently (e.g., instructions for the network processor to execute). In this particular example, the two memory connections are chosen because the network processor described in the next section has interfaces for both SRAM and SDRAM.

20.10 Chip-Level Architecture

We said that a chip-level architecture describes the internal structure of a single integrated circuit. As an example, consider the network processor in the board-level architecture illustrated in Figure 20.5. The figure uses a rectangle to depict a network processor. If we move to a chip-level architectural description, we can examine the internal structure of the chip. Figure 20.6 shows the chip-level architecture of an Intel network processor.

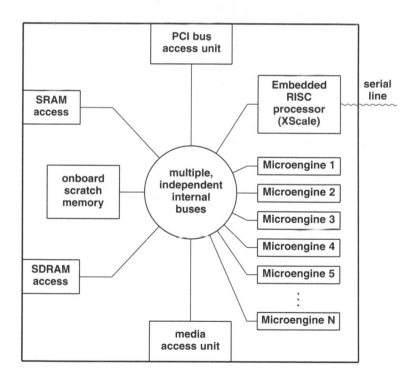

Figure 20.6 Example of a chip-level architecture that shows the major internal components of an Intel network processor. Access units provide connections outside the chip.

It is important to remember that the entire figure refers to a single integrated circuit. Surprisingly, the Intel network processor chip contains many items. For example, the chip contains various external interfaces, an onboard *scratch* memory that provides high-speed storage, and multiple, independent processors. In particular, the chip contains a set of programmable RISC processors, known as *microengines†*, that operate in parallel as well as an *XScale* RISC processor. The XScale provides a general-purpose processor that manages other processors and provides a management interface. When the network processor operates, the XScale runs a conventional operating system, such as *Linux*. To indicate that processors are part of an integrated circuit, we say they are *embedded*.

Details of the network processor and each of the processors are irrelevant. The important point is to understand that more detail is revealed at each architectural level. In this case, we have seen that although a single integrated circuit can contain many functional units, the structure of the circuit is only revealed in a chip-level diagram; the structure remains hidden in a board-level description. We can summarize:

> *A chip-level architecture reveals details about the internal structure of an integrated circuit that are hidden in a board-level architecture.*

20.11 Structure Of Functional Units On A Chip

Figure 20.6 illustrates how it is possible to describe the interconnection of major components on a single chip. Interestingly, it is possible to provide more details than are found in a chip-level architecture. We can examine each of the subunits on a chip. For example, consider the SRAM access unit shown in Figure 20.7. Although the chip-level architecture does not show the details, the internal structure of the memory access unit is quite complex. Figure 20.7 illustrates the structure.

---

†Intel manufactures multiple models of their chip. The IXP2400 contains eight microengines, and the IXP2800 contains sixteen microengines.

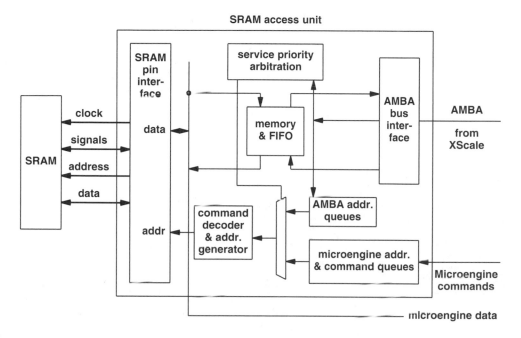

Figure 20.7 The internal structure of the SRAM access unit that remains hidden in Figure 20.6. Each level of architecture reveals further details and structure.

20.12 Summary

The architecture of a digital system can be viewed at several levels of abstraction. A system-level architecture shows the structure of an entire computer system, a board-level architecture shows the structure of each board, and a chip-level architecture shows the internal structure of an integrated circuit. At each successive level, details are revealed that remain hidden in previous levels.

We considered a hierarchy of architectures that shows the structure of a personal computer, the structure of a LAN interface board used in a personal computer, and the structure of a network processor that can be used on a LAN interface board. Finally, we saw that a chip-level architecture can be further refined by looking at the architecture of each embedded unit.

20.13 Hierarchy Beyond Computer Architectures

Levels of hierarchy occur outside the realm of computer architecture. For an interesting examination of hierarchy, see:

http://micro.magnet.fsu.edu/primer/java/scienceopticsu/powersof10/index.html

Appendix 1

Lab Exercises For A Computer Architecture Course

A1.1 Introduction

This Appendix presents a set of lab exercises for an undergraduate computer architecture course. The labs are designed for students whose primary educational goal is learning how to build software, not hardware. Consequently, after a few weeks of introduction to digital circuits, the labs shift emphasis to programming.

The facilities required for the lab are minimal: a small amount of hardware is needed for the early weeks, and access to computers running a version of the Unix operating system (e.g., Linux) is needed for later labs. A RISC architecture works best for the assembly language labs because instructors find that CISC architectures absorb arbitrary amounts of class time on assembly language details.

One lab asks students to write a C program that detects whether an architecture is big endian or little endian. Few additional resources are needed, however, because most of the coding and debugging can be performed on one of the two architectures, with only a trivial amount of time required to port and test the program on the other.

A1.2 Digital Hardware For A Lab

The hardware labs covered in the first few weeks of lab require each student to have the following:

- Solderless breadboard
- Wiring kit used with breadboard (22-gauge wire)
- Five-volt power supply
- Light-Emitting Diode (used to measure output)
- NAND and NOR logic gates

None of the hardware is expensive. To handle a class of 70 students, for example, Purdue University spent less than $1000 on hardware. Smaller classes or sharing in the lab can reduce the cost further. As an alternative, it is possible to institute a lab fee or require students to purchase their own copy of the hardware.

A1.3 Solderless Breadboard

A *solderless breadboard* is used to rapidly construct an electronic circuit without requiring connections to be soldered. Physically, a breadboard consists of a block of plastic (typically three inches by seven inches) with an array of small holes covering the surface.

The holes are arranged in rows with a small gap running down the center and extra holes around the outside. Each hole on the breadboard is a socket that is just large enough for a copper wire — when a wire is inserted in the hole, metal contacts in the socket make electrical contact with the metal wire. The size and spacing of the sockets on a breadboard are arranged to match the size and spacing of pins on a standard integrated circuit (IC), and the gap on the breadboard matches the spacing across the pins, which means that one or more integrated circuits can be plugged into the breadboard. The pins on an IC plug directly into the sockets.

The back of a breadboard contains metal strips that interconnect various sockets. For example, the sockets on each side of the center in a given row are interconnected. Figure A1.1 illustrates sockets on a breadboard and the electrical connections among the sockets.

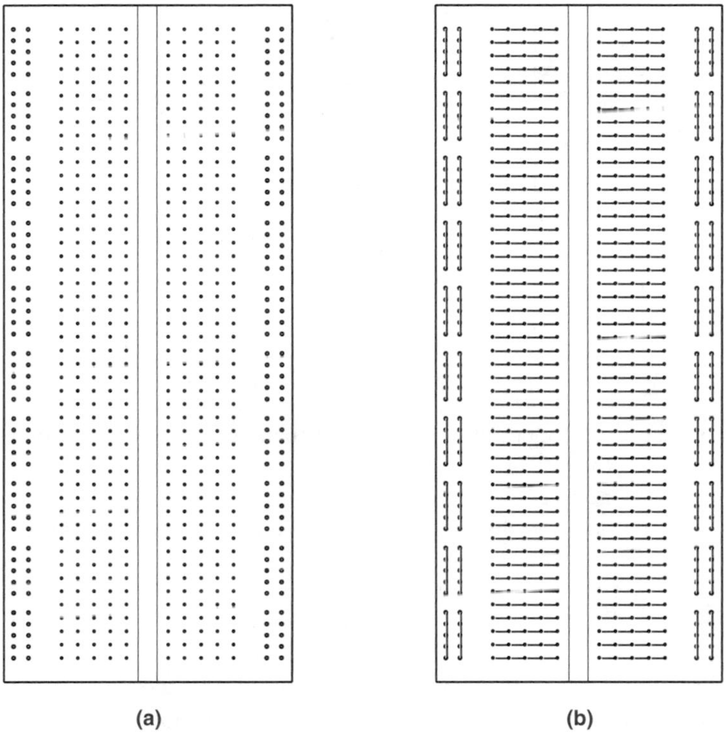

(a)   (b)

Figure A1.1 (a) Illustration of a breadboard with sockets into which wires can be inserted, and (b) blue lines showing the electrical connections among the sockets.

A1.4 Using A Solderless Breadboard

To use a breadboard, an experimenter plugs integrated circuits onto the breadboard along the center, and then uses short wires to make connections among the ICs. A wire plugged into a hole in a row connects to the corresponding pin on the IC that is plugged into the row. To make the connections, an experimenter uses a set of pre-cut wires known as a *wiring kit*. Each individual wire in the wiring kit has bare ends that plug into the breadboard, but is otherwise insulated. Thus, many wires can be added to a breadboard because the insulated area on a wire can rub against the insulation of other wires without making electrical contact.

Figure A1.2 illustrates part of a breadboard that contains a 7400 IC, with wires connecting some of the gates on the IC.

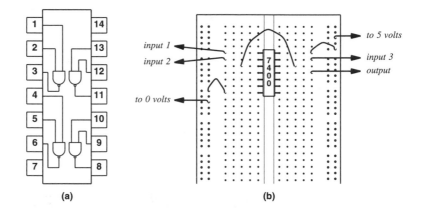

Figure A1.2 Illustrations of (a) the internal connections on a 7400 chip, and (b) part of a breadboard with blue lines indicating wires connecting a 7400 chip. Using a set of sockets to connect power and ground wires allows additional connections to be added.

A1.5 Testing

Beginners often find it easiest to construct a circuit in stages, and test each part of the circuit as building proceeds. For example, after connecting power and ground to a chip, a gate on the chip can be tested to verify that the chip is working. Similarly, after a particular gate has been connected, the input(s) and output(s) of the gate can be measured to determine whether the connections are working.

An easy and inexpensive way to test digital logic consists of using a *Light Emitting Diode* (*LED*). The LED glows when its input wire connects to logical one (i.e., five volts), and is off when its input wire connects to logical zero (i.e., zero volts). For example, to test the circuit in Figure A1.2, an LED can be connected between the output (pin 11 of the integrated circuit) and ground (zero volts)†.

A1.6 Power And Ground Connections

When multiple chips are plugged into a breadboard, each chip must have connections to *power* and *ground* (i.e., five volts and zero volts). To ensure that the power and ground connections are convenient and to keep the wires short, many experimenters choose to devote the outer sets of sockets on both sides of the breadboard to power and ground. To do so, jumper wires are added that interconnect the outer columns. Figure A1.3 illustrates the wiring.

The wires used to connect power and ground are semi-permanent in the sense that they can be reused for many experiments. Thus, experimenters often use the color of a

---

†Note: the LED must have electrical characteristics that are appropriate for the circuit — an arbitrary LED can draw so much electrical power that it will cause a 7400-series integrated circuit to burn out.

wire to indicate its purpose, and choose colors for power and ground that are not used for other connections. For example, red wires can be used for all power connections, black wires can be used for all ground connections, and blue wires can be used for other connections. Of course, the wires themselves do not differ — the color of the insulation merely helps a human understand the purpose of the wire. When disassembling a breadboard after an experiment is finished, the experimenter can leave the power and ground connections for a later experiment.

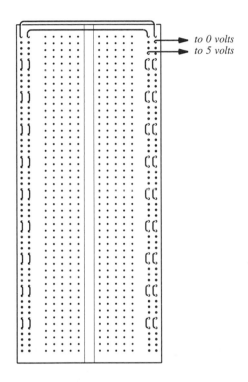

Figure A1.3 A breadboard with semipermanent jumper wires added to connect the outer two rows of sockets on each side of the board to power and ground. The outer row of sockets connects to ground (zero volts), and the next row of sockets connects to five volts.

A1.7 Lab Exercises

The next pages contain a series of lab exercises. Although each writeup specifies the steps to be taken in lab, additional details that pertain to the local environment or computer system must be supplied by the lab instructor. For example, the first lab asks students to establish their computer account, including environment variables. Because the set of directories to be included on the path depend on the local computer system, the set of actual paths must be supplied for each environment.

Lab 1

Introduction And Account Configuration

Purpose

To learn about the lab and set up a computer account for use in lab during the semester.

Background Reading And Preparation

Read about the *bash shell* available with Linux, and find out how to set Linux environment variables.

Overview

Modify your lab account so your environment will be set automatically when you log in.

Procedure And Details (checkmark as each is completed)

_____ 1. Modify your account startup file (e.g., *.profile* or *.bash_profile*) so your PATH includes directories as specified by your lab instructor.

_____ 2. Log out and log in again.

_____ 3. Verify that you can reach the files and compilers that your lab instructor specifies.

Notes

Lab 2
Digital Logic: Use Of A Breadboard

Purpose

To learn how to wire a basic breadboard and use an LED to test the operation of a gate.

Background Reading And Preparation

Read Chapter 2 to learn about basic logic gates and circuits, and read the beginning sections of this Appendix to learn about breadboards. Attend a lecture on how to properly use the breadboard and related equipment.

Overview

Place a 7400 chip on a breadboard, connect power and ground from a five-volt power supply, connect the inputs of a gate to the four possible combinations of zero and one, and use an LED to observe the output.

Procedure And Details (checkmark as each is completed)

_____ 1. Obtain a breadboard, power supply, wiring kit, and parts box with the necessary logic gates. Also verify that you have a copy of the textbook or a data sheet that specifies the pins on a 7400 (quad, two-input NAND gate).

_____ 2. Place the 7400 on the breadboard as Figure A1.2† shows.

_____ 3. Connect the two wires from a five-volt power supply to two separate sets of sockets near the edge of the board.

_____ 4. Add a wire jumper that connects pin 14 on the 7400 to five volts.

_____ 5. Add a wire jumper that connects pin 7 on the 7400 to zero volts. NOTE: be sure not to reverse the connections to the power supply or the chip will be damaged.

_____

†Figure A1.2 can be found on page 334.

_____ 6. Add a wire jumper that connects pin 1 on the 7400 to zero volts.

_____ 7. Add a wire jumper that connects pin 2 on the 7400 to zero volts.

_____ 8. Connect the LED, from the lab kit, between pin 3 on the 7400 and ground (zero volts). NOTE: the LED must be connected with the positive lead attached to the 7400.

_____ 9. Verify that the LED is lit (it should be lit because both inputs are zero which means the output should be one).

_____ 10. Move the jumper that connects pin 2 from zero volts to five volts, and verify that the LED remains lit.

_____ 11. Move the jumper that connects pin 2 back to zero volts, move the jumper that connects pin 3 from zero volts to five volts, and verify that the LED remains lit.

_____ 12. Keep the jumper from pin 3 on five volts, move the jumper that connects pin 2 to five volts, and verify that the LED goes out.

Optional Extensions (checkmark as each is completed)

_____ 13. Wire the breadboard as shown in Figure A1.2 (pin 3 connected to pin 12, and pin 13 acting as an additional input).

_____ 14. Connect the LED between pin 11 and ground.

_____ 15. Record the LED values for all possible combinations of the three inputs.

_____ 16. What Boolean function does the circuit represent?

Lab 3

Digital Logic: Building An Adder From Gates

Purpose

To learn how basic logic gates can be combined to perform complex tasks such as binary addition.

Background Reading And Preparation

Read Chapter 2 about basic logic gates and circuits, and read the beginning sections of this Appendix to learn about breadboards.

Overview

Build a half adder and full adder circuit using only basic logic gates. Combine the circuits to implement a two-bit binary adder with carry output.

Procedure And Details (checkmark as each is completed)

_____ 1. Obtain a breadboard, power supply, wiring kit, and parts box with the necessary logic gates as well as lab writeups that describe both the chip pinouts and the logic diagram of an adder circuit.

_____ 2. Construct a binary half adder as specified in the logic diagram that your lab instructor provides.

_____ 3. Connect the outputs to LEDs, the inputs to switches, and verify that the results displayed on the LED are the correct values for a one-bit adder.

_____ 4. Construct a binary full adder as specified in the logic diagram that your lab instructor provides.

_____ 5. Connect the outputs to LEDs, the inputs to switches, and verify that the results displayed on the LED are the correct values for a full adder.

_____ 6. Chain the half adder circuit to the full adder circuit to make a two-bit adder. Verify that the circuit correctly adds a pair of two-bit numbers and the carry out value is correct.

Optional Extensions (checkmark as each is completed)

_____ 7. Draw the logic diagram for a three-bit adder.

_____ 8. Draw the logic diagram for a four-bit adder.

_____ 9. Give a formula for the number of gates required to implement an n-bit adder.

Notes

Lab 4

Digital Logic: Clocks And Demultiplexing

Purpose

To understand how a clock controls a circuit and allows a series of events to occur.

Background Reading And Preparation

Read Chapter 2 to learn about basic logic gates and clocks. Concentrate on under-standing how a clock functions.

Overview

Use a switch to simulate a clock, and arrange for the clock to operate a demulti-plexor circuit.

Procedure And Details (checkmark as each is completed)

_____ 1. Obtain a breadboard, power supply, wiring kit, and parts box with the neces-sary logic gates as well as lab writeups that describe both the chip pinouts and the logic diagram of a demultiplexing circuit.

_____ 2. Use a switch to simulate a slow clock.

_____ 3. To verify that the switch is working, connect the output of the switch to an LED, and verify that the LED goes on and off as the switch is moved back and forth.

_____ 4. Connect the simulated clock to the input of a four-bit binary counter (a 7493 chip).

_____ 5. Use an LED to verify that each time the switch is moved through one cycle, the outputs of the counter move to the next binary value (modulo four).

_____ 6. Connect the four outputs from the binary counter to the inputs of a demultiplexor chip (a 74154).

_____ 7. Use an LED to verify that as the switch moves through one cycle, exactly one output of the demultiplexor becomes active. Warning: the 74154 is counter-intuitive because the active output is low (logical zero) and all other outputs are high (logical one).

Optional Extensions (checkmark as each is completed)

_____ 8. Use a 555 timer chip to construct a 1Hz clock, and verify that the clock is working.

_____ 9. Replace the switch with the clock circuit.

_____ 10. Use multiple LEDs to verify that the demultiplexor continually cycles through each output.

Notes

Lab 5
Representation: Testing Big Endian Vs. Little Endian

Purpose

To learn how the integer representation used by the underlying hardware affects programming and data layout.

Background Reading And Preparation

Read Chapter 3 to learn about big endian and little endian integer representations and the size of an integer.

Overview

Write a C program that examines data stored in memory to determine whether a computer uses big endian or little endian integer representation.

Procedure And Details (checkmark as each is completed)

_____ 1. Write a C program that creates an array of bytes in memory, fills the array with zero, and then stores integer 0x04030201 in the middle of the array.

_____ 2. Examine the bytes in the array to determine whether the integer is stored in big endian or little endian order.

_____ 3. Compile and run the program (without changes to the source code) on both a big endian and little endian computer, and verify that it correctly announces the integer type.

_____ 4. Add code to the program to determine the integer size (hint: start with integer 1 and shift left until the value is zero).

_____ 5. Compile and run the program (without changes to the source code) on both a thirty-two bit and a sixty-four bit computer, and verify the program correctly announces the integer size.

Optional Extensions (checkmark as each is completed)

_____ 6. Find an alternate method of determining the integer size.

_____ 7. Implement the alternate method to determine integer size, and verify that the program works correctly.

_____ 8. Extend the program to announce the integer format (i.e., one's complement or two's complement).

Notes

Lab 6

Representation: A Hex Dump Program In C

Purpose

To learn how values in memory can be presented in hexadecimal form.

Background Reading And Preparation

Read Chapter 3 on data representation, and find both the integer and address sizes for the computer you use†. Ask the lab instructor for an exact specification for the output format.

Overview

Write a C procedure that produces a hexadecimal dump of memory in ASCII. The lab instructor will give details about the format for a particular computer, but the general form is as follows:

```
Address          Words In Hexadecimal          ASCII characters
---------- -------- -------- -------- -------- ----------------
aaaaaaaa  xxxxxxxx xxxxxxxx xxxxxxxx xxxxxxxx cccccccccccccccc
```

In the example, each line corresponds to a set of memory locations. The string *aaaaaaaa* denotes the starting memory address (in hexadecimal) for values on the line, *xxxxxxxx* denotes the value of a word in memory (also in hexadecimal), and *cccccccccccccccc* denotes the same memory locations when interpreted as ASCII characters. Note: the ASCII output only displays printable characters; all other characters are displayed as blanks.

Procedure And Details (checkmark as each is completed)

_____ 1. Create a procedure, *mdump* that takes two arguments that each specify an address in memory. The first argument specifies the address where the dump should start, and the second argument specifies the highest address that needs to be included in the dump. Test to ensure that the starting address is less than the ending address.

---

†On most computers, the address size equals the integer size.

_____ 2. Modify both arguments so each value specifies an appropriate word address (i.e., an exact multiple of four bytes). For the starting address, round down to the nearest word address; for the ending address, round up.

_____ 3. Test the procedure to verify that the addresses are rounded correctly.

_____ 4. Add code that uses *printf* to produce headings for the hexadecimal dump, and verify that the headings are correct.

_____ 5. Add code that iterates though the addresses and produces lines of hexadecimal values.

_____ 6. To verify that procedure *mdump* outputs correct values, declare a *struct* in memory, place values in fields, and invoke the procedure to format the values.

_____ 7. Add code that produces printable ASCII character values for each of the memory locations, as shown above.

_____ 8. Verify that only printable characters are included in the output (i.e., verify that a non-printable character such as 0x01 is mapped into a blank).

Optional Extensions (checkmark as each is completed)

_____ 9. Extend the dump program to start and stop on a byte address (i.e., omit leading values on the first line of output and trailing values on the last line).

_____ 10. Change the program to print values in decimal instead of ASCII character form.

_____ 11. Modify the dump program so instead of printing ASCII values, the program assumes the memory corresponds to machine instructions and gives mnemonic opcodes for each instruction. For example, if the first word on the line corresponds to a *load* instruction, print *load*.

_____ 12. Add an argument to procedure *mdump* that selects from among the various forms of output (ASCII characters, decimal, or instructions).

Lab 7

Processors: Learn A RISC Assembly Language

Purpose

To gain first-hand experience with an assembly language and understand the one-to-one mapping between assembly language instructions and machine instructions.

Background Reading And Preparation

Read Chapters 4 through 6 and 8 to learn the concepts of instruction sets and operand types. Read about the specific instruction set available on your local computer. Consult the assembler reference manual to learn the syntax conventions needed for the assembler. Also read the assembler reference manual to determine the conventions used to call an external procedure.

Overview

Write an assembly language program that shifts an integer value to the right and then calls a C procedure to display the resulting value in hexadecimal.

Procedure And Details (checkmark as each is completed)

_____ 1. Write a C procedure, *int_out*, that takes an integer argument and uses *printf* to display the argument value in hexadecimal.

_____ 2. Test the procedure to ensure it works correctly.

_____ 3. Write an assembly language program that places the integer 4 in a register, shifts the contents of the register right one bit.

_____ 4. Extend the program to pass the result of the previous step as an argument to external procedure *int_out*.

_____ 5. Verify that the program produces 0x2 as the output.

_____ 6. Instead of using 4 as the initial integer, use 0xBD5A, and verify that the output is correct.

Optional Extensions (checkmark as each is completed)

_____ 7. Rewrite the external procedure *int_out* and the assembly language program to pass multiple arguments.

Notes

Lab 8

Processors: Function That Can Be Called From C

Purpose

To learn how to write an assembly language function that can be called from a C program.

Background Reading And Preparation

Read Chapter 8 to learn about subroutine calls in assembly languages, and read the C and assembler reference manuals to determine the conventions that C uses to call a function on your local computer.

Overview

Write an assembly language function that can be called from a C program to perform the *exclusive or* of two integer values.

Procedure And Details (checkmark as each is completed)

_____ 1. Write a C program that calls function *xor* with two integer arguments and displays the result of the function.

_____ 2. Create an assembly language function, *xor*, that takes two integer values as arguments, computes the *exclusive or* of the two arguments, and returns the result as the value of the function.

_____ 3. Add a *printf* call to the *xor* function to verify that the function correctly receives the two values that the C program passes as arguments (i.e., argument passing works correctly).

_____ 4. Add a *printf* call to the C function to verify that the *xor* code returns the correct value.

Optional Extensions (checkmark as each is completed)

_____ 5. Modify the C program and the *xor* function so the C program passes a single structure as an argument instead of two integers. Arrange for the structure to contain two integer values.

Notes

Lab 9

Memory: Row-Major And Column-Major Array Storage

Purpose

To understand storage of arrays in memory and the difference between row-major order and column-major order.

Background Reading And Preparation

Read Chapters 9 through 11 to learn about basic memory organization and the difference between storing arrays in row-major order and column-major order.

Overview

Instead of using built-in language facilities to declare two-dimensional arrays, implement two C functions, *two_d_store* and *two_d_fetch*, that use linear storage to implement a two-dimensional array. Function *two_d_fetch* takes six arguments: the base address in memory of a region to be used as a two dimensional array, the size (in bytes) of a single entry in the array, two array dimensions, and two index values. For example, instead of the two lines:

```
int  d[10,20];
x = d[4,0];
```

a programmer can code:

```
char  d[200*sizeof(int)];
x = two_d_fetch(d, sizeof(int), 10, 20, 4, 0);
```

Function *two_d_store* has seven arguments. The first six correspond to the six arguments of *two_d_fetch*, and the seventh is a value to be stored. For example, instead of:

```
int  d[10,20];
d[4,0] = 576;
```

a programmer can code:

```
char  d[200*sizeof(int)];
two_d_store(d, sizeof(int), 10, 20, 4, 0, 576);
```

Procedure And Details (checkmark as each is completed)

_____ 1. Implement function *two_d_store*.

_____ 2. Create an area of memory large enough to hold an array, initialize the entire area to zero, and then call *two_d_store* to store specific values in various locations. Use the hex dump program created in Lab 6 to display the result, and verify that the correct values have been stored.

_____ 3. Implement function *two_d_fetch*.

_____ 4. Verify that your implementation of *two_d_fetch* works correctly.

_____ 5. Test *two_d_store* and *two_d_fetch* for boundary conditions, such as the minimum and maximum array dimensions.

Optional Extensions (checkmark as each is completed)

_____ 6. Verify that functions *two_d_store* and *two_d_fetch* work correctly for an array that stores: characters, integers, or double-precision items.

_____ 7. Extend *two_d_store* and *two_d_fetch* to work correctly with any range of array index. For example, allow the first index to range from -5 to +15, and allow the second index to range from 30 to 40.

Lab 10

Input / Output: A Buffered I/O Library

Purpose

To learn how buffered I/O operates and to compare the performance of buffered and unbuffered I/O.

Background Reading And Preparation

Read Chapters 13 through 15 to learn about I/O in general, and read Chapter 16 to learn about buffering.

Overview

Build three C procedures, *buf_in*, *buf_out*, and *buf_flush* that implement buffered I/O. On each call, procedure *buf_in* delivers the next byte of data from file descriptor zero. When additional input is needed from the device, *buf_in* reads sixteen kilobytes of data into a buffer, and allows successive calls to return values from the buffer. On each call, procedure *buf_out* writes one byte of data to a buffer. When the buffer is full or when the program invokes procedure *buf_flush*, data from the buffer is written to file descriptor one.

Procedure And Details (checkmark as each is completed)

_____ 1. Implement procedure *buf_in*.

_____ 2. Verify that *buf_in* operates correctly for input of less than sixteen kilobytes (i.e., less than one buffer of data).

_____ 3. Redirect input to a large file, and verify that *buf_in* operates correctly for input that spans multiple buffers.

_____ 4. Implement procedures *buf_out* and *buf_flush*.

_____ 5. Verify that *buf_out* and *buf_flush* operate correctly for output of less than one buffer.

_____ 6. Verify that *buf_out* and *buf_flush* operate correctly for output that spans multiple buffers.

Optional Extensions (checkmark as each is completed)

_____ 7. Compare the performance of procedures *buf_in*, *buf_out*, and *buf_flush* to the performance of unbuffered I/O (i.e., *read* and *write* of one byte) for various size files. Plot the results.

_____ 8. Measure the performance of *buf_in*, *buf_out*, and *buf_flush* for various size buffers when copying a large file. Use buffers that range in size from 4 bytes to 100 Kbytes, and plot the results.

Notes

Lab 11
A Hex Dump Program In Assembly Language

Purpose

To gain experience coding assembly language.

Background Reading And Preparation

Review Chapters 4 through 6, Chapter 8, and assembly language programs written in earlier labs.

Overview

Rewrite the hex dump program from Lab 6 in assembly language.

Procedure And Details (checkmark as each is completed)

_____ 1. Rewrite the basic hex dump procedure in assembly language.

_____ 2. Verify that the assembly language version gives the same output as the C version.

Optional Extensions (checkmark as each is completed)

_____ 3. Extend the dump procedure to start and stop on a byte address (i.e., omit leading values on the first line of output and trailing values on the last line).

_____ 4. Change the program to print values in decimal instead of ASCII character form.

_____ 5. Modify the dump program so instead of printing ASCII values, the program assumes the memory corresponds to machine instructions and gives mnemonic opcodes for each instruction. For example, if the first word on the line corresponds to a *load* instruction, print *load*.

_____ 6. Add an argument to the dump procedure that selects from among the various forms of output (ASCII characters, decimal, or instructions)

Notes

Bibliography

AGERE SYSTEMS [Sept. 1999], The Challenge for Next Generation Network Processors, *White Paper*.

FLYNN, M. J., K. W. RUDD [March 1996], Parallel architectures, *ACM Computing Surveys*, v28:1, p.67-70.

HENNESSY, J. L. and D. A. PATTERSON [2002], *Computer Architecture a Quantitative Approach*, 3rd edition, Morgan Kaufmann, San Francisco.

SPARC INTERNATIONAL [Nov. 1994], *The SPARC Architecture Manual, v8,* Prentice Hall Technical Reference, Upper Saddle River, New Jersey, ISBN 0-13-825001-4.

WILKES, M. V. [April 1965], Slave memories and dynamic storage allocation, *IEEE Transactions on Electronic Computers* 14(2), 270-271.

Index